教学型本科院校商务英语系列教材

# 国际财经术语（双语版）

徐　凡　主编

对外经济贸易大学出版社
中国·北京

**图书在版编目（CIP）数据**

国际财经术语：双语版：汉、英 / 徐凡主编. —北京：对外经济贸易大学出版社，2022.1

教学型本科院校商务英语系列教材

ISBN 978-7-5663-2282-1

Ⅰ. ①国… Ⅱ. ①徐… Ⅲ. ①经济–名词术语–高等学校–教材–汉、英 Ⅳ. ①F-61

中国版本图书馆 CIP 数据核字（2021）第 113131 号

**国际财经术语**（**双语版**）

徐　凡　**主编**

**责任编辑**：董　黛

出版发行：对外经济贸易大学出版社

社　　址：北京市朝阳区惠新东街 10 号

网　　址：www.uibep.com

资源网址：www.uibepresources.com

邮政编码：100029

邮购电话：010－64492338

发行部电话：010－64492342

E-mail：uibep@126.com

成品尺寸：185mm×260mm

印　　张：12

字　　数：277 千字

ISBN 978-7-5663-2282-1

印　　刷：北京时代华都印刷有限公司

版　　次：2022 年 1 月北京第 1 版

印　　次：2022 年 1 月第 1 次印刷

定　　价：42.00 元

# 出 版 说 明

随着经济全球化浪潮的日益高涨，中国与世界各国之间的经贸往来日益密切，既掌握娴熟英语又具有扎实商务专业知识的复合型人才已成为市场的主要需求。根据教育部发布的《国家中长期教育改革和发展规划纲要》，“建立高校分类体系，实行分类管理”的要求，对外经济贸易大学出版社专门针对教学型本科院校组织编写了这套“教学型本科商务英语系列教材”。

现如今，我国的高等院校分为大致可分为研究型、教学研究型、教学型三大类。不同类型高等院校在人才培养类型、创新贡献和服务社会方面都应有各自的定位，与之相应的，其适用教材也各有不同。教学型高校作为我国高等教育的主力，量大面广、层次多、类型多，是培养应用型高级人才的主要力量。教学型高校以培养应用型、复合型人才为出发点，按“基础扎实，知识面宽，应用能力强，素质高，有较强的创新精神”的要求，以人为本，使学生“会学习”“会创新”“会做人”。既加强通识教育，同时也为终身教育做准备、打基础。

本系列教材面向全国教学型本科院校，目标群体明确，教材选题和内容均根据全国教学型本科院校课程设置而定，作者队伍也拟联合全国教学型本科院校的优秀一线师资，适用于全国教学型本科院校商务英语专业、财经专业和英语专业校商务/应用/外贸外语方向的学生。

本套“教学型本科商务英语系列教材”适用于全国应用型本科院校商务英语专业、英语专业的商务/应用/外贸英语方向以及财经类专业的学生，内容包括《商务英语综合教程》《商务英语听说》《商务英语阅读》《商务英语写作》《商务英语函电》《商务英语翻译》《商务英语口译》《商务知识导读》《英语财经报刊阅读》《跨文化交际基础》《国际商务礼仪》《进出口贸易实务》《国际商务制单》《国际贸易理论与实务》等。

本系列的编撰者们不仅具有丰富的语言教学经验，而且具备商务活动的实践经验，他们集教学经验和专业背景于一身，这是本套商务英语系列教材编撰质量的有力保证。

此外，本套教材配有辅导用书或课件等立体化教学资源，供教师教学参考（可登录我社资源网 www.uibepresources.com 下载）。

对外经济贸易大学出版社
外语图书事业部
2022 年 1 月

# 前　言

本教材依托对外经济贸易大学硕士研究生公选课程“国际财经术语（英）”，是本课程开设三年以来章节课件、随堂讨论、课后练习及同行反馈的系统总结与整理，内容涉及现代国际财经体系证券、信托、银行、保险等业务常用术语和基本原理，在题材、体例方面呈现两个突出特征：其一，涵盖国际财经系列题材、实务术语及相关理论，选题设置与21世纪商务英语学科演绎同步而行，与经济全球化下中国商务人才培养规划相得益彰；其二，结构立体严谨，突破传统商务英语类教材体例，综合国际财经五大门类最核心术语，立足国际财经媒体例句语境释义术语应用。

本教材共分为股票篇、债券篇、信托篇、银行篇、保险篇五大章节，每章主体结构由导读、术语中英文定义、术语英文例句与中文翻译、关联术语辨析、易混淆概念比较五部分构成。除此之外，每条术语还配有概括性中文释义，并以注释形式延伸阐述，既便于高效掌握语用模式、行业惯例、演绎规律等知识要点，又兼顾培养举一反三能力，所有英文例句均遴选自近年国际财经期刊并标注来源出处。

本教材采用中英双语模式，适用于全国高等院校国际商务、国际金融、商务英语、国际贸易等专业硕士课内外使用，亦可作为国际财经从业者参考用书。全书结构完整、内容充实，理论与实务要点配比相得益彰，有助于系统掌握国际财经术语应用规范、核心原理及文化惯例，力求在知识结构和实操方法方面突破传统谋篇体例，着重培养实用跨国商务沟通能力，所收录术语、定义、相关经典理论及释义均符合国际财经行业规范，并集合专业性、时效性、普适性三位于一体，致力弥补国内相关课程双语教材空白。

结合我国商务英语课程及学科机制建设规划，本教材从选题设计、体例构建、课件融合到教材立项，以及选题必要性和可行性跟踪论证，至今业已经历多年课堂积累与总结，在章节编写阶段将科学性、专业性、准确性放在首位，兼顾约定俗成的语义特点，同时侧重诠释术语在国际商务语境之下的时代内涵。教材顾问委员会由国内商务英语、世界经济、国际金融等专业一线教授，以及中国人民银行、中国银行和商务部资深专家共同构成。

**主　编**

**2022年1月**

# Contents

# Chapter 1

# Terminologies of Stock
# （股票篇）

股票（Stock）是股份公司发行的所有权凭证，是股份公司为筹集资金而发行给各个股东作为持股凭证并借以取得股息和红利的一种有价证券。每股股票都代表股东对企业拥有一个基本单位的所有权。同一类别的每股股票所代表的公司所有权是相等的。股票是股份公司资本的一项构成，可以转让、买卖，是资本市场主要的长期信用工具，但股东不能要求公司返还其出资。

## 1.1 Chinese Stock Market（中国股票市场）

中国股票市场这一章内容包括股票、股票分类、股票市场、股票市场参与者、股票市场地位与功能。

中国股票市场即中华人民共和国股票市场。1989 年作为试点，本着“试得好就上、试不好就停”的理念建立，因而政策消息对其运作影响较大。后受“3.27 国债期货事件”影响，经过 1995 年中国期货市场全面的整顿清理，中国股市成为扶持的对象，由此迎来了真正利好的大发展时期。

### 1.1.1 证券及证券市场相关概念

证券（security）是多种经济权益凭证的统称，也指专门的种类产品，是用来证明券票持有人享有的某种特定权益的法律凭证。主要包括资本证券、货币证券和商品证券等。

**1. A-share　A 股**

The A-share market offers a lot of upside potential for value investors with a mid to long-term horizon. (http://www.quamnet.com/mob/newscolumnistcontent.action?articleId=4702123&authorCode=COL_CHL)

A 股市场为具有中长期偏好的价值投资者提供很多上行潜力。

注：value investors 价值投资者一般是指希望成为长期股东的价值投资者。这里的长期是指 5～10 年的股票持有期。

相关术语：trend investors 趋势投资者；individual investors 个人投资者；institutional investors 机构投资者；speculators 投机者

A-Shares are shares of the Renminbi currency that are purchased and traded on the Shanghai and Shenzhen stock exchanges.

A 股是指在沪深证券交易所购买和交易的人民币计价股票。

注：Shanghai and Shenzhen stock exchanges 沪深证券交易所；2019 年全球前五证券交所(按市值)：(1)New York Stock Exchange 纽约证券交易所；(2)Nasdaq Stock Exchange 纳斯达克证券交易所；（3）Tokyo Stock Exchange 东京证券交易所；（4）Shanghai Stock Exchange 上海证券交易所；（5）Hong Kong Stock Exchange 香港证券交易所

**2. At-the-money option (ATM)　平价期权**

ATM options are consequently more expensive than OTM options. (http://www.options-trading.com/options-moneyness-atm-itm-and-otm-options/)

因此，平价期权比价外期权更为昂贵。

注：at the money 平价期权，指执行价格与个人外汇买卖实时价格相同的期权；out of the money 价外期权，指期权行使价格高于股票当前价格的期权；in the money 价内期权，指执行价格与基础工具的现行远期市场价格相比较为有利的期权。

At-the-money option is an option whose current stock price is equal to the strike price.

非货币期权/平价期权是目前股价等于执行价的期权。

注：stock price 股票价格，指股票在证券市场上买卖时的价格；strike price 成交价，是经由买卖双方充分参与，在一定的撮合原则下，由市场供需决定的公平、合理的价格，亦是产品最终的交易价格。

股票成交价原则：价格优先原则、成交时间优先顺序原则及成交的决定原则。

**3. B-share　B 股**

B-Shares trading seats are divided into tangible seats and intangible seats according to the way offers are made. (http://english.sse.com.cn/tradmembership/tradingsystem/trading/)

根据报价方式，B 股股票交易席位分为有形席位和无形席位。

注：trading seats 交易席位，证券商参与证券交易必须首先购买席位，席位购买后只能转让，不能撤销；tangible seats 有形席位，指在证券交易所或交易厅内有实际工作位置的席位，它属于一种场内报盘；intangible seats 无形席位，指在证券交易所无实际工作位置的席位，它属于一种场外报盘。

席位分类：（1）报盘方式：有形席位、无形席位。
（2）证券种类：A 股席位、B 股席位。
（3）业务种类：代理席位、自营席位。

B-shares (officially domestically listed foreign investment shares) on the Shanghai and Shenzhen stock exchanges refers to those that are traded in foreign currencies.

上海和深圳证券交易所的 B 股（正式上市外商投资股票）是指以外币交易的股票。

注：B-shares B 股，人民币特种股票。它是指以人民币标明面值，以外币认购和买卖，在中国境内证券交易所上市的外资股。B 股公司的注册地和上市地都在境内。

foreign currencies 外币

**4. Bull market 牛市**

Many people think that they ring a bell at the top of a bull market. (http://www.mauldineconomics.com/the-10th-man/how-bull-markets-end)

许多人认为他们可以在牛市鼎盛时刻敲响警钟。

注：bull market 牛市，指价格长期呈上涨趋势的证券市场；bear market 熊市，指价格长期呈下跌趋势的证券市场。

A bull market is a financial market in which stock prices are rising or are expected to rise.

牛市是指股价上涨或预计将上涨的金融市场。

注：financial market 金融市场的分类：

（1）交易的标的物：货币市场，资本市场，外汇市场，黄金市场。

（2）金融资产的发行和流通特征：初级市场，二级市场，第三市场，第四市场。

（3）交割方式：现货市场，衍生市场。

**5. Blue chip 蓝筹股**

Qualified insurance companies will be allowed to invest up to 10 percent of their assets in a single blue chip. (http://health.cnr.cn/jkgdxw/20150708/t20150708_519120208.shtml)

合格保险公司最多可以将其资产的 10%投资于单一蓝筹股。

注：blue chip 蓝筹股，指股票市场上的那些在所属行业内占有重要支配性地位、业绩优良、红利优厚的大公司股票；insurance companies，指采用公司组织形式来经营保险业务的保险人。保险公司享有收取保险费、建立保险费基金的权利。当保险事故发生时，负有赔偿被保险人的经济损失的义务。

A blue chip is stock in a corporation with a national reputation for quality, reliability, and the ability to operate profitably in good and bad times.

蓝筹股是指一家公司的股票，该公司在质量、可靠性方面享有全国声誉，并有能力在好的时候和坏的时候盈利。

注：junk stock/garbage stock 垃圾股，指经营亏损或违规的公司的股票。在美国，junk bonds 比 garbage bonds 使用更频繁。

**6. Bullet loan 子弹贷款**

After this, the central government can conduct buy-backs in 0.25% bullet loan in 2018.

在此之后，中央政府可以在 2018 年回购 0.25%子弹贷款。

注：bullet loan 子弹贷款/小额贷款，指借款人在贷款期结束时一次性偿还本金的贷款模式。

In banking and finance, a bullet loan is a loan where a payment of the entire principal of the loan, and sometimes the principal and interest, is due at the end of the loan term.

在银行和金融方面，子弹贷款是指在贷款期限结束时支付贷款全部本金，有时支付本息和的贷款。

注：贷款种类：

（1）经营属性：自营贷款，委托贷款，特定贷款。

（2）使用期限：短期贷款，中长期贷款。

（3）主体经济性质：国有及国家控股企业贷款，集体企业贷款，私营企业贷款，个体工商业者贷款。

**7. Bearer stock　无记名股票**

According to investigation and study, many countries or regions have adopted plans to eliminate bearer stocks. (www.chinanews.com/ga/2014/10-28/6724029.shtml)

许多国家或地区已经通过了消除无记名股票的计划

注：bearer stock 无记名股票，指在股票上不记载股东姓名或名称的股票，发行、流通手续简单。在我国，对社会公众发行的股票，可以为记名股票，也可以为无记名股票。

Bearer stocks refer to the voting that does not record the names of shareholders on the stock par and the stock company's list of shareholders.

无记名股票是指在票面上不记载股东名额和股票公司股东名录的股票。

注：inscribed stock 记名股票，指在股票上记载股东姓名或名称的股票。此类股票有利于公司了解、掌握股东的人数及股票的流向。在我国，公司向发起人、法人发行的股票，应当为记名股票。

**8. Bubble economy　泡沫经济**

At the same time, central banks have a legitimate role to play in controlling bubble economies. (http://www.gold-eagle.com/article/role-central-bank-bubble-economy-section-i)

与此同时，中央银行肩负着管控泡沫经济的职责。

注：bubble economy 泡沫经济，指资产价值超越实体经济，极易丧失持续发展能力的宏观经济状态。泡沫经济经常会因为支撑投机活动的市场预期破灭而导致资产价值迅速下跌。

central bank 中央银行，是国家居主导地位的金融中心机构，是国家干预和调控国民经济发展的重要工具，负责制定并执行国家货币信用政策，独具货币发行权并实行金融监管。

全球主要央行：

中国：中国人民银行 The People's Bank of China

日本：日本银行 The Bank of Japan

英国：英格兰银行 The Bank of England

美国：美国联邦储备系统 The Federal Reserve System

欧盟：欧盟中央银行 European Central Bank

An economic bubble or asset bubble is trade in an asset at a price or price range that strongly exceeds the asset's intrinsic value.

经济泡沫或资产泡沫是指以明显超过资产内在价值的价格或价格范围进行的资产交易。

注：financial crisis 经济危机，是指资本主义在生产过程中周期性爆发的生产过剩危机。这种生产过剩不是绝对过剩而是相对过剩，即相对于劳动人民有支付能力的需求和

资本价值增值需要而言的过剩。

asset bubble 资产泡沫，指在没有显著基本面变化情况下，资产价格持续上升从而产生的现象。

通货膨胀 inflation vs. 资产泡沫 asset bubble

通货膨胀指一般物价水平持续上涨过程，是过多货币追逐较少商品的结果；而资产泡沫则是某种资产的市场价格水平相对于理论价格非平稳性向上偏移的过程，是不符合经济现实的买卖行为所导致的资产价格高估。

**9. Bonus issue 股票红利**

Stock splits and bonus issues are two common corporate actions that publicly listed companies undertake. (http://stockresearchasia.com/stock-split-vs-bonus-issue.html)

股票分割和股票红利是上市公司采取的两种常见行为。

注：bonus issues 股票红利，指以股东赠送的形式发放股利的股票。股东对股份的占有比例并未发生变化。

stock splits 股票分割，是公司“购回”其发行在外的股份，再将原来的一股分割成两股或更多股，按持股比例分配给各股东，分割后的股票面值或设定价值将会降低。

A bonus issue, also known as a scrip issue or a capitalization issue, is an offer of free additional shares to existing shareholders.

股票红利，也就是股票发行或资本化发行，是向现有股东免费提供额外股票。

注：share issuance 股票发行，是公司新股票的出售过程。新股票一经发行，经中间人或径自进入应募人之手，应募人认购，持有股票，即成为股东。

**10. Hang Seng index 恒生指数**

The Hang Seng index in Hong Kong followed the mainland higher, advancing 0.9 percent to 21, 237.43. (www.ftchinese.com)

香港恒生指数随内地股市走高，上涨 0.9%，至 21 237.43 点。

注：Hang Seng index 恒生指数，由若干只成份股（即蓝筹股）市值计算得出。

全球重要股指：

NASDAQ 纳斯达克，DowJones 道琼斯，S&P 标准普尔，FTSE100 英国富时 100，CSI300 沪深 300，Euro Stoxx 50 欧洲斯托克 50 指数

Hang Seng index is a figure indicating the relative price of shares on the Hong Kong Stock Exchange.

恒生指数是一个数字，显示港交所股票相对价格。

注：Hong Kong Stock Exchange 香港交易所，是全球主要交易所集团之一，也是一家在香港上市的控股公司。

**11. Financial institution 金融机构**

A certain financial institution may concentrate these foreign currency savings and invest them in Hong Kong's stock market. (www.dictall.com)

一家金融机构可将外汇集中起来投资于香港股市。

注：金融机构是指从事金融相关的金融中介机构，为金融体系的一部分，金融业包

括银行、证券、保险、信托、基金等行业。

Institution is an establishment consisting of a building or complex of buildings where an organization for the promotion of some cause is situated.

机构是由促进某种事业的组织所在的建筑物或建筑群组成的。

注：investor 投资人，指投入现金购买某种资产并期望获取利益的自然人和法人。

**12. In the tank　跳水**

The stock price is in the tank nowadays.

目前，股票价格在急剧下跌。

注：in the tank（股市中）跳水，指股市大盘或某支股票不顾一切大幅度迅猛下跌，即走势像高台跳水一样在短时间内直线向下，该说法也适用于线性图表。

相关词汇：lose ground 股市下跌；rally 价格止跌；regain ground 重新获得利润；plunge 大幅下跌；plummet 大幅下跌

In the tank means a sharp fall in stock prices.

跳水意味着股价大幅下跌。

注：punch down 冲高回落，指当日股票急速无量上涨，然后带量下跌，分时图走势为先扬后抑。

**13. Market share　市场占有率**

Hewlett-Packard remains the largest vendor, with 17.7% market share, up from 17.3% a year ago. (*Forbes*: PC Sales Grew 3.2% In Q3, Gartner Says)

惠普仍然是最大的供应商，市场份额从一年前的 17.3%上升到 17.7%。

注：market share 市场份额，指某企业某一产品（或品类）的销售量（或销售额）在市场同类产品（或品类）的销售总额中所占比重。

Market share is the percentage of a market (defined in terms of either units or revenue) accounted for by a specific entity.

市场份额指特定实体所占市场百分比（以单位或收入来定义）。

注：市场份额的三种基本测算方法：

（1）总体市场份额，指某企业销售量（额）在整个行业中所占比重。

（2）目标市场份额，指某企业销售量（额）在其目标市场，即其所服务的市场中所占比重。

（3）相对市场份额，指某企业销售量与市场上最大竞争者销售量之比，若高于 1，表明其为这一市场的领导者。

**14. Market value　市场价值**

Google’s market value has been sagging, but this week brought some good news for Google investors. (NPR: Google’s Android Makes Phones Act like PCs)

虽然谷歌的市场价值一直在下降，但是本周谷歌投资者获得了一些好消息。

注：market value 企业的市场价值，即指企业本身的价值，是企业有形资产和无形资产价值的市场评价。由于企业商誉的存在，通常企业的实际市场价值远远超过账面资产价值。

Market value or OMV (Open Market Valuation) is the price at which an asset would trade in a competitive auction setting.

市场价值或公开市场估值（OMV）是指资产在竞争性拍卖环境中的交易价格。

注：company value 公司价值，指某个商业实体的市值。公司价值是对所有声明的证券的价值的总和，包括债券、优先股、普通股和其他证券。

**15. Maturity date　到期日**

He recommends investors look at long-term bonds with 10 years or more between the bond's call date and maturity date. (WSJ: SmartMoney: Watch Out! These Municipal Bonds Come with a Bit of a Kick)

他建议投资者关注在债券赎回日和到期日之间有 10 年或更长时间的长期债券。

注：maturity date 到期日指偿还本金的日期。

In finance, maturity or maturity date refers to the final payment date of a loan or other financial instrument, at which point the principal (and all remaining interest) is due to be paid.

在金融行业中，到期或到期日是指贷款或其他金融工具的最后付款日期，此时应支付本金（和所有剩余利息）。

注：last trading day 最后交易日，指期货或期权合约允许的交收月份最后截止日，合约的最后交易日必须以现货、金融工具或根据期货合约协议作结算。

## 1.1.2　融资手段

**融资手段（financing means）**，是企业融通资金的一种具体形式，融资方式越多意味着可供企业选择的融资机会就越多，它可以分为两类：债务性融资和权益性融资，前者包括银行贷款、发行债券和应付票据、应付账款等，后者主要指股票融资。

**1. Arm's length principle　公平交易原则**

This arm's length principle is in fact not new—it existed in the Income Tax Act 1970, as section 17. (http://www.jamaicaobserver.com/business/Transfer-pricing-Keeping-transactions-at-arm-s-length_54704)

事实上，这种公平交易原则并非新鲜出炉，早在 1970 年版的《所得税法》第 17 部分就已出现。

The arm's length principle (ALP) is the condition or the fact that the parties to a transaction are independent and on an equal footing. Such a transaction is known as an "arm's-length-transaction".

公平交易原则（ALP）是指交易各方独立且平等的条件或事实，此类交易被称为"独立交易"。

注：公平交易的概念使市场能够确保交易双方都为各自利益行事，并且不受对方的压力或胁迫并向第三方保证，买卖双方之间没有串通。

**2. Back-door listing　反向收购**

It is referred to as a reverse takeover or backdoor listing and provides an alternative method of listing to the more conventional initial public offering (IPO). (https://www.asx.com.

au/education/investor-update-newsletter/201508-ipos-v-backdoor-listings-rules-and-risks.htm)

它被称为反向收购或借壳上市，为传统首次公开发行（IPO）提供一种可供选择的上市方式。

A back-door listing is one way for a private company to go public if it doesn't meet the requirements to list on a stock exchange. Essentially, the company gets on the exchange by going through a back door.

如果不符合在证券交易所上市的要求，则后门上市是私人公司公开上市的一种方式。本质为该公司通过后门进入交易所。

注：（1）reverse takeover 反向兼并，指一家非上市公司在投资银行顾问公司的帮助下获得一家上市壳公司的绝对控股权，又作 reverse takeover，reverse buyout，reverse acquisition。（2）上市途径有首发股票上市（IPO 上市）和买壳上市两种。

**3. Capital raising　募集资金**

After the private placement, ABC's (Agricultural Bank of China) capital raising overhang will be removed. (http://hk.jrj.com.cn/2018/03/13111624232557.shtml)

私募之后，中国农业银行融资过剩情况将会得到改善。

Capital raising is a company raising money from investors, creditors or other related individuals or institutes to run itself.

募集资金是指从投资者、债权人或其他相关个人或机构中筹集资金以运营自己的公司。

注：（1）私募（private placement）是将股票或债券出售给预先选定的投资者和机构，而不是在公开市场上出售。

（2）公募（public offering）是国际债券发行的一种方式。借款人先与国际性大银行或证券公司联系，初步确定债券发行条件并选定牵头银行，然后组成银行集团或证券公司向投资者推销。

（3）相关术语：中国六大银行：中国农业银行（Agricultural Bank of China，简称 ABC，农行）；中国工商银行（Industrial and Commercial Bank of China，简称 ICBC，工行）；中国银行（Bank of China，简称 BOC，中行）；中国建设银行（China Construction Bank，简称 CCB，建行）；中国邮政储蓄银行（Postal Savings Bank of China，简称 PSBC，邮储银行）；交通银行（Bank of Communications，简称 BCM，交行）。

**4. IPO　首次公开募股**

Almost all of China's largest state-owned banks have sold shares to foreign strategic investors and listed on stock markets in Hong Kong and Shanghai. (www.ftchinese.com)

几乎所有中国最大的国有银行都将股份出售给外国战略投资者，并在香港和上海的股票市场上市。

Initial public offerings (IPO) refers to the initial issuance of shares by companies to investors through stock exchanges, with a view to raising the process of financing for enterprise development.

首次公开募股（IPO）指公司通过证券交易所向投资者首次发行股票，以期为企业发展筹集资金的过程。

注：银行是金融机构之一，按类型分为：中央银行 central bank，政策性银行 policy lender/non-commercial bank，商业银行 commercial bank，投资银行 investment banks，世界银行 world bank，它们的职责各不相同。

（1）中央银行：中国人民银行 The People's Bank of China，英文简称 PBOC，是我国的中央银行。

（2）国有政策性银行：包括中国进出口银行（The Export-Import Bank of China）、中国农业发展银行（Agricultural Development Bank of China）、国家开发银行（China Development Bank）。

（3）国有商业银行：包括中国工商银行、中国农业银行、中国银行、中国建设银行、中国邮政储蓄银行、交通银行等。

（4）投资银行：包括高盛集团（Goldman Sachs）、摩根士丹利（Morgan Stanley，NYSE：MS）、花旗集团（Citigroup）、富国银行（Wells Fargo）、瑞银集团（Union Bank of Switzerland）、法国兴业银行（Social General）等。

## 1.2 Overseas Stock Market（海外股票市场）

海外股票市场分为美国股票市场、亚洲（除中国）股票市场和欧洲股票市场三种。

本章重点是掌握股票及股票市场基础知识，包括股票、股票分类、股票市场、股票市场参与者、股票市场的地位与功能。

### 1.2.1 美国股票市场

#### 1.2.1.1 证券及证券市场相关概念

**1. Amortization 摊销**

Taking out amortization of intangible assets and share-based compensation, Non-GAAP earnings per ADS were US$0.20 for the second quarter of fiscal year 2011. (http://news.imeigu.com/a/1305808937637.html)

扣除无形资产摊销和股份补偿，2011 财年第二季度非美国通用会计准则下每股美国存托股收益为 0.20 美元。

Amortization is paying off an amount owed over time by making planned, incremental payments of principal and interest.

摊销是指通过按计划、递增地支付本金和利息来偿还一段时间内所欠的金额。

注：（1）intangible assets 无形资产，指长期使用的非有形资产；tangible assets：有形资产，指用于公司运营的有形资产和可测量资产。

（2）non-GAAP earnings：非 GAAP 收入是衡量公司收入的另一种会计方法。非 GAAP 收入是备考数字，不包括“一次性”交易（例如组织重组）。相关术语：GAAP：公认会计准则，是公司及其会计师在编制财务报表时必须遵循的一套通用的公认会计准则、标准和程序。

（3）ADS：美国存托股票，指可以在美国证券交易所购买的以美元计价的外国公司股票。相关术语：ADR：美国存托凭证，是由美国存托银行发行的可转让凭证，特定数量（或少至一股）的投资于外国公司的股票。

（4）fiscal year：会计年度，是指公司或政府基于会计目的和准备财务报表的一年时间。相关术语：① a calendar year：日历年，是根据常用的公历从 1 月 1 日开始到 12 月 31 日结束的一年。②a tax year：纳税年度，指特定纳税申报表涵盖的年份。在美国，个人纳税年度为 1 月 1 日至 12 月 31 日，其中包括该年度应纳税所得额。

（5）principal and interest：本金和利率

**2. Current liabilities　流动负债**

Bob Evans Farms total current liabilities overstated by $458.8 mln. (https://xw.qq.com/c/finance/20141205031000)

鲍勃・埃文斯农场虚报了 4.588 亿美元流动性负债。

Current liabilities are short-term financial obligations that the company expires within one year or within the normal operating cycle.

流动负债是公司在一年内或正常运营周期内到期的短期财务债务。

**3. January effect　一月效应**

Subsequent researchers have made refinements and produced ingenious explanations, but the main interest in the January effect is as a challenge markets hypothesis. (www.ftchinese.com)

后来研究人员对其进行提炼，并给出创造性的解释，但对于一月效应，人们主要兴趣在于，它是对市场假说的一种挑战。

The January effect is a common phenomenon in analyzing stock market movements from a statistical point of view, meaning that the rate of return in January is often “positive”.

从统计角度来看，一月效应是分析股票市场走势的常见现象，这意味着一月份的回报率通常是“正”的。

注：the rate of return（RoR）回报率，指定时间段内一项投资的净损益占投资初始成本的比例。相关术语：（1）Net Present Value（NPV）净现值，是一段时间内现金流入的现值和现金流出的现值之差；（2）Internal Rate of Return（IRR）内部收益率，是资本预算中用来估算潜在投资获利能力的指标，是使来自特定项目的所有现金流的净现值等于零时的折现率。

**4. Joint account　联名账户**

US citizens are obliged to declare all their accounts; but the Swiss lawyers said it was not uncommon for a US citizen to omit to declare a joint account held with a non-US partner. (www.ftchinese.com)

美国公民有义务申报其全部银行账户；但瑞士律师表示美国公民不申报与非美国籍伴侣联名账户的做法并不罕见。

account 相关术语：

account type 账户种类；individual account 个人账户；joint account 联名账户；cash account 现金账户；margin account 保证金账户；investment immigration cash account 资本投资者入境计划账户

美国的商业银行账户类别：check account 支票账户（相当于活期账户，基本没有利息）；saving account 储蓄账户（利息非常低）

Joint account refers to the joint opening of two or two or more (five or less) individual customers, the deposit is not restricted, the withdrawal of the foreign currency personal current settlement account or the deposit and consolidation of the regular savings deposit account to be handled in accordance with the agreement.

联名账户是指由两个或两个以上（五个以下）客户共同开立，存款不受限制，支取须按约定方式办理的本外币个人活期结算账户或整存整取定期储蓄存款账户。

注：savings deposit account 个人储蓄账户，指自然人凭个人有效身份证件以自然人名称在银行储蓄机构开立的办理资金存取业务的人民币储蓄存款账户。

存款类别：current deposit account/ demand account 活期存款；fixed-term deposit account 定期存款；large amount deposit receipts 大额储蓄存单；structural deposits 结构性存款

personal current settlement account 个人结算账户，指个人专门的账户用来办理转账汇款、刷卡消费、投资、贷款等各项支付结算业务，可以对他人或单位转账，也可接受转账。

**5. Garbage bonds 垃圾债券**

Credit ratings of CCC or below are reserved for garbage bonds with the highest risk of default. (www.ftchinese.com)

信用评级在 CCC 或以下的债券为具有最高违约风险的垃圾债券。

注：Securities Credit Rating 证券信用评级，包括长期债券、短期融资券、优先股、基金、各种商业票据等的信用评级。

债券等级一般由高到低分为 AAA、AA 等九个等级。AAA 级表示债券发行者偿债能力很强，投资者基本不承担任何风险；C 级则表示债券发行者处于破产边缘。

Garbage bonds are also known as “high-interest bonds”, a non-investment-grade bond issued by American companies.

垃圾债券亦称“高息债券”，是美国公司发行的一种非投资级债券。

注：junk stock 垃圾股，经营亏损或违规的公司的股票。在美国 junk bonds 比 garbage bonds 使用更频繁。

**6. Large-cap 大型股票**

Favorite small-cap stocks rests on the presumption that large-cap emerging market stocks represent export-oriented and globally oriented businesses (www.ftchinese.com)

对小型股偏好是基于一种假设：即新兴市场大型股代表出口导向型和全球导向型企业。

注：small-cap stock 小型股，又称细价股，指相对来说发行数比较少的股票（总市值在 7 亿元以下的公司股票），价格易飙升、波动大且风险较高。

export-oriented business 出口导向性企业，指以生产出口产品为主要经营方式，生产要素与盈利多寡取决于国际市场需求且受世界经济影响较大的外向型加工企业。

Shares issued by large companies with a capital amount of more than 1 billion yuan are large-cap.

资本额在十亿元以上的大公司发行的股票就是大型股票。

注：资本额：amount of capital; capital sum

**7. Lead underwriter　主承销商**

He worked alongside bankers from Merrill Lynch the lead underwriter who invited him to join them. (www.ftchinese.com)

他与邀请他加入的主承销商美林（Merrill Lynch）的银行家们一起工作。

注：Merrill Lynch，世界最著名的证券零售商和投资银行之一，总部位于美国纽约。2008 年被美国 Bank of America Corp. 收购，合并后成为银行巨头。

2008 年以前的华尔街五大投行一般是指高盛 Goldman Sachs、摩根士丹利 Morgan Stanley、美林 Merrill Lynch、雷曼 Lehman Brothers 和贝尔斯登 Bear Stearns Cos.。

2008 年金融海啸之后，雷曼兄弟宣布破产，这也是美国历史上最大的破产案。

美国第三大投行美林公司（Merrill Lynch）被美国银行（Bank of America）收购。

美联储宣布批准美国第一大投行高盛（Goldman Sachs）和第二大投行摩根士丹利（Morgan Stanley）实施业务转型，转为银行控股公司，即普通商业银行。

贝尔斯登被摩根大通收购。

The lead/principal underwriter is the underwriting Director-General. The underwriter in the underwriting group who is responsible for the overall affairs, assumes the main duties and signs the underwriting agreement with the issuing company on behalf of the underwriting group.

主承销商（lead underwriter）是在承销团中负责全面事务、承担主要职责并代表承销团与发行公司签署承销协议书的承销商。

注：underwriting 证券包销、承销，指一家投资银行（或证券公司）将发行人的证券按照协议全部购入或在承销期结束时将售后剩余证券全部自行购入的承销方式。证券包销具有如下特点：① 证券所有权发生转移；② 发行人可以迅速、可靠地获得证券价款；③ 承销人要承担全部发行风险；④ 费用比较高。

securities distribution 分销，即产品通过一定渠道销售给消费者。从这个角度来讲，任何一种销售方式都可以称为分销，即分销是产品由生产地点向销售地点运动的过程，产品必须通过某一种分销方式才能到达消费者手中。

securities broker/dealer 证券经纪人，是在证券交易中，代理客户买卖证券，从事中介业务的个人或机构。在证券交易中，广大的证券投资人相互之间不是直接买卖证券的，而是通过证券经纪人来买卖证券的，经纪人向双方收取交易手续费（佣金）。

**8. Listing application　上市申请书**

However, E&Y then resigned as auditor in 2010 due to “certain inconsistencies in documentation” and the group withdrew its listing application soon afterwards, according to the SFC. (www.ftchinese.com)

然而据 SFC 称，2010 年安永因“文档存在某些不一致”不再担任审计机构，不久该公司撤销上市申请。

注：E&Y 安永会计师事务所（Ernst & Young）是一家总部位于英国伦敦的跨国性专业服务公司。

四大国际会计师事务所：普华永道（PwC）、德勤（DTT）、毕马威（KPMG）、安永（E&Y）。

SFC（Securities and Futures Commission）香港证券及期货事务监察委员会（证监会），是独立于政府公务员架构之外的法定组织，负责监管香港证券期货市场的运作。

A listing application is a approval document submitted by a limited company to a stock Exchange Listing committee requesting permission to trade its publicly issued shares on a stock exchange.

上市申请书是具备股票上市法定条件的股份有限公司，向证券交易所上市委员会提交的批准文件，请求准许其公开发行的股票在证券交易所交易。

注：目前中国正在从审核制（verification system）向注册制（registered system）改革。

publicly issued（shares）公开发行，指没有特定的发行对象，面向广大投资者公开推销的发行方式。发行人通过中介机构向不特定的社会公众广泛地发售证券。在公募发行情况下，所有合法的社会投资者都可以参加认购。公开发行的股票不一定要求上市，但是上市必须要求公开发行股票。

IPO, Initial Public Offering 首次公开募股，指股份有限公司首次向社会公众公开招股的发行方式。

private placements 私募（非公开发行股），在中国多被称为定向发行。在国际资本市场上，私募（private placements）与公募（public offering）相对应，指发行人或证券承销商通过自行安排将股票、债券等证券产品销售给其熟悉的或联系较多的合格投资者，从而避免证券监管部门审批或备案的一种证券发行方式。它与公开售股、配股（公开发行）等共同构成上市公司发行股票的主要工具。

**9. Long position 多头持仓**

We might suggest a corollary to Keynes' irrationality principle: the shorts can remain short longer than you can continue holding a long position at such a depressed price. (www.fortunechina.com)

参照凯恩斯非理性原则，我们或许可以提出一个推论：在如此低迷的价格下，空头可以继续做空，而不是继续持有多头头寸。

注：Keynes' irrationality principle 凯恩斯非理性原则：资本主义社会里，由于经济前景的动荡不定，人们对未来掌握很少，如果前期实际价格低于本期预期价格，悲观情绪者的预期价格将下降，预期利润率降低，导致投资减少，进而一国的就业与收入水平下降，反之亦然。

shorts 空头，是投资者或股票商认为虽然现时股价较高，但对股市前景看坏，预计股价将会下跌，于是把股票卖出，待股价跌至某一价位时再买进，以获取差额收益（先

卖出后买进、从中赚取差价）的投机方式。相关词汇：sale short 做空

long hedging 多头，期货交易所中投机方式之一。投机者估计证券、商品等有涨价的趋势，先期买进，企图涨价后售出。这种投机方式以先买进为基础，投机者于未售出前手头多有了一笔证券或商品，故称“多头 bulls”，与“空头 bears”相对。

In stock index futures trading, the position held by investors after buying stock index futures contracts is called long positions, referred to as bulls.

在股指期货交易中，投资者在购买股指期货合约后持有的仓位称为多头持仓，简称多头。

注：Share Price Index Futures 股指期货，英文简称 SPIF，股票价格指数期货，指以股价指数为标的物的标准化期货合约。双方约定在未来的某个特定日期按照事先确定的股指大小进行标的指数的买卖，到期后通过现金结算差价来进行交割。股指期货交易与普通商品期货交易基本相同。

**10. Loan syndication　银团贷款**

The San Francisco-based lender earned most of its investment banking fees in the US from capital markets activity and loan syndication. (www.okread.info)

总部在旧金山的富国银行，其在美国本土投行业务佣金大部分来自资本市场活动和银团贷款。

注：富国银行 Wells Fargo，总部设在旧金山，是美国唯一一家获得 AAA 评级的银行，由巴菲特重仓持股。

A syndicated loan is a foreign currency loan or credit business provided by two or more banks to a borrower through a correspondent bank on the basis of the same loan terms, in accordance with the same loan contract, in accordance with the agreed time and proportion.

银团贷款是指由两家及以上银行基于相同贷款条件，依据同一贷款合同，按约定时间和比例，通过代理行向借款人提供本外币贷款或授信业务。

注：credit business 授信业务，指商业银行向非金融机构客户直接提供的资金，或者对客户在有关经济活动中可能产生的赔偿、支付责任做出的保证，包括贷款、贸易融资、票据融资、融资租赁、透支及各项垫款等。

correspondent bank 代理行，指与其他国家建立往来账户，代理对方的一些业务，为对方提供服务的银行。对一家银行来说，代理行实际上不附属于本银行，代理行关系是不同国家银行之间建立的结算关系。

**11. Lockup period　锁定期**

The promise may help to ease market fears of excessive share dumping after the lockup period. (www.chinadaily.com.cn)

这一承诺可能有助于缓解市场对锁定期后过度抛售股票的担忧。

注：相关术语：open an account with the stockbroker 开户；completion of a business transaction 交割；transferring ownership 过户；date declare 宣布日；date of record 股权登记日；date payable 派息日；share interest（dividend）股息；bonus 红利；bear raiders 大量抛空者

A legally binding contract between an lockup underwriter and an insider who makes an initial public listing, providing that such person cannot sell any of the company's shares for a specified period of time.

锁定期是指承销商与首次公开上市的内幕人士之间具有法律约束力的合约，规定在特定时期内，这些人士不可出售任何该公司股票。

注：Initial Public Offering 首次公开募股 vs. Initial Public Listing 首次公司上市：

（1）首次公开发行是股票成功第一阶段：一家企业要上市需要由一家券商进行保荐并通过证监会的审核，经过一系列的路演、询价等程序。

（2）首次公开上市是第二阶段：首次公开发行股票完成后申请到证券交易所（SE）或报价系统挂牌交易的过程。

相关术语：issue stocks 发行股票；subscribe stocks 认购股票

**12. financial repression　金融抑制**

In the years after the Second World War, central banks effectively lost their independence, when the West embarked on financial repression. (www.ftchinese.com)

在二战后几年，当时西方实行金融抑制政策，央行实际上已经丧失独立性。

注：central bank 中央银行，是一个国家居主导地位的金融中心机构，是国家干预和调控国民经济发展的重要工具，负责制定并执行国家货币信用政策，独具货币发行权，实行金融监管。

Financial repression means that the government inhibits the development of the financial system through excessive intervention in financial activities and the financial system, and the lag of the development of the financial system hinders the development of the economy, which results in financial repression and economic backwardness.

金融抑制（financial repression），指政府通过对金融活动和金融体系过多干预抑制金融体系发展，而金融体系发展滞后又阻碍经济发展，从而造成金融抑制和经济落后。

注：金融抑制的手段有压制利率（名义利率限制 nominal interest rate）、实行信贷配给（credit rationing）、高估本币汇率、维持进口数量和增加对低效产业的财政补贴等。

**13. Double top　双顶**

The double top chart pattern is considered to be an indicator of an intermediate- or long-term reversal in price. (Investopedia/Jun.8,2017/DoubleTophttps://www.investopedia.com/terms/d/doubletop.asp#ixzz5C2N9ndv4)

双顶图模式被认为是价格中期或长期逆转指标（指下跌）。

相关术语：advance-decline theory 涨跌理论；bullish 行情看涨；congestion area 震荡区；bearish 行情看跌

Dual Top commonly known as M head Graphics, is when the price in a certain period of time in a row to rise to the height of the meeting to form the price trend of the pattern.

双顶（Double Top）俗称 M 头图形，是当价格在某时段内连续两次上升至相近高度时而形成的价位走势图。

注：双顶是一种常见的顶部反转信号，一旦形成，股价下跌几乎成为定局。因此，一旦股价出现构筑双重顶的势头，投资者及时停损离场是最佳操作策略。

**14. Double bottom　双底**

The double bottom pattern always follows a major or minor down trend in a particular security, and signals the reversal and the beginning of a potential uptrend. (Investopedia/Jun.8, 2016/DoubleBottomhttps://www.investopedia.com/terms/d/doublebottom.asp#ixzz5C2N9ndv4)

双底模式总是遵循特定证券主要或次要下降趋势，并表示反转和潜在上升趋势的开始。

注：分析人士认为，double bottom 形态一旦形成，不用多久就会上扬，此时是投资者入市的很好时机。其他几种价位走势图形有：Triple Top 三重顶；Triple Bottom 三重底；Head and Shoulders Top 头肩型

The rise succeeded in surpassing the highs of the first rally, marking the formation of a double-bottomed form.

这次上涨成功超越第一次反弹时的高点，标志着双底形态形成。

注：A double bottom pattern is a technical analysis charting pattern that describes a change in trend and a momentum reversal from prior leading price action. It describes the drop of a stock or index, a rebound, another drop to the same or similar level as the original drop, and finally another rebound. The double bottom looks like the letter "W".

双底形态是一种技术分析图表形态，描述了之前的主导价格走势所产生的势头反转和趋势变化。它描述了一只股票或指数的下跌、反弹、再次下跌至与原始下跌水平相同或相似，以及最后一次反弹的过程。双底形似字母"W"。

**15. Deleverage　去杠杆**

Deleverage may be a red flag to investors who require growth in their companies. (Investopedia/Jun.8,2016/Deleragehttps://www.investopedia.com/terms/d/deleverage.asp#ixzz5C2N9ndv4)

对于那些要求公司成长的投资者来说，去杠杆化可能是一个警示。

Deleveraging is to append the borrowed currency to the available funds for the investment.

将借入的货币追加到投资的可用资金中。

注：Deleveraging is when a company or individual attempts to decrease its total financial leverage. In other words, it is the reduction of debt.

去杠杆，指公司或个人试图降低其总财务杠杆即减少债务。

leverage ratio 杠杆率，资产与银行资本（bank capital）的比率。

补充内容：

和公司的杠杆不同，期货杠杆是期货采用保证金交易，以 10%的保证金来说，就是 10 倍杠杆。对应期货合约价格波动 2%，体现在保证金上的盈亏上就会放大 10 倍。

**16. Dow Jones Industrial Average 道琼斯工业平均指数**

Holiday shopping is also important to the stock market. That report helped the Dow Jones Industrial Average to close above ten-thousand for the first time in eighteen months. (voa/2013/12/18/www.21voa.com/VOA_Special_English_2003/Economics_Report_1352.html)

假日购物对股票市场也很重要。这份报告使得道琼斯工业平均指数 18 个月以来首次收于 10 000 点以上。

注：stock market 股票市场，是已发行的股票转让（transfer）、买卖和流通的场所，包括交易所市场和场外交易（curb exchange）市场两大类别。由于它是建立在发行市场基础上的，因此又称作二级市场（secondary market)。股票市场比发行市场（一级市场）的结构和交易活动更为复杂，其作用和影响力也更大。

通常所说的道琼斯指数一般指道琼斯四组指数中的第一组。

道琼斯四种股价平均指数分别是：

（1）以 30 家著名的工业公司股票为编制对象的道琼斯工业股价平均指数（Dow Jones Industrial Average, DJIA）；

（2）以 20 家著名的交通运输业公司股票为编制对象的道琼斯运输业股价平均指数（Dow Jones Transportation Average, DJTA）；

（3）以 15 家著名的公用事业公司股票为编制对象的道琼斯公用事业股价平均指数（Dow Jones Utility Average, DJUA）；

（4）以上述三种股价平均指数所涉及的 65 家公司股票为编制对象的道琼斯股价综合平均指数。

The Dow was first compiled in 1884 by Charles Henry Dow, the founder of Dow Jones, an arithmetic average stock price index Charles Henry Dau.

道琼斯指数（Dow Jones Industrial Average）最早是在 1884 年由道琼斯公司创始人查尔斯·亨利·道（Charles Henry Dow 1851—1902 年）开始编制的一种算术平均股价指数。

**17. Dead cat bounce 报复性反弹**

GLIMMER of recovery or a dead-cat bounce? Confidence in economic prospects has picked up slightly among chief financial officers around the world. (*The Economist*/2009/3/11/http://club.topsage.com/thread-1448791-1-1.html)

是复苏迹象还是报复性反弹？世界首席财务官对经济前景的信心略有回升。

The stock market tends to generate retaliatory gains after the collapse of continuity, which is known as "dead cat bounce."

股市往往会在连续性暴跌后产生报复性上涨行情，这种行情被称为“报复性反弹”。

注：Cisco Systems Inc.思科系统公司（NASDAQ：CSCO）的股价曾在 2000 年 3 月达到峰值，为每股 82 美元。而在互联网泡沫破灭之际，在 2001 年 3 月跌至 15.81 美元，并在随后的几年经历了多次报复性反弹（dead cat bounce）。到 2001 年 11 月，该股票恢复到 20.44 美元；到 2002 年 9 月，又跌至 10.48 美元；截至 2016 年 6 月，其股价为每股 28.47 美元，仅为 2000 年技术泡沫时期最高价格的三分之一；到 2019 年，其股价已高达 $ 47.50。

**18. Equity index　股票指数**

The integration of China into the world's financial markets took another step as MSCI, an index provider, decided to include shares of 222 companies listed in Chinese mainland in its widely followed emerging-markets equity index.(*The Economist*/2017/6/5/http://mp.weixin.qq.com/s?__biz=MzA5OTg1MjYzMg%3D%3D&idx=3&mid=2651024046&sn=aa99a8b78b4796a86f2e6b3bdc72a2bd)

随着指数提供商摩根士丹利资本国际（MSCI）决定将在中国内地上市的 222 家公司的股票纳入其广受关注的新兴市场股票指数，中国融入全球金融市场的进程又迈出了一步。

注：纳入的是中国 A 股。MSCI 是全球领先并受人关注最多的各类金融市场指数生成和分析公司之一，其新兴市场指数涉及约 1.5 万亿美元。中国之前已经占据了该指数 26.8%的份额，绝大多数得益于在香港和纽约上市的公司，A 股的完全加入将使这一比率提高到 39%。据《英国金融时报》数据，这将对 A 股产生约 1 800 亿美元的潜在买入。中国上市公司的股票有 A 股、B 股、H 股、N 股和 S 股等。

The stock price index is a relative number of share price statistics compiled to measure and reflect the overall price level of the stock market and its changing trend.

股票价格指数是指为度量和反映股票市场总体价格水平及其变动趋势而编制的股价统计相对数。

**19. Equity　股权**

If the firms do well, they buy back the equity in cash, which goes to the shareholders, with a cut for the fund. (*The Economist*/2013/6/7/http://www.kekenet.com/menu/201306/243323. shtml)

如果公司运作良好，他们就会用现金买回股权给予股东，并分给基金一份利润。

注：share repurchase 股权回购，近几十年来，股权回购　近几十年来，股票回购已超过股息成为向股东返还现金的首选方式。回购部分或全部已发行股票可以是以一种简单的方式来偿还投资者并降低总体资本成本，同时也保存了股票价值。

Equity is a comprehensive right of the shareholders of a limited liability company or a Joint Stock Co., Ltd. to the personal and property rights and interests enjoyed by the company.

股权是有限责任公司或者股份有限公司股东对公司享有人身和财产权益的一种综合性权利。

注：股东资产收益权包括分红权、股权增值权和剩余财产分配权。

SARs（Stock Appreciation Rights）股权增值权，指股东投资公司后，除了可以分得利润，还可能因为公司收益变高，其对应的股权价值增长，比如股票涨价就是股权增值权的一种具体体现。剩余财产分配权是指公司解散时，如果还有剩余财产的情况下，股东有权分得剩余财产。

dividend 股息，指股份公司按股票份额的一定比例支付给股票持有者的收入。股息是股份公司把每股投资应得的收入也就是所得利息分配给股东。股息一般以三种形式存放，主要是现金股息、股票股息和财产股息。

bonus 分红，指股份公司在赢利中每年按股票份额的一定比例支付给投资者的红利，是上市公司对股东的投资回报。分红是将当年的收益在按规定提取法定公积金、公益金等项目后向股东发放，是股东收益的一种方式。

相关术语：year-end bonus 年终分红

**20. Equity kicker 权益**

He also wrote that PEM Group would be paid interest and an "equity kicker" in the deal. (cuyoo.com)

他还写了道保盛丰将从这项交易中获得利息和分享权益。

相关术语：compound interest 复利；simple interest 单利；accrued interest 应计利息

Equity in accounting refers to assets. The interest that belongs to all is called the owner's interest, and the interest belonging to the creditor is called the creditor's interest. Both are always referred to as equity.

在会计学上权益是指资产，属于所有人权益时称为所有者权益，属于债权人权益时称为债权人权益。两者总称为权益。

An equity kicker is a type of equity incentive typically issued in combination with privately placed subordinated or mezzanine debt to improve the return for subordinated debtholders. Equity kickers can have a convertible feature exchangeable for shares or warrants to purchase shares at a set price at some point in the future.

权益是一种股权激励，通常与私人配售的次级债或夹层债结合发行，以提高次级债持有人的回报。股权溢价可转换为股票或权证从而能在未来某个时间以一个固定的价格购买股票。

owner's equity 所有者权益 vs. creditor's equity 债权人权益

所有者权益在企业经营期内可供企业长期、持续地使用，企业不必向投资人返还资本金。而负债须按期返还给债权人。

企业所有者有行使企业经营管理权，或者授权管理人员行使经营管理权的权利。而债权人并没有经营管理权。

企业所有者凭其对企业投入的资本享有税后分配利润的权利。所有者权益是企业分配税后净利润的主要依据。而债权人除按规定取得利息外，无权利分配企业的盈利。

企业的所有者对企业的债务和亏损负有无限责任或有限责任，而债权人与企业的其他债务无关，一般不承担企业的亏损。

**21. Equity market segmentation 股票市场分割现象**

But equity market segmentation has been severe due to systematical and institutional factors. (www.fabiao.net)

但由于体制和制度设计原因，股票市场分割现象十分严重。

注：（1）Equity Market Segmentation 股票市场分割现象十分严重，表现为在同一市场上同时存在 A 股、B 股、H 股，股票的价格差异很大，使得投资者的利益受损，且信息失真，市场约束力弱化，影响股票市场功能的发挥。

（2）A 股、B 股、H 股的区别：

A 股，正式名称是人民币普通股票（RMB ordinary shares）。由我国公司发行，供境内机构、组织或个人（不含台、港、澳）以人民币认购和交易的普通股股票。

B 股，以人民币标明面值，以外币认购和买卖，在境内（上海、深圳）证券交易所上市交易的股票。投资人限于：外国的自然人、法人和其他组织等。

H 股，即注册地在内地，上市地在香港的外资股。

纽约和新加坡上市的股票就分别叫做 N 股和 S 股。

（3）不同股票：

equity share, common stock, ordinary shares 普通股

普通股是指在公司的经营管理、盈利及财产分配上享有普通权利的股份。现在上海和深圳证券交易所进行交易的股票都是普通股。

preference shares 优先股

优先股在利润分红及剩余财产分配的权利方面具有优先的股票，与普通股相对应。

reserved stock 后配股

后配股一般是在普通股分配之后，对剩余利益进行再分配的股票。

junk stock 垃圾股

垃圾股是指经营亏损或违规的公司的股票。

blue chip 蓝筹股

股票市场上，在其所属行业内占有重要支配性地位、业绩优良、成交活跃以及红利优厚的大公司股票称为蓝筹股。

China's stock market has a distinct institutional characteristics of government-driven growth, showing the phenomenon of structural segmentation in the arrangement of ownership structure, trading system and management.

中国股票市场具有明显的政府主导型增长的制度特征，在股权结构安排、交易制度和经营管理等方面呈现出结构性分割现象。股票市场属于资本市场，债券、房地产市场也算资本市场

注：ownership/stock right/shareholding structure 股权结构

trading system 股票交易制度：binding transaction 定期交易，actual purchase 连续交易

**22. Face value　票面价值**

Those speculators who bought Nakheel's debt at half its face value have been vindicated.（*The Economist*/2009/10/29: Dubai's debt mountain/http://club. topsage.com/thread-1475978-1-1.html）

那些以票面价值的一半买入纳希切特债券的投机者已经被证明是正确的。

注：face value 票面价值 vs. book value 账面价值

股票票面价值又称股票票值、票面价格，是股份公司在所发行的股票票面上标明的票面金额，它以元/股为单位，主要功用是确定每股股票在公司股票中所占份额。在我国上海和深圳证券交易所流通的股票面值均为每股 1 元。

股票账面价值又称股票净值或每股净资产，是每股股票所代表的实际资产的价值。

每股账面价值等于公司净资产减去优先股账面价值后除以发行在外的普通股票的股数。

Face value is the amount indicated above the shares issued by the enterprise.

票面价值是指在企业所发行股票上面所标明的金额。

**23. Futures 期货**

This project studies the analysis of fundamental drivers for the prices of crude oil futures. The report first presents a summarization of the crude oil basics, including types, futures trading and modeling approaches. (cs.uic.edu/http://xueshu. baidu. com/s?wd=paperuri)

本项目研究对原油期货价格基本驱动因素的分析。该报告首先概述原油的基本情况，包括类型、期货交易和建模方法。

注：（1）futures 期货 vs. actuals 现货

期货是买卖双方通过签订标准化合约（期货合约），同意按指定的时间、价格与其他条件，交收指定数量的现货，包括金融工具或未来交割销售的实物商品。

现货（actuals）也称实物商品。可供交割的现货是指可在近期或远期基础上换成现金，或先付货然后买方在极短期限内付款的商品的总称。现货是期货的对称。

（2）options 期权 vs. futures 期货

权利和义务不同，期权是单向合约，期货是双向合约。

期权只需卖方缴纳保证金；期货双方都需要缴纳保证金。

（3）futures market 期货市场 vs. stock market 股票市场

空头方面：期货市场不需要拥有现货就可以抛空，只要在合约到期以前买回同额的商品即可成交；股票市场投资人必须向证券公司借入股票才可以抛空。

时间方面：期货契约有其时间性，在契约到期前，必须冲销，否则法律上就得提运实质商品；证券市场没有时间限制。

风险方面：期货市场保证金低，风险大，利润大；证券市场风险小，周转率大约为30%。

（4）全球主要期货交易所

芝加哥商业交易所（CME）近年来先后并购了芝加哥期货交易所（CBOT）、纽约商品交易所（NYMEX）组建成芝加哥商业交易所集团，成为全球霸主。

印度国家证券交易所（NSE）

洲际交易所（ICE）

莫斯科交易所（Moscow Exchange）

欧洲期货交易所（EUREX）

上海期货交易所（SHFE）

纳斯达克（NASDAQ）

大连商品交易所（DCE）

Futures are not mainly goods, but a certain mass products such as cotton, soybeans, oil and other financial assets such as stocks, bonds and other standardized tradable proof.

期货主要不是指货物，而是以棉花、大豆或石油等某种大众产品及股票、债券等金融资产为标的标准化可交易合约。

期货分为两大类，分别是商品期货（commodity futures）和金融期货（financial futures）。

商品期货有金属商品、能源商品、农产品等。

金融期货主要指传统的金融商品或工具，如股指、国债、利率、汇率等。

stock index futures 股指期货，是指以股价指数为标的物的标准化期货合约，目前主要沪深 300、中证 500、上证 50 三大产品。

treasury bond futures 国债期货，是一种高级的金融衍生工具，2013 年 9 月 6 日，国债期货正式在中国金融期货交易所上市交易，目前主要产品有两年期国债、五年期国债、十年期国债。

interest rate futures 利率期货，指以债券类证券为标的物的期货合约，一般可分为短期利率期货和长期利率期货。

currency futures 外汇期货，又称为货币期货，是指以汇率为标的物的期货合约，用来规避汇率风险。它是金融期货中最早出现的品种。

**24. Fundamental analysis　基本分析**

There are two main ways to analyze financial markets—either through fundamental analysis or technical analysis. (*Forbes*: Crude Oil Wants To Slip Below $80 Again, Test $78)

分析金融市场有两种主要方法—通过基本分析或技术分析。

注：（1）technical analysis 技术分析，指以市场行为为研究对象，以判断市场趋势并跟随趋势的周期性变化来进行股票及一切金融衍生物交易决策的方法的总和。技术分析认为市场行为包容消化一切信息、价格波动、历史重演。（2）自股票市场产生以来，人们就开始对股票投资理论进行探索，形成了多种多样的理论成果。实际上，技术分析是 100 多年前蒙昧时期创建的股票投资理论（Stock Investment Theory），是精明的投资者对股价变化进行长期观察并积累经验，逐步归纳总结出来的有关股市波动的若干所谓的“规律”。

The basic analysis (fundamental analysis) is based on the intrinsic value of the enterprise as the main research object, through a detailed analysis of the macroeconomic situation that determines the value of the enterprise and the impact of the stock price, the development prospects of the industry, the operating conditions of the enterprise, etc.

基本分析是以企业内在价值作为主要研究对象，通过对决定企业价值和影响股票价格的宏观经济形势、行业发展前景、企业经营状况等进行详尽分析。

注：（1）intrinsic value 企业的内在价值，指企业自身所具有的价值，又称为非使用价值，是一家企业在其余下的寿命之中可以产生的现金的折现值。内在价值是一个非常重要的概念，它为评估投资和企业的相对吸引力提供了唯一的逻辑手段。（2）相关术语：value in use 使用价值

**25. Frozen account　冻结账户**

Bidders should have a good commercial credit without having been ordered to rectify business, take over, frozen account or bankrupt. (www.dlztb.com)

投标人应具有良好的商业信用，且未被责令整顿业务、接管、冻结账户或破产。

注：commercial credit 商业信誉，简称商誉，指商业主体即商业企业或商人在频繁的商品交换中所形成的顾客对企业或商人的一种信赖关系。

Freezing assets is an asset that an enterprise is not allowed to withdraw or transfer in the bank according to law.

冻结资产是企业依法不得在银行提取或转移的资产。

注：（1）enterprise 企业，指以盈利为目的，运用各种生产要素（土地、劳动力、资本、技术和企业家才能等）向市场提供商品或服务，实行自主经营、自负盈亏、独立核算的法人或其他社会经济组织。分为独资企业、合伙企业和公司三类基本形式。（2）相关术语：sole proprietorship 独资企业；partnership enterprise 合伙企业；company 公司

#### 1.2.1.2 融资手段

**1. Dumping 抛售，倾销**

Here's why I dumped all my shares of Apple. (Business Insider/Apr. 17, 2012,10: 28AM/http://www.businessinsider.com/finance-guru-damodaran-dumped-apple-2012-4)

这是我抛售苹果公司所有股票的原因。

注：dump 倾倒；丢下；猛地放下；（向国外）倾销

In particular, dumping is the sale of surplus goods abroad is lower than the domestic market price.

倾销特指用低于国内市场的价格向国外销售过剩商品。

注：（1）倾销：如果在正常的贸易过程中，一项产品从一国出口到另一国，该产品的出口价格低于在其本国内消费的相同产品的价格，也即以低于其正常价值的价格进入另一国的商业渠道，则该产品将被认为是倾销。（2）相关术语：short-run dumping 短期倾销；intermittent dumping 间歇性倾销；persistent dumping 持续性倾销

**2. Equity carve-out 分拆**

As a strategic decision, the equity carve-out contains compound real options, which enhances the value of itself. (www.dictall.com)

分拆上市作为一项战略决策，股权分拆包含复合实物期权，从而提高了自身的价值。

注：复合期权主要有四种类型：基于某个看涨期权的看涨期权；基于某个看涨期权的看跌期权；基于某个看跌期权的看涨期权；基于某个看跌期权的看跌期权。

Equity carve-out refers to the legal and organizational separation of the operation of a subsidiary from the operation of the parent company by a parent company that distributes its shares in the subsidiary to the shareholders of the existing parent company in a proportional manner.

股权分拆是指母公司将其在子公司的股份按比例分配给现有母公司的股东，将子公司的经营与母公司的经营在法律上和组织上分离。

注：在国际商务中，母公司是指以母国为基地，通过对外直接投资对海外经济实体进行有效控制的总公司。大多数跨国公司的母公司为一个国家的资本所建立，但在少数情况下也可能由两个或更多国家的资本联合建立。

**3. Free-riding　投机**

Ratings would have to be confidential to prevent investors from free-riding on each other. (Forbes: Rethinking Credit Ratings)

评级必须保密，以防止投资者相互投机。

注：confidential 机密的，表示信任的，获信任的

Speculation refers to the trading behavior that uses the spreads in the market to buy and sell profits from them.

投机是指利用市场差价买卖进行买卖从中获得利润的交易行为。

注：free-riding 搭便车，指经济中某个体消费的资源超出他的公允份额，或承担的生产成本少于他应承担的公允份额。

## 1.2.2　亚洲股票市场

**1. Current assets　流动资产**

Current assets in Cambodia's banking and financial institutions had risen to 25.6 billion US dollars by June 2016. (http://www.xinhuanet.com/english/2016-08/23/c_135627583.htm)

截至 2016 年，柬埔寨银行和金融机构流动资产已增至 256 亿美元。

Current asset is any asset which can reasonably be expected to be sold, consumed, or exhausted through the normal operations of a business within the current fiscal year or operating cycle.

流动资产，指在当前会计年度或运营周期内，通过企业的正常运营可以合理预期出售、消耗或耗尽的任何资产。

注：exhaust 使筋疲力尽，耗尽；fiscal year 会计年度，（美）财政年度，亦称预算年度，或预算期，指预算有效的起讫时间。

**2. Last trading day　最后一个交易日**

Stocks in Japan and South Korea ended the last trading day of the year yesterday by notching up annual falls of more than 40 per cent, their worst yearly result since records began. (www.ftchinese.com)

昨日是日本和韩国股市今年最后一个交易日，其年度跌幅均超过 40%，为有史以来最糟糕的结果。

注：（1）notch up 完成，创下，达到；（2）kick it up a notch 升级；（3）step up a notch 加剧

The final cut-off date for the month of settlement allowed for a futures or options contract.

最后一个交易日是期货或期权合约允许交收月份的最后截止日。

**3. Financial trading　金融交易**

India last year banned financial trading in most agricultural commodities but prices continued to rise. (www.ftchinese.com)

印度去年禁止大多数农业商品的金融交易，但是农产品价格继续上涨。

注：农产品（agricultural commodities），包括 mushrooms 香菇，burdock 牛蒡，broccoli 青花菜，carrot 胡萝卜，beans 毛豆，asparagus 芦笋，strawberry 草莓等。

Financial transactions refer to all transactions involving changes in the ownership of financial assets of institutional units, including the generation and liquidation of financial claims and liabilities.

金融交易，指涉及机构单位金融资产所有权变更的所有交易，包括金融债权和负债的产生和清偿。

注：liabilities（法律上对某事物的）责任；义务；负债；债务指企业过去的交易或者事项形成的，预期会导致经济利益流出企业的现时义务。

**4. Flash crash 瞬间暴跌**

An investigation found that a poorly executed algorithmic trade was at the root of the "flash crash". (www.ebigear.com)

一项调查发现，执行不力的算法交易是"瞬间暴跌"的根本原因。

注：algorithmic trade 算法交易：也称为自动交易，黑盒交易，是利用电子平台，输入涉及算法的交易指令，以执行预先设定好的交易策略。算法中包含许多变量，包括时间，价格，交易量，或者在许多情况下，由"机器人"发起指令，而无需人工干预。

Cliff-style plunge, also known as cliff-type decline, cliff-style decline, the standard definition is to jump long yin fall, is a stock term.

瞬间暴跌，也叫断崖式下跌、断崖式下滑，标准定义就是跳空长阴下跌，是一个股票术语。

注：大阴线又称长阴线，是股票交易术语，特征是当天几乎以最高价开盘，最低价收盘。中国股市在实行涨跌停板制度下，最大的日阴线实体可达当日开盘价的 20%，即以涨停板开盘，跌停板收盘。

**5. Price-earnings (P/E) ratio 市盈率**

The IMF reckons that the price-earnings (p/e) ratio of the market's top20 firms is 73.3%, way above anything seen invother emerging markets, now or during the Asian boom that ended almost a decade ago. (http://www.finweb.com/)

据 IMF 估算，股市排名前 20 位公司的股价收益比率为 73.3%，不管是在大约十年前亚洲繁荣时期还是在当今新兴市场中都可谓遥遥领先。

注：emerging markets 新兴市场，是市场经济体制逐步完善、经济发展速度较高、市场发展潜力较大的市场。

The price-earnings ratio (P/E ratio) is the ratio for valuing a company that measures its current share price relative to its per-share earnings.

市盈率（P/E 比率）是衡量公司当前股价相对于每股收益的比率。

注：earnings per share 公司的每股的盈利，而 dividend 是发给股东的股息。一般成熟的公司会在 earnings per share 里拨出作为 dividend。股利收益率是 dividend 除以市价，市盈率是市价除以 earnings per share。

**6. Paired shares　配对股票**

Paired shares (STAY)'s underwent a drastic change in their shares price and moved 0.61% during the last trading session. TSN thestocks news）

配对股票（停留）的价格发生巨大变化，并在最后一个交易日上涨了 0.61%。

注：trading session 交易时段；股市交易时间为每周一到周五上午 9:30-11:30，下午 13:00-15:00。周六、周日及上海证券交易所、深圳证券交易所公告的休市日不交易。

The stock of two separate companies are under the management or supervision of a single corporation. Paired shares are traded as if they are one stock and are sold as one unit.

两家独立公司的股票由一家公司管理或监督。配对股票被当作一只股票进行交易，并作为一个单位出售。

注：（1）supervision 监督，管理；（2）financial supervision 金融监管；（3）词义辨析：supervision vs oversight：supervision 不仅仅是单纯的监督，还含有督导的意思，oversight 有纵观全局监督的含义。

## 1.2.3　欧洲股票市场

### 1.2.3.1　证券及证券市场相关概念

**1. Bad loan　不良贷款**

Spain's bad loan ratio had peaked in December 2013, when it had reached 13.61 percent with a total of 197.04 billion euros of bad debt as a result of the country's financial crisis, real estate sector debt and high unemployment. (http://www.xinhuanet.com/english/2017-09/26/c_136640516.htm)

西班牙的不良贷款率在 2013 年 12 月达到顶峰，当时由于该国的金融危机、房地产部门的债务和高失业率，西班牙的不良贷款率达到 13.61%，总计 1970.4 亿欧元。

相关术语：immovable property=real estate=real property 不动产；compensation for demolition 拆迁补偿费；removal expense 拆迁费用；urban housing provident fund 城镇住房公积金；low-cost housing 低价住房；property ownership certificate 房产证

Bad loan is one that have passed the payment period and cannot be recovered after reminder, it may become bad debts.

不良贷款是指逾期不能收回的贷款，有可能成为坏账。

注：（1）bad debts= irrecoverable debts 坏账；（2）allowance for uncollectible accounts= provision for bad debt= bad debt reserves 坏账准备，指企业的应收款项（含应收账款、其他应收款等）计提的，是备抵账户。

**2. Lender of last resort　最后贷款者**

The ECB must also act as a lender of last resort and provide liquidity to support Eastern European currencies. (www.ftchinese.com)

欧洲央行也必须作为最后贷款者，提供流动性以支撑东欧货币。

注：The European Central Bank (ECB) 欧洲中央银行（欧洲央行），总部位于德国法

兰克福，成立于 1998 年 6 月 1 日，负责欧盟欧元区的金融及货币政策，是为适应欧元发行流通而设立。

The lender of last resort, the last lender, also known as the final lender, is the Lender (usually the central bank) responsible for meeting the demand for funds in the event of a crisis or liquidity shortage.

最后贷款者即最后贷款人，又称最终贷款人，即在出现危机或者流动资金短缺时负责满足资金需求的贷款人（通常是中央银行）。

注：（1）liquidity 流动资产比率=流动资产/流动负债 × 100%；（2）相关术语：liquidity surplus 流动性过剩；liquidity risk 流动性风险；liquidity level 流动性水平；liquidity management 流动性管理；liquidation 清算

**3. Long-term liabilities　长期债务**

Such investors have long coveted the accompanying inflation-linked investment returns, which match their long-term liabilities.

长期以来，这些投资者一直渴望获得与通胀挂钩的投资回报，这与他们的长期负债持平。

注：通胀挂钩债券（inflation-indexed bond）是香港政府发行为期三年的零售债券。通胀挂钩债券每手面值 10 000 港元，每半年派息一次，其息率分浮息及定息，浮息与香港最近六个月的通胀率（以综合消费物价指数为准）挂钩，定息为一厘，最终派息率以高者为准。

Long-term debt is a loan or financial liability that requires interest, a period of more than 1 years.

长期债务是指需要支付利息、年期超过一年的贷款或金融负债。

注：（1）short-term debt 短期债务/短期负债，指需要在短时间内（一般为一年以内）清偿的各种债务；（2）相关术语：foreign debt 外债；debt restructuring 债务重组；debt financing　债务融资；debt chain 债务链

**4. Liquidation　清算**

Without rarely granted special approval, registered capital may not be withdrawn prior to liquidation. (www.ftchinese.com)

在未得到政府特别批准（这种情况相当罕见）的情况下，注册资本不能在清算之前撤出。

注：（1）registered capital 注册资本/法定资本，是公司制企业章程中规定的全体股东或发起人认缴的出资额或认购的股本总额，并在公司登记机关依法登记；（2）相关术语：minimum registered capital 最低注册资本；crime of misstating the registered capital 虚报注册资本；validation of registered capital 验证注册资本

Liquidation is a procedure, including calculation, verification, etc., to put an end to the existing legal relationship, to dispose of its surplus property and to destroy it.

清算是结束现有法律关系、处理和销毁剩余财产的程序，包括计算、核实等。

注：狭义上，清算与结算（settlement）不同，清算不涉及债权债务的转移，而结算

是债权债务关系的转移。广义上，清算是结算的推广。

**5. Liquidity　流动性**

Hedge funds have cut their borrowings sharply, reducing the amount of liquidity being provided to the financial system. (www.ftchinese.com)

对冲基金大幅削减借款规模，从而减少了提供给金融体系的流动性。

注：（1）financial system 金融系统，是有关资金的流动、集中和分配的一个体系。它是由连接资金盈余者和资金短缺者的一系列金融中介机构和金融市场共同构成的一个有机体。（2）相关术语：financial intermediary 金融中介；financial market 金融市场；financial institution 金融机构；financial instrument 金融票据

Liquidity refers to the ability of banks to pay their debts due.

流动性是指银行到期偿付债务的能力。

注：hedge fund 对冲基金，也称避险基金或套期保值基金，是指金融期货和金融期权等金融衍生工具与金融工具结合后形成的以营利为目的的金融基金。

**6. Credit line　信贷额度**

Austria's Oberbank will grant one billion euro of credit line for financing investment projects in Iran. (http://www.xinhuanet.com/english/2017-06/12/c_136359728.htm)

奥地利中央银行将为伊朗的投资项目提供 10 亿欧元的信贷额度。

注：奥地利第一储蓄银行（Erste Group Bank）；奥地利中央合作银行（Raiffeisen Zentralbank）；奥地利联合信贷银行（UniCredit Bank Austria AG）；巴瓦克银行（BAWAG P.S.K.）

A credit line is credit source extended to a government, business or individual by a bank or other financial institution.

信贷额度是银行或其他金融机构向政府、企业或个人提供的信贷来源。

注：extend 推迟（原承诺的债务偿还期）；延期归还（贷款、抵押借款等），宽限

**7. Derivatives　衍生品**

The London Stock Exchange and Deutsche Börse formally announced their intention to merge, which would boost their businesses in derivatives, clearing houses and other financial services. (economist/2016/3/19/http://blog.sina.com.cn/s/ blog_44ced7990102w0rf.html)

伦敦证券交易所和德意志证交所正式宣布合并意向，这将推动它们在衍生品、清算所和其他金融服务领域的业务。

注：（1）clearing house 清算所，指金融机构交换支付指令或者其他金融证券的一个中心地点或者一种中央处理机制。金融机构根据清算所的章程和办法在指定的时间交换要结算的凭证。在一些情况中，清算所作为清算系统的重要订约方，或承担清算系统的金融及风险管理的责任。

（2）merge：合并，并购

（3）相关术语：acquisition 收购；takeover 接管；leveraged buyout 融资收购

Derivative products are a financial instrument, generally manifested as an agreement between two subjects whose price is determined by the price of other basic products.

衍生产品是一种金融工具，一般表现为两个主体之间的协议，其价格由其他基本产品的价格决定。

注：（1）financial instrument 金融工具，亦称“信用工具”或“交易工具”，指资金缺乏部门向资金盈余部门借入资金或发行者向投资者筹措资金时，依一定格式做成的书面文件，上面确定债务人的义务和权利，是具有法律效力的契约。

（2）常见种类：security 证券类（bills，commercial paper）；其他现金类（存款、定存）；交易所交易的金融衍生品类（short term interest rate futures）；柜台金融衍生品类（forward rate agreement，interest rate swap）

**8. Hover 徘徊**

Demand for German 10-year bunds is so heavy that their yields hover above 1% and the government bonds of once crisis-wracked Spain are near 200-year lows. (www.kekenet.com)

市场对德国 10 年期国债的需求是如此之大，以至于其收益率徘徊在 1% 以上，而一度遭受危机重创的西班牙国债收益率则接近 200 年低点。

注：（1）government bonds 政府债券，是政府为筹集资金而向出资者出具并承诺在一定时期支付利息并偿还本金的债务凭证，包括国家债券即中央政府债券、地方政府债券和政府担保债券等。美国联邦政府发行的各种债券，包括国库券（treasury bill）、国库本票（treasury notes）和联邦政府公债（treasury bonds）。

（2）yield 收益；yield curve 收益曲线；direct hours yield 直接工时产出率

If something such as price, value, or score hovers around a particular level, it stays at more or less that level and does not change much.

如果价格、价值或分数等东西徘徊在某一特定水平上，它或多或少会停留在这个水平上，变化不大。

**9. Holder of record 注册股票持股人**

Holder of Record Owner of stock recorded in a company's books as of a certain date.

在某一日期登记在公司账目上的注册股票持股人（也是股东）。

The holder of a stock has ownership of part of the capital of a joint-stock company.

股票持有者对股份公司部分资本拥有所有权。

注：joint-stock company=stock corporation 股份有限公司，指公司资本为股份所组成的，股东以其认购的股份为限对公司承担责任的企业法人。

**10. Holding the market 托盘**

Holding the market is hard to pull off these days because any one person would have to have very deep pockets to make a significant impact on a security's price. (www.investopedia.com)

如今托盘很难成功，因为任何一个人都必须拥有非常雄厚的资金才能对证券价格产生重大影响。

注：（1）security 证券，是多种经济权益凭证的统称，也指专门的种类产品，是用来证明券票持有人享有某种特定权益的法律凭证，主要包括资本证券、货币证券和商品证券等。（2）相关术语：security-based swap agreement 以证券为基础的互换协议；stock index futures 股票指数期货；financial futures 金融期货；financial derivative instrument 金融衍

生工具；spot market 现货市场

A pallet is a medium that transforms static goods into dynamic goods, a cargo platform, and a platform for activity, or removable ground.

托盘是将静态货物转换为动态货物、货物平台和活动平台或可移动地面的媒介。

**11. Growth stocks 成长型股票**

The 40m GLG Technology Equity fund (formerly SG Technology) favours small-cap growth stocks. (www.ftchinese.com)

掌管 4 000 万英镑的 GLG 科技股本基金（GLG Technology Equity，以前名为 SG 科技基金）青睐小盘成长型股票。

注：GLG 科技股本基金，基金经理：休·格里夫斯（Hugh Grieves）。

Growth stocks usually refer to stocks with fast growth rate and great potential for future development, and their price-to-earnings ratio and market net rate are usually higher.

成长型股票通常指收益增速快、未来发展潜力大的股票，其市盈率、市净率通常较高。

注：Price to Earnings ratio，“股价收益比率” 或 “市价盈利比率（简称市盈率）”，市盈率是最常用来评估股价水平是否合理的指标之一。

**12. Investment grade 投资级别**

Their investment grade ratings of many subprime mortgage-backed securities were a primary cause of the current financial crisis. (www.ftchinese.com)

对许多次级抵押贷款证券化的投资评级是当前金融危机的主要原因。

注：（1）mortgage backed securities 抵押贷款证券化（2）相关术语：financial turmoil 金融危机；Freddie Mac 房地美（联邦住房抵押公司）；Fannie Mae 房利美（联邦国民抵押贷款协会）；Office of Federal Housing Enterprise Oversight（OFHEO）美国联邦住房企业监督办公室；Government Sponsored Enterprises（GSE）政府发起企业；credit crunch 信贷紧缩；foreclosure 止赎权，丧失赎取权；lagged effect 滞后影响；swap lines 互惠额度

Standard & amp; Poor’s has rated bonds at four level 12: AAA, AA, A, BBB, BB, B, CCC, CC, C, DDD, DD, D.

标准普尔公司把债券评级（investment grade）定为四等 12 级，即：AAA、AA、A、BBB、BB、B、CCC、CC、C、DDD、DD、D。

注：（1）标准普尔（Standard & Poor’s）由亨利·瓦纳姆·普尔先生（Mr Henry Varnum Poor）于 1860 年创立，是普尔出版公司和标准统计公司 1941 年合并而成的世界权威金融分析机构，总部位于美国纽约市。

（2）纳斯达克（NASDAQ，National Association of Securities Dealers Automated Quotations）是美国全国证券交易商协会于 1968 年着手创建的自动报价系统名称的英文简称，特点是收集和发布场外交易非上市股票的证券商报价。

**13. Overheating 过热经济**

Worried about overheating, her government is trimming 50 billion real from this year’s budget. (*The Economist*: Measuring Brazil’s Economy)

担心经济过热，本年度政府财政预算缩减500亿雷亚尔。

注：（1）budget guideline ratio 财政预算案准则；budget proposal 财政预算案建议；budget revenue 财政预算案收入；budgetary criterion 开支预算准则；budgetary deficit 财政预算赤字

（2）Real 雷亚尔，是1993年巴西发行的新货币，之前的货币克鲁塞罗雷亚尔只流通了一年半的时间。雷亚尔在1994年7月1日正式采用，1雷亚尔等于2 750克鲁塞罗雷亚尔，之后又有所回升。

An overheating economy is one that has too much domestic demand for its own good. To grow, an economy needs investment. Growth achieved is a function of savings and the capital output ratio.

过热的经济是一个为了自身利益而拥有过多内需的经济。为了增长，一个经济体需要投资。实现的增长是储蓄和资本产出比率的函数。一个经济体要想增长就需要投资，所实现的增长是储蓄和资本产出比率函数。

注：增量资本产出率（the Incremental Capital Output Ratio）是衡量投资效率的主要经济指标，反映增加经济产出所需要的投资增量，即投资与经济产出增量之比。增加产出所需的投资越低越好，亦即增量资本产出率越小，投资效率则越高。

**14. Offering date　发行日期**

Under a look-back provision, the stock price is keyed to the offering date or the purchase date, whichever is lower. (WSJ: Getting Going: Buying Stock From the Boss)

在一项回购条款中，股票会以发行日价格或购买日价格更低者来定价。

The offering date is the date on which a new set of stocks or bonds will first be sold to the public.

发行日期是一套新股票或债券首次向公众出售的日期。

注：（1）issue shares 发行股票，指符合条件的发行人以筹资或实施股利分配为目的，按照法定程序，向投资者或原股东发行股份或无偿提供股份的行为；（2）go public 股票上市，指已经发行的股票经证券交易所批准后在交易所公开挂牌交易的法律行为。股票上市是连接股票发行和股票交易的“桥梁”；（3）相关术语：share price 股价；earnings per share 每股收益

**15. Near money　近钱**

It is weakly overseen without an independent audit and thus is able to intermediate the transformation of bad, liquid assets into money (and near money) and then back again into valuable financial assets, all done secretly and anonymously. (*Forbes*: Is the Federal Reserve Using Money-Laundering Techniques to Cleanse Banks' Balance Sheets?)

在没有独立审计的情况下达不到有效监管，因此能够将不良资产、非流动性资产转化为货币（或者准货币），然后再转变为有价的金融资产，这些都是在秘密和匿名的情况下进行的。

Near money is a kind of liquid asset that can be converted to cash very quickly, such as a bank deposit or bill of exchange.

近钱是一种流动性资产，可以很快转换为现金，如银行存款或汇票。

注：（1）审计是由国家授权或接受委托的专职机构和人员，依照国家法规、审计准则和会计理论，运用专门的方法对被审计单位的财政、财务收支、经营管理活动及其相关资料的真实性、正确性、合规性、合法性、效益性进行审查和监督，评价经济责任，鉴证经济业务，以此维护财经法纪、改善经营管理、提高经济效益的一项独立性的经济监督活动。（2）四大会计师事务所：世界上著名的四个会计师事务所有普华永道（PwC）、德勤（DTT）、毕马威（KPMG）和安永（E&Y）；（3）相关术语：internal audit 内部审计；external audit 外部审计；audit report 审计报告；audit committee 审计委员会

**16. Overvalue　高估**

These recurring extremes of yield establish undervalue and overvalue price levels. (*Forbes*)

这些反复出现的极端情况导致价格被低估和价格被高估。

To overvalue something, often a cost or rate of exchange means to place its value at too high a level compared with other similar things.

高估某种事物，往往是指与其他类似事物相比，它价值过高。

注：（1）资产评估是对资产在某一时点的价值进行估计的行为或过程。具体地讲，资产评估是指符合国家有关规定的专门机构和人员，依据国家的有关规定，为了特定的评估目的，遵循适用的评估原则，选择适当的价值类型，按照法定的评估程序，运用科学的评估方法，对特定资产的价值进行估算的过程。（2）相关术语：overvalue assets 资产评估过高

**17. Open interest　未平仓利率**

He said the current net-long position is roughly 43% of the total open interest in futures. (*Forbes*: FOCUS: Speculators Add To Bullish Gold, PGM Positions For Seventh Straight Week—CFTC Data)

他表示，目前净多头头寸约占期货交易未结算权益的 43%。

Open interest is the number of “open” contracts of derivatives like futures and options that have a time limit after which they expire. Open interest in a derivative is the sum of all contracts that have not expired, been exercised or physically delivered.

未平仓利率是指期货和期权等衍生品“未平仓”合约的数量，这些合约在到期后有时限。衍生品未平仓权益是所有尚未到期、未行使或未实际交付合同总和。

注：（1）derivatives 金融衍生品，指一种金融合约，其价值取决于一种或多种基础资产或指数，合约的种类包括远期、期货、掉期（互换）和期权。金融衍生品还包括具有远期、期货、掉期（互换）和期权中一种或多种特征的混合金融工具。（2）相关术语：futures 期货；options 期权

**18. Management fee　管理费**

Ackman charges his investors an annual management fee of 1.5% and, importantly, a 20% performance fee. (*Forbes*: The Most Serious Accusation Carl Icahn Made Against Bill Ackman In Their CNBC Deathmatch)

阿克曼向投资者收取每年 1.5%的经办费，重要的是，还同时收取 20%的绩效费。

In the investment advisory industry, a management fee is a periodic payment that is paid by investors in; a pooled investment fund to the fund's investment adviser for investment and portfolio management services. Usually, the fee is calculated as a percentage of assets under management.

在投资咨询行业，管理费是由集合投资基金的投资者定期支付给基金投资顾问，用于投资和投资组合管理服务的费用。通常情况下，费用是按所管理资产的百分比计算。

注：（1）投资银行是与商业银行相对应的一类金融机构，主要从事证券发行、承销、交易、企业重组、兼并与收购、投资分析、风险投资、项目融资等业务的非银行金融机构，是资本市场上的主要金融中介。投资银行是美国和欧洲大陆的称谓，英国称之为商人银行，在日本则指证券公司。（2）知名投行：Goldman Sachs；Morgan Stanley；J.P. Morgan；UBS Investment Bank；The Blackstone Group；（3）相关术语：application fee 申请费；professional fee 专业费；sponsorship fee 赞助费；registration fee 注册费；primary market 一级市场

#### 1.2.3.2 融资手段

**1. Bear raid 抛空**

The practice of bear raid has its roots in the 17th-century Dutch Republic (https://en.wikipedia.org/wiki/Bear_raid)

大量抛空做法起源于 17 世纪荷兰共和国。

A bear raid is a type of stock market strategy, where a trader (or group of traders) attempts to force down the price of a stock to cover a short position.

抛空是一种股市策略，交易者（或交易者群体）试图压低股票价格以弥补空头头寸。

注：short position 证券或外汇交易中未补抛空差额、欠缺的头寸。

空头是空头头寸的简称，指因预料价格会下跌而卖出或使卖出大于买入的头寸。头寸即款项、资金之意。

**2. Dilution 摊薄**

To see the effect of stock disposals and dilution, consider eight founder-run firms: Alibaba, Alphabet, Amazon, Facebook, Netflix, Tencent, Tesla and SoftBank. (*The Economist*/ 2017/12/19/ https://item.btime.com/m_2s1cmatho1e)

要看股权出售和摊薄影响，我们来看八家创始人运行的公司：阿里巴巴、Alphabet、亚马逊、Facebook、Netflix、腾讯、特斯拉和软银。

As a result of the issuance of new shares and so on, the spread of profits to each share accordingly reduced.

由于增发新股等原因使得分摊到每一股的利润相应减少。

注：stock disposals 股票出售

**3. New issue 新股发行**

Italy raised 5bn euros from a new issue of bonds on Thursday, but had to pay an interest rate of 6.087% to borrow the money for one year. (BBC: Eurozone's growth has stalled, says EU)

意大利周四发行新债券筹集了 50 亿欧元，但必须为一年期债券支付 6.087%的利率。

New issue is an issue of shares being offered to the public for the first time.

新股发行是首次向公众发行股票。

注：interest rate 利率

补充：基准利率

基准利率是金融市场上具有普遍参照作用的利率，其他利率水平或金融资产价格均可根据这一基准利率水平来确定。

基准利率是利率市场化的重要前提之一，在利率市场化条件下，融资者衡量融资成本，投资者计算投资收益，以及管理层对宏观经济的调控，客观上都要求有一个普遍公认的基准利率水平作参考。所以，从某种意义上讲，基准利率是利率市场化机制形成的核心。

# Chapter 2

# Terminologies of Bond
# （债券篇）

## 2.1 Government Bond（政府债券）

导读

政府债券，政府为筹集资金而向出资者出具的并承诺在一定时期内支付利息并偿还本金的债务凭证，具体包括国家债券即中央政府债券、地方政府债券和政府担保债券等。

本章主要介绍政府债券概念；其次引出现代政府债券分类，简要介绍现代政府债券不同分类依据和主要种类；最后强调对政府债券管理的手段。

### 2.1.1 政府债券相关概念

**1. Bond credit rating 债券信用评级**

Therefore, our bond credit rating will still be a hard and important work for us. (http://www.doc88.com/p-1436988873410.html)

所以，我国在企业债券评级方面的研究仍然任重道远。

In investment, the bond credit rating represents the credit worthiness of corporate or government bonds. It is not to be confused with an individual's credit score. The ratings are published by credit rating agencies and used by investment professionals to assess the likelihood the debt will be repaid.

在投资方面，债券信用评级代表企业或政府债券的信用价值。这不能与个人信用评分相混淆。评级由信用评级机构公布，并由投资专业人员用于评估偿还债务的可能性。

注：credit worthiness 信贷可靠性；信誉；信贷价值

**2. Bond vigilante 债券民团**

The notion that the "bond vigilantes" can impose some restraint on fiscal and monetary policy is a bad idea that should die, writes Caroline Baum. (www.marketwatch.com)

卡罗琳鲍姆写道，"债券保民"可以对财政和货币政策施加一些约束的想法是一个应该消亡的坏主意。

A bond vigilante is a bond market investor who protests monetary or fiscal policies he considers inflationary by selling bonds, thus increasing yields. In the bond market, prices move inversely to yields. When investors perceive that inflation risk or credit risk is rising they demand higher yields to compensate for the added risk.

bond vigilante 债券治安维持者，指通过出售债券来抗议通货膨胀的货币或财政政策。债券民团是抗议通过出售债券来通胀货币或财政政策，从而提高收益率的债券市场投资者。在债券市场上，价格与收益率成反比。当投资者意识到通胀风险或信用风险正在上升时，他们会要求更高的收益率来补偿增加的风险。

注：fiscal and monetary policy 财政金融政策

财政政策是国家制定的指导财政分配活动和处理各种财政分配关系的基本准则。它是客观存在的财政分配关系在国家意志上的反映。在现代市场经济条件下，财政政策又是国家干预经济，实现宏观经济目标的工具。

货币政策也就是金融政策，指中央银行为实现其特定的经济目标而采用的各种控制和调节货币供应量和信用量的方针、政策和措施的总称。货币政策的实质是国家对货币的供应根据不同时期的经济发展情况而采取“紧”“松”或“适度”等不同的政策趋向。

**3. Discount rate　贴现率**

The State Bank of Pakistan (SBP) has raised its key discount rate by 25 basis points to 6 percent, the first increase in four years. (*Global Times*/2018/1/27)

巴基斯坦国家银行（SBP）将其关键贴现率提高 25 个基点至 6%，这是四年来首次增长。

The discount rate is the interest rate charged to commercial banks and other depository institutions on loans they receive from their regional Federal Reserve Bank's lending facility—the discount window.

贴现率是指对商业银行和其他存款机构从其区域联邦储备银行的贷款设施（贴现窗口）获得的贷款收取的利率。

注：Federal Reserve Bank 联邦储备银行

美国联邦储备银行是美国联邦储备系统所属的私营区域性金融机构。根据 1913 年《联邦储备法》规定，全美国划分为 12 个联邦储备区，每区设立一家联邦储备银行并以所在城市命名。它是执行货币政策的机构。美国的中央银行在组织形式上与其他西方国家的中央银行有所不同，它并不是一家单独的银行，而是由联邦储备委员会、12 个地区的联邦储备银行、联邦公开市场委员会和联邦咨询委员会等组成的执行中央银行职能的金融系统。其职能是发行货币、代理国库、调节货币流通、监督私人银行和管理金融机构、组织票据清算等。

**4. Carry trade　套利交易**

If done in enough volume, this so-called carry trade would then push down the value of the affected currencies. (*Global Times*/2018/3/25)

如果交易量足够大，这种所谓的套利交易将会压低受影响货币的价值。

The carry trade is a strategy in which traders borrow a currency that has a low interest rate and use the funds to buy a different currency that is paying a higher interest rate.

套利交易是一种策略，交易员借入一种利率较低的货币，然后利用这些资金购买另一种利率较高的货币。

注：carry trade 套利交易；套息交易；利差交易；息差交易

套利交易又叫套期图利，指利用不同国家或地区短期利率的差异，将资金由利率较低的国家或地区转移到利率较高的国家或地区进行投放，以从中获得利息差额收益的一种外汇交易。期货市场的套利交易是指同时买进和卖出两张不同种类的期货合约。

**5. Coupon rate　息票利率**

With a term of three years and coupon rate of 5.0 percent, the yuan-denominated bond issue attracted orders of as much as 9.22 billion yuan, or more than six times the offer. (*Global Times*/2018/3/20)

以人民币计价的债券发行期限为三年，票面利率为 5.0%，吸引了高达 92.2 亿元人民币订单，是该发行价格的六倍多。

A coupon rate is the yield paid by a fixed-income security; a fixed-income security's coupon rate is simply just the annual coupon payments paid by the issuer relative to the bond's face or par value.

息票利率是由固定收益证券支付的收益率；固定收益证券息票利率仅仅是发行人相对于债券面值或票面价值支付的年利率。

注：par value 面值；票面价值；平价

票面价值是企业发行的股票上面所标明的金额，有的企业发行的股票上有票面价值，也有企业发行的股票不标明票面价值。票面价值的作用之一是可以确定每一股份对企业占有的一定比例。假如一个企业发行在外的总票面价值是 100 万元，每一股的票面价值是 100 元，则每一股表示拥有企业万分之一的所有权。票面价值的大小，除了从企业所需资产和投资前景来考虑外，有时还受税收问题的影响。如果按票面价值的大小征税，企业就会减小其票面价值，进入较低的征税等级。当股票在市场上发行时，其价值往往与票面价值不一致，往往高于或低于票面价值。

**6. Credit risk　信用风险**

Local governments are encouraged to set up credit risk compensation funds to increase support for small and medium-sized enterprises and start-ups. (*Global Times*/ 2017-7-28)

鼓励地方政府建立信用风险补偿基金加大对中小企业和创业企业的支持力度。

A credit risk is the risk of default on a debt that may arise from a borrower failing to make required payments.

信用风险是由于借款人未能支付所需款项而产生的债务违约风险。

注：small and medium-sized enterprises 中小型企业

中小型企业是相对于微型企业而言的生产规模更大的企业，即劳动力、劳动手段、劳动对象和产品生产集中程度高的企业。中小型企业在国民经济中起着十分重要的作用，是国家建设的重点，它符合生产社会化和科学技术进步的客观要求，在投资和生产经营上能带来明显的经济效益。中小型企业是实施大众创业、万众创新的重要载体，在增加就业、促进经济增长、科技创新与社会和谐稳定等方面具有不可替代的作用，对国民经济和社会发展具有重要的战略意义。

**7. Dead loan　死贷**

However, its dead loan reserve fund reached 13.54 billion yuan, compared with 9.57 billion yuan from a year earlier. (*Global Times*/ 2009-10-21)

然而，其呆账（死贷）储备基金达到 135.4 亿元，而去年同期为 95.7 亿元。

Dead loan refers to the loan that is overdue (including 3 years) for collection and loan management, which is confirmed as bad account loss, not approved, and ready to be cancelled.

死贷指已逾期（含 3 年）进行收款和贷款管理，确认为坏账损失，未经批准准备注销的贷款。

注：collection 托收

托收指在进出口贸易中，出口方开具以进口方为付款人的汇票，委托出口方银行通过其在进口方的分行或代理行向进口方收取货款的一种结算方式，包括 D/P（付款交单），与 D/A（承兑交单）。

**8. Effective interest method　有效利率**

Borrowings are recognised initially at fair value, net of transaction costs incurred, and subsequently stated at amortised cost using the effective interest method. (http://www.youdao.com/w/eng/Effective%20interest%20method/#keyfrom=dict2.index)

借款按公允价值扣除交易成本后的金额进行初始计量，并采用实际利率法按摊余成本进行后续计量。

The effective interest rate is a method used by a bond buyer to account for accretion of a bond discount as the balance is moved into interest income, and to amortize a bond premium into an interest expense. The effective interest rate uses the book value, or the carrying amount of the bond, to calculate interest income, and the difference between interest income and the bond's interest payment is the amount of the accretion or amortization posted each year.

有效利率是债券买家在余额转入和利息收入时，用来核算债券贴现增加的一种方法，并将债券溢价摊销成利息支出。实际利率使用账面价值或债券账面金额来计算利息收入，利息收入与债券利息支付之间的差额是每年入账的增值或摊销金额。

注：fair value 公允价值；公平价格

公允价值亦称公允市价、公允价格，指熟悉市场情况的买卖双方在公平交易和自愿的条件下所确定的价格，或无关联的双方在公平交易的条件下买卖一项资产或者清偿一项负债的成交价格。在公允价值计量下，资产和负债按照公平交易中熟悉市场情况的交易双方自愿进行资产交换或者债务清偿的金额计量。购买企业等合并业务需要运用公允价值的信息。在实务中，通常由资产评估机构对被并企业的净资产进行评估。

**9. Effective rate　债务收益率**

So with income tax at 45% and surtax at 52.5%, the effective rate was 147.5%. https://www.forbes.com/sites/robertwood/2012/09/29/best-french-exports-bread-brie-fashion-and-taxes/#3b3d6a045a7f)

所得税税率为 45%，附加税税率为 52.5%，有效税率为 147.5%。

The yield rate on bonds based on the purchase price is a more accurate measure of bond investment returns than simple coupon payments. It is calculated using price appreciation capital gain and bond yield.

与简单息票支付相比，根据购买价格计算的债务收益率更能准确衡量债券投资回报，以及计算使用价格升值资本收益和债券收益。

注：surtax 附加税

附加税是“正税”的对称。随正税加征的税。中华人民共和国成立之前，附加税名目繁多，仅国民党时期的盐税就有中央附加、地方附加、外债附加、建设专款等，附加税额课重往往超过正税的几倍乃至二十余倍。中华人民共和国成立后，国民党的种种附加税被废除，仅保留了少量的地方附加，属于预算外收入，用于地方公益事业，如农业税附加、外国企业所得税附加等，附加比例都比较低。

**10. Arirang Bond 阿里郎债券**

This study contrasts the development of the Republic of Korea's market for won-denominated foreign bonds (Arirang) with similar markets in the Asia-Pacific region. (https://academic.oup.com/wbro/article-abstract/22/2/165/1714103)

这项研究对比了以韩元计价的外国债券（阿里郎）为主导的韩国市场与亚太地区类似市场的发展情况。

注：（1）foreign bond 外国债券，指外国借款人，即政府、私人公司或国际金融机构所在国与发行市场所在国具有不同的国籍并以发行市场所在国的货币为面值货币发行的债券。（2）相关术语：domestic bond 本国债券

An Arirang bond is a won-denominated bond issued by a foreign entity in Korea. The name refers to “Arirang”, a Korean folk song.

阿里郎债券是由韩国一家外国实体发行的以韩元结算的债券。阿里郎债券的名字指是韩国民歌《阿里郎》。

注：（1）foreign entity 外国实体；（2）其他由外国实体发行的外国债券：Yankee bond 扬基债券；Panda bond 熊猫债券；Uridashi bonds 武士债券；Kimchi bond 泡菜债券

**11. Bond 债券**

Sure, the stock and bond holders will get wiped out, but the infrastructure will still be there. (http://dict.youdao.com/search?q=bond&keyfrom=hao360)

当然，股票和债券持有人将被消灭，但基础设施仍将存在。

注：bond holders 债券持有人，指在采用发行债券的方式筹措长期资金时的资金贷方

Bond, in finance, is a type of debt security.

债券在金融领域是一种债务担保。

注：（1）debt security 债务担保；（2）债务担保指的是一种债务工具，包括 government bond 政府债券；municipal bond 市政公债；corporate bond 公司债券；certificate of deposit 存单

**12. Build America Bonds (BABs)　构建美国债券**

Build America Bonds are a new form of taxable bonds to be issued by municipalities in lieu of tax-free municipal bonds. (https://www.bestcashcow.com/bonds/buildamerica)

BABs 债券是一种新型应税债券，由市政当局发行，以代替免税市政债券。

注：municipal bond 市政债券，又称市政证券，是指由州、地区、所属地及行政区划所发行的债券。

Build America Bonds are taxable municipal bonds that carry special tax credits and federal subsidies for either the bond issuer or the bondholder. Build America Bonds were created under Section 1531 of Title I of Division B of the American Recovery and Reinvestment Act that US President Barack Obama signed into law on February 17, 2009. The program expired December 31, 2010.

BABs 债券是应纳税市政债券，为债券发行人或债券持有人提供特殊税收抵免和联邦补贴。构建美国债券是根据《美国复苏和再投资法案》B 部分第一篇第 1531 条创建的，美国总统奥巴马于 2009 年 2 月 17 日签署成为法律。该计划于 2010 年 12 月 31 日到期。

注：（1）bond issuer 债权发行人；（2）债券发行人包括 firms 公司；government 政府；supranational entities 超国家实体；regions and municipalities 区域和自治市；special projects and SPVs 特殊项目及目的机构/公司

**13. Collateralized Loan Obligations (CLOs)　抵押贷款债券**

The central bank launched a pilot program in 2005 to allow banks to package loans into bond-like securities known as collateralized loan obligations (CLO). (*China Daily*/2013-11-01)

2005 年，中国央行启动一项试点计划，允许银行将贷款打包成债券型证券，即所谓抵押贷款债券（CLO）。

注：bond-like security 债券性证券，指由发行企业或政府机构发行并规定还本付息的时间与金额的债务凭证，包括国库券、金融债券和其他公司债券，表明企业拥有证券发行单位的债权。

Collateralized loan obligations (CLOs) are a form of securitization where payments from multiple middle-sized and large business loans are pooled together and passed on to different classes of owners in various tranches. A CLO is a type of collateralized debt obligation.

抵押贷款债券是将多个中型和大型商业贷款汇集在一起证券化后，然后卖给不同级别的所有者。抵押贷款债券是担保债务凭证的一种。

注：（1）securitization 证券化；（2）其他证券化的形式：住房抵押贷款证券（Mortgage-Backed Security, MBS）

**14. Dual currency bond　双币种债券**

China Agricultural Bank is also selling dual-currency bonds denominated in the yuan and the dollar in London. (*Global Times*/2015-10-13)

中国农业银行也在伦敦出售以人民币和美元计价的双币种债券。

注：（1）China Agricultural Bank 中国农业银行，是中国金融体系的重要组成部分，

提供各种公司银行和零售银行的产品和服务，同时开展金融市场业务及资产管理业务。（2）相关术语：central bank 中央银行

A dual-currency-bond is a debt instrument in which the coupon and principal payments are made in two different currencies.

双重货币债券是一种债务工具，其中息票和本金支付以两种不同货币支付。

注：（1）debt instrument 债务工具；（2）常用的债务工具：US treasuries 美国国库证券；municipal bonds 市政债券；corporate bonds 公司债券；alternative structured debt security products 可选择的结构性债务证券

**15. Book-entry discount treasury bonds 账面贴现国债**

The Ministry of Finance said Friday it would issue two batches of short-term book-entry discount treasury bonds next week. (*Global Times*/ 2010-6-12)

财政部周五表示，将于下周发行两批短期账面贴现国债。

注：（1）the Ministry of Finance 中华人民共和国财政部，是中华人民共和国国务院组成部门，其前身为 1949 年 10 月 1 日成立的中央人民政府财政部。（2）a batch of 一批，后可接 cakes, letters, recruits, bonds。

**16. Exchequer bonds 国库债券**

Following the debate, MPs approved a motion allowing the exchequer to raise funds to cover any costs resulting from the successful passage of the Sports Grounds Safety Authority Bill, a private member's bill which has secured government support. (BBC/November/15/2010/http://news.bbc.co.uk/democracylive/hi/house_of_commons/newsid_9181000/9181617.stm)

辩论结束后，议员们批准了一项议案，允许财政部筹集资金，以支付成功通过《运动场安全委员会法案》所产生的任何费用。该法案是一项获得政府支持的私人议员法案。

注：the Sports Grounds Safety Authority Bill《运动场安全委员会法案》，此法案赋予足球执照颁发机构更多权力，并给予对其进行修改名称的权力。

A British government interest-bearing bond constituting part of the unfunded debt.

英国政府计息债券（exchequer bonds）构成无准备金债务的一部分。

注：（1）unfunded debt 无准备金债务；（2）funded debt 准备金债务；（3）准备金债务包括 bonds with maturity dates of more than a year 到期日超过一年的债券；convertible bond 可转换公司债券；long-term notes payables 长期应付票据；debenture 信用债券

**17. Extendible bond 可扩展债券**

To tap financial markets, borrowers have a broad range of instruments from which to choose. Puttable and extendible bonds are one example. (World Bank/Oct. 2003 /http://www.imf.org/external/pubs/ft/wp/2003/wp03201.pdf)

为挖掘金融市场，借款人可以选择各种各样工具。上市债券和可延伸债券就是其中一例。

注：puttable bond 上市债券，指经由政府管理部门批准，在证券交易所内买卖的债券，也叫挂牌券。

Extendible bond (or extendable bond) is a complex bond with the embedded option for a holder to extend its maturity date by a number of years. Such a bond may be considered as a portfolio of a straight, shorter-term bond and a call option to buy a longer-term bond. This relatively rare type of bond works to the advantage of investors during periods of declining interest rates.

可扩展债券是一种复杂债券，持有人可以将其到期日延长数年。债券持有人可选择将债券到期日延长至数年。这种债券可以被视为一种由短期直接债券和购买长期债券的看涨期权组成的投资组合。这种相对罕见的债券在利率下降期间对投资者有利。

注：（1）short-term bond 短期债券；（2）通常，根据基金投资组合中债券的平均到期期限，可分为三个部分：① short-term (less than 5 years) 短期（不超过五年）；② intermediate-term (5 to 10 years) 中期（五到十年）；③ long-term (more than 10 years) 长期（超过十年）

**18. Government bond　政府债券**

Previously, the lower 30-year US government bond rates were used to calculate lump-sum pension values. (*Forbes*/December 8, 2009/https://www.forbes.com/2009/12/08/lump-sum-pension-retirement-annuity-personal-finance-bernicke_print.html/)

此前，较低的 30 年期美国国债利率用于计算养老金的总价值。

注：pension 养老金，也称退休金、退休费，是一种最主要的社会养老保险待遇，主要用于保障职工退休后的基本生活需要。

A government bond or "sovereign bond"' is a bond issued by a national government, generally with a promise to pay periodic interest payments and to repay the face value on the maturity date.

政府债券或“主权债券”是国家政府发行的债券，一般承诺定期支付利息，并在到期日偿还面值。

注：（1）periodic interest 定期利息；（2）periodic interest rate 定期利率；（3）利率分类：the nominal interest rate 名义利率；the effective interest rate 实际利率

**19. Government debt　政府债务**

However, the report warned that developed economies still needed to watch levels of government debt. (BBC/ April 12, 2011/ https://www.bbc.co.uk/news/business-13050017/)

然而，据报告警示，发达国家仍需要注意政府债务的杠杆率。

注：（1）developed economy 发达国家；（2）developing economy 发展中国家

Government debt (also known as public debt and national debt) is the debt owed by a central government.

政府债务（也称为公共债务和国债）是中央政府所欠债务。

注：（1）public debt 公共债务；（2）美国国债包括 ① treasury bills 国库券；② notes 票据；③ bonds 债券

**20. Guaranteed bond　担保债券**

Mainly a firmer commitment to pay its debts, probably through some form of mutually guaranteed bond, and much tighter coordination of budgetary and broader economic policy. (*Wall Street Journal*/ September 23,2011/ https://cn.wsj.com/GB/20110923/ecb100451.asp/)

主要是更加坚定地承诺偿还债务，具体办法可能是设立某种形式共同担保债券，或是在财政政策和总体经济政策方面大大加强协作。

注：（1）budgetary policy 财政政策，是国家制定的指导财政分配活动和处理各种财政分配关系的基本准则。它是客观存在的财政分配关系在国家意志上的反映。（2）cooperation vs. coordination: cooperation 合作，被描述为共同合作或实施符合标准的行为，以实现共同目标。合作是自愿的活动，这个过程是自然发生的，交流是大家心照不宣的；coordination 协调，对各种管理要素的系统安排，以确保顺利运作。协调是管理过程的一部分，交流是公开的。

A guaranteed bond is a debt security that offers a secondary guarantee that interest and principal payments will be made by a third party, should the issuer default due to reasons such as insolvency or bankruptcy.

担保债券是一种债务担保，提供一种二级担保，即如果发行人因资不抵债或破产等原因违约，利息和本金将由第三方支付。

注：（1）principal payment 本金；（2）可以在多种情况下支付本金：partial amounts of the amount due 本金可以是应付款项的部分金额；the full amount of the loan 本金可以是贷款的全部金额

**21. Gross debt　总债务**

That Gross Debt would cross 100% of GDP, equal to our entire economy, in 2020. (*Forbes*/April 19, 2013/https://www.forbes.com/sites/peterferrara/2013/04/19/president- obamas-predictable-budget-more-spending-more-tax-increases/)

总债务将在 2020 年达到国内生产总值的 100%，相当于我们整个经济体。

注：Gross Domestic Product 国内生产总值，是指按市场价格计算的一个国家或地区所有常驻单位在一定时期内生产活动的最终成果，常被公认为衡量国家经济状况的最佳指标。

Gross debt is the general amount of debt a government has.

总债务是政府拥有一般债务的数额。

注：2018 年中国政府债券为 180 711 亿元。

**22. Government borrowing　政府借贷**

Change will come slowly at first, meaning high levels of government borrowing will continue. (*Forbes*/ August 30,2012/ https://www.forbes.com/sites/rickferri/2012/08/30/the- next-10-years/)

改革一开始会很慢，意味着政府借贷还会继续维持较高数额。

注：（1）相关术语：government debt 政府债务；（2）政府借贷分为：internal debt (owed to lenders within the country) 内部债务；external debt (owed to foreign lenders) 外部债务

Government borrowing is money that the government borrows to spend on public services.

政府借贷是政府借入的公共服务资金。

注：（1）public service 公共服务；（2）公共服务主要包括：electricity 电；education 教育；emergency services 紧急服务；environmental protection 环境保护；health care 医疗；military 军事；public transportation 公共交通

**23. Guaranteed debt　担保债务**

This includes debt guaranteed by the federal government, like money market funds and bank CDs, and the obligations of government agencies like Ginnie Mae, Freddie Mac and Fannie Mae mortgage debt. (*Forbes*/July 25, 2011/ http://www.forbes.com/sites/kenrapoza/2011/07/25/is-us-debt-downgrade-inevitable/2/)

这包括联邦政府担保的债务，如货币市场基金和银行存单，以及诸如美国政府国民抵押协会，联邦住房贷款抵押公司和联邦全国抵押协会抵押债务等政府机构债务。

注：（1）money market funds 货币市场基金，指投资于货币市场短期有价证券的一种投资基金。该基金资产主要投资于国库券、商业票据、银行定期存单、银行承兑汇票、政府短期债券、企业债券等短期有价证券。（2）guarantee vs. warranty: ① guarantee 通常承诺退款，类似质保，而 warranty 通常只负责修理，类似保修；② guarantee 通常没有时限，与质量有关，如 lifetime guarantee（寿命保证），而 warranty 一般注明 12 个月或 24 个月等，并且可以延期；③ guarantee 可以用于口头也可用于书面，往往来自制造商，而 warranty 用于书面上，往往来自销售商。

**24. Good debt　良好债务**

Mortgage debt is good debt, so long as the interest payments are tax deductible. (*Forbes*/June 24, 2011/https://www.forbes.com/forbes/welcome/?toURL=https://www.forbes.com/sites/investor/2011/06/24/in-hard-times-mortgage-debt-can-set-you free/&refURL=http://dict.youdao.com/w/good%20debt/&referrer=http://dict.youdao.com/w/good%20debt/)

只要利息可以免税，抵押贷款债务就是良好债务。

注：interest payments 利息支出，指临时借款的利息支出。在以收付实现制作为记账基础的前提条件下，所谓支出应以实际支付为标准，即资金流出，标志着现金、银行存款的减少。

Good debt is debt that can help you generate income and increases you net worth. It takes money to make money.

良好债务可以帮助你创造收入和增加净资产。赚钱需要钱。

注：（1）net worth 净值；（2）net worth=assets–liablities 企业估值等于总资产减总负债

**25. Going rate　现行利率**

In such a market, anyone can borrow or lend as much as they want at the going rate of interest. (*The Economist*/http://www.economist.com/node/4424648/email?sort=1/)

在这样市场中，任何人都可以按照现行利率任意借贷。

注：interest 利率，指一定时期内利息额与借贷资金额即本金的比率。利率是决定企业资金成本高低的主要因素，同时也是企业筹资、投资的决定性因素，对金融环境的研

究必须注意利率现状及其变动趋势。

Going rate is the established interest rate based on prevalent market.

现行利率是基于大众市场的既定利率。

注：the established interest rate 既定利率

**26. General fund 普通基金**

It is part of the Treasury Department's general fund and has been since the Johnson administration. (*Forbes*/September 17, 2008/https://www.forbes.com/2008/09/17/banking-rtc-treasury- biz- beltway-cx_lm_0918rtc_print.htm/)

自约翰逊政府以来，它一直是财政部普通基金的一部分。

注：（1）Johnson administration 约翰逊政府，美国第36任总统。继任后，约翰逊提出有关人权、减税、反穷困和资源保护的立法，得以批准。（2）administration vs. government：前者偏重于"行政当局"，即政府中最为明显的一个组成部分，是行动中的政府，它代表政府中行政的、实施的、最显著的一边；后者偏重于完整意义上的"政府"。

A general fund is a financial term referring to a nonprofit entity's financial pool of resources. This term traditionally refers to a fund used by a government or university, because for-profit businesses use a general ledger to monitor finances.

普通基金是一个金融术语，指非营利实体的金融资源池。这一术语传统上指的是政府或大学使用的基金，因为营利性企业使用总分类账来监控财务状况。

注：（1）general ledger 总分类账；（2）general journal（普通）日记账；（3）日记账可包括：sales journal 销售日记账；cash receipts journal 现金收入日记账；purchases journal 采购日记账；cash disbursements journal 现金支出日记账

**27. High interest rate 高利率**

Ohio begins a deal today that could help some homeowners get out of high interest rate mortgages. (NPR/April 2, 2007/https://www.npr.org/templates/story/story.php?storyId=9277330/)

俄亥俄州今天开始一项可以帮助一些房主摆脱高利率抵押贷款的交易。

注：mortgage 抵押，指抵押人和债权人以书面形式订立约定，不转移抵押财产的占有，将该财产作为债权的担保。当债务人不履行债务时，债权人有权依法以该财产折价或者以拍卖、变卖该财产的价款优先受偿。

An interest rate is the rate at which interest is paid by borrowers (debtors) for the use of money that they borrow from lenders (creditors).

利率是借款人（债务人）使用从贷款人（债权人）处借入的资金支付利息的利率。

注：（1）borrower/debtor 债务人；（2）lender/creditor 债权人

**28. Bond issuance 债券发行**

Corporate bond issuance in emerging market currencies has surged to record levels this year, deepening the local sources of capital for companies. (FTchinese/Apr 26,2017/http://www.ftchinese.com/story/001072320)

今年，以新兴市场货币发行的公司债券已飙升并创下纪录，加深了公司在当地的资本来源。

注：（1）emerging market 新兴市场，是市场经济体制逐步完善、经济发展速度较高、市场发展潜力较大的市场。具有低投资，高成长、高回报以及反经济周期的特点；市场规模普遍偏小；且投机者和追涨杀跌的投资者占多数。（2）词义辨析 currency vs. money：currency 指流通中的货币，是全部流通的货币的总称；money 是钱的通称，范围较 currency 更广，且具有财富、资产等更宽泛的含义。（3）相关术语：developed market 发达市场，是市场体系发育完备，市场手段现代化，能够充分发挥市场机制作用的市场。发达市场是一个相对的范畴。比如，城市市场相对于农村市场为发达市场。

Bond issuance is a debt instrument issued by government agencies or corporations to raise money. The issuer must pay a fixed amount each year until the certificate of debt reaches its predetermined maturity date.

债券发行是政府机构或公司为筹集资金而发行的债务工具。发行人必须每年支付固定金额，直到债务凭证达到预定到期日。

注：（1）debt instrument 债务工具，是金融工具中会形成债权债务的一类工具，如各种债券、银行对企业的信贷、商业票据等，属于固定收益证券。其持有者的要求权是获得固定的支付，它具有具体的支付条款，如期限、利息、息票率等。

（2）债务工具与权益工具的区别：① 债务工具是金融工具中会形成债权债务的一类工具；如各种债券、持有至到期投资、可供出售金融资产（债券）等都是债务工具；② 权益工具是金融工具中形成股权的一类工具；一般就是指股权投资、长期股权投资、交易性股票、可供出售股票等。

**29. Matured bonds　到期债券**

For example, JP Morgan (JPM) or Bank of America (BAC) took in Spanish bonds as collateral that MF Global had just purchased and made a loan that matured concurrently with the bond maturity date. (*Forbes*/Aug27, 2012/https://www.forbes.com/sites/richardfinger/2012/08/27/mr-jon-corzine-criminal-or-just-plain-old-fashioned-stupid/#132ac1961141)

例如，摩根大通（JPM）或美国银行（BAC）吸收了西班牙债券作为 MF Global 刚购买的抵押品，并发放了与债券到期日同时到期的贷款。

注：collateral 抵押品，又称“担保品”，指银行发放贷款时作为抵押的实物，主要有土地、房屋、有价证券和商品等。作为贷款的抵押品，一般应具备下列条件：价值比较稳定，市场价格波动较小；易售性较强，有广大市场，可以随时变卖；易于保管，不易变质损失；进行鉴定所需要的技术不是很复杂。

The maturity of a bond is determined by factors such as the turnover period of the issuer's use of funds, the habit of the market, the trend of the interest rate, the reputation level of the issuer and the demand for the investment by the holder.

债券到期日是由发行人使用资金周转期、市场习惯、利率趋势、发行人声誉水平和持有人投资需求等因素决定的。

注：（1）turnover period 周转期；（2）相关术语：inventory turnover period 存货周转期，指企业从取得存货开始，至消耗、销售为止所经历的天数，周转天数越少，说明存

货变现的速度越快；cash turnover period 现金周转期，指从购买存货支付现金到收回现金这一期间的长度。

**30. Interest bond 利息债券**

That means contributions to 401(k)s and other retirement plans, as well as itemized deductions for charitable giving, mortgage interest and state and local taxes would be hit by the 28% limit and municipal bond interest would only be exempt at the 28% rate. (*Forbes*/Apr10,2013/https://www.forbes.com/sites/janetnovack/2013/04/10/obama-budget-aims-to-raise-580-billion-in-new-taxes-from-old-ideas-targeting-rich/#29d692644228)

这意味着对 401（k）计划和其他退休计划的供款，以及慈善捐赠、抵押贷款利息、州和地方税的逐项扣除额将受到 28%的限制，市政债券利息将仅以 28%的利率豁免。

注：（1）hit：达到某个时间点、状态或水准；

（2）词义辨析 rate vs. ration：rate 强调部分与整体的关系，ration 强调两件相似事物的比例；

（3）相关术语：tax-exempt income 免税收入；tax-exempt interest 免税利息；tax-exempt items 免税项目

Interest bond mainly refers to Treasury bonds, local government bonds, policy related financial bonds and central bank bills. As the bond interest rate fluctuate with the market interest rate, the floating rate bond form can avoid any significant difference between the actual rate of return and the market rate of return, which makes the cost of the issuer and the income of the investor consistent with the trend of the market change.

利息债券主要指国债、地方政府债券、政策性金融债券和央行票据。由于债券利率随市场利率波动，浮动利率债券形式可以避免实际收益率与市场收益率之间的任何显著差异，这使得发行人的成本和投资者的收入与市场变化趋势一致。

注：（1）floating rate bond 浮动利率债券，指发行时规定债券利率随市场利率定期浮动的债券，也就是说，债券利率在偿还期内可以进行变动和调整。浮动利率债券往往是中长期债券。

（2）fixed rate bond 固定利率债券，又称“普通债券”，是“浮动利率债券”的对称，其利率在发行时就被固定。这种债券通常在票面上印制有固定利息息票和到期日，发行人每半年或一年支付一次利息。在市场利率变动不大时比较通行，但当市场利率不稳定甚至急剧变动时，其发行受到极大限制。

**31. Joint and several liabilities 连带责任**

It is unclear why in China's present civil procedure law there is a compulsory requirement that parties with joint and several liabilities or claims thereof be united in a single lawsuit. (www.dictall.com)

目前尚不清楚为什么在现行的中国民事诉讼法中，强制要求承担连带责任或其索赔的多个当事方合并在一个诉讼中。

注：（1）joint action 共同诉讼，指当事人一方或双方为两人以上的诉讼。在某些纠纷中，当事人一方或双方均为两人以上，形成诉讼时，原告或被告一方或双方均是多数，

这就形成了一种特殊的诉讼形态——共同诉讼。其意义在于简化诉讼程序，避免法院在同一事件处理上作出矛盾的判决。

（2）词义辨析 liabilities vs. debt：liabilities 的复数形式时具有“债务”的意思，具有法律上的意义；debt 作可数名词时指具体所欠的财物，也可指抽象的“负债的状况”或所欠的“人情”，这种情况下是不可数名词。

Joint and several liabilities is the liability of more than one person for which each person is liable to pay back the entire amount of a debt or damages.

连带责任是指债权人可就两个以上债务人所欠的债务同时对所有债务人提起诉讼，也可单独就其中某一债务人提起而要求其归还所有其他人所欠债务，一旦归还，其他债务人也就免去自己的债务。

相关术语：joint liability 共同责任/共同负债，指两个或两个以上债务人共同对第三人的负债，或在侵权案件中两个或两个以上的侵权人对被侵权人应负的责任，债务人或责任人在诉讼中有权要求其共同债务人或共同责任人作为本诉的共同被告，且要求他们共同偿还债务或赔偿损失。

**32. Income mortgage bonds　收入抵押债券**

The majority of these investments are in fixed income securities like government and corporate bonds and the remainder in equity securities, mortgage loans, policy loans and other investment securities. (*Forbes*/Dec7,2010/https://www.forbes.com/sites/greatspeculations/2010/12/07/metlife-eyes-50-per-share-if-investment-returns-pick-up/#5430351670e3)

这些投资大部分是固定收益证券，如政府债券和公司债券，其余是股票证券、抵押贷款、政策性贷款和其他投资证券。

注：remainder 继受权，指在英美物权法体系中，若受让人或继受人能够在不动产自然到期时成为所有人，且该不动产处于同一条约下，那么就可以获得其远期收益。

An income mortgage bond is a bond secured by a mortgage or pool of mortgages. These bonds are typically backed by real estate holdings and real property such as equipment. In a default situation, mortgage bondholders have a claim to the underlying property and could sell it off to compensate for the default.

收入抵押债券是由抵押贷款或抵押贷款池担保的债券。这些债券通常得到房地产持有量和设备等不动产的担保。在违约情况下，抵押债券持有人对相关财产享有债权，并可以出售其抵押财产以补偿违约。

注：mortgage pool 抵押贷款池，指信托基金以抵押品形式所持有的一系列抵押贷款，从而提高抵押贷款证券的安全性。

## 2.1.2　政府债券管理

**1. Interest rate policy　利率政策**

The European Central Bank plans to revamp its system for guiding interest rate policy to take better account of credit and money supply data, as well as threats posed by asset price bubbles. (http://www.ftchinese.com/story/001028590?archive)

欧洲央行（ECB）计划改革其利率政策指导机制，以更好地考虑信贷和货币供应数据，以及资产价格泡沫带来的威胁。

注：（1）bubble 经济泡沫，是指一系列资产（尤其是虚拟资本）价格膨胀，即在一个连续过程中大幅度上涨，使其市场价格远远超过了它实际代表的价值，形成虚假繁荣和含有过多“泡沫”的经济总量。产生经济泡沫的两个主要原因是：投机成为一种潮流，在它的推动下，资产价格持续上升；资产具有过度的、异常的评价收益。这种过高的评价收益使资产的市场价格远远脱离了它实际代表的价值即经济的真实基础。

（2）相关术语：economic crisis 经济危机；economic turmoil 经济动荡 hyperinflation 恶性通胀

Interest rate policy refers to the central bank's policies and measures to control and regulate market interest rates to influence the supply and demand of social funds. It is an important means for the central bank to indirectly control the credit scale.

利率政策是指央行控制和调节市场利率以影响社会资金供求的政策和措施。它是央行间接控制信贷规模的重要手段。

注：（1）credit 信贷，指以偿还和付息为条件的价值运动形式。通常包括银行存款、贷款等信用活动，狭义上仅指银行贷款，广义上同“信用”通用。信贷是社会主义国家用有偿方式动员和分配资金的重要形式，是发展经济的有力杠杆。

（2）相关术语：bank credit/bank loan 银行信贷；standby credit 备用信贷；terms of credit 信贷条款；restriction of credit 信贷管制；credit funds 信贷资金；credit squeeze 收紧信贷

**2. Joint financing　共同融资**

Recently, I have read a book called *The Technological and Social Significance of Joint Financing*.

最近我读了一本书，书名叫《论联合资助的科技与社会意义》。

注：（1）social significance，有时也可以被认为是 social benefit 社会效益，指最大限度地利用有限的资源满足社会上人们日益增长的物质文化需求。人的行动自由只能在必要的公共利益范围内才得以限制。往往在一段比较长的时间后才能发挥出来。广义的社会效益是相对于经济效益而言的，包括政治效益、思想文化效益、生态环境效益等。狭义的社会效益，亦与经济效益相对称，还与政治效益、生态环境效益等相并列。（2）相关术语：political efficacy 政治效益

Joint financing is a form of investment activities in different regions, different departments,different ownership of legal organizations or natural persons jointly funded by certain agreements or articles of association.

联合融资是指在不同地区、不同部门、不同所有权的法律组织或自然人之间通过某些协议或章程共同出资进行的投资活动。

注：（1）investment activities 投资活动；（2）相关术语：long-term investments 长期投资；securities 证券投资；property 资产投资；equipment 设备投资；cash flow 现金流

**3. SEC (Federal Securities and Exchange Commission)　美国证券交易委员会**

Critics say the SEC has been dragging its feet on tighter rules on short-selling. (*Forbes*: Curbing Short-Selling Abuse)

批评人士称，美国证券交易委员会一直在拖延执行更严格的卖空交易规定。

注：（1）short-selling 卖空，指卖出并未拥有或借入的证券。是股票期货市场常见的一种操作方式，操作为预期股票期货市场会有下跌趋势，操作者将手中筹码按市价卖出，等股票期货下跌之后再买入，以赚取中间差价。

（2）相关术语：

① short 空头，又称放空、做空、买空卖空，是多头的相反，指投资人在手中不持有证券的情况下，向券商借入证券以卖出。放空的部位须于当日内回补，否则收盘后无法交割，交付买方其买入之证券，即构成违约交割。

② short hedge：卖出套期保值，又称“空头套期保值”，是为了防止现货价格在交割时下跌的风险而先在期货市场卖出与现货数量相当的合约所进行的交易方式。持有空头头寸，来为交易者将要在现货市场上卖出的现货从而进行保值。因此，卖出套期保值又称为“卖空保值”或“卖期保值”。

The US Securities and Exchange Commission (SEC) is an independent agency of the United States federal government.

美国证券交易委员会（SEC）（证交会）是美国联邦政府的一个独立机构。

注：（1）agency 代理，指代理人在代理权限内，以被代理人的名义实施民事法律行为，由此产生的民事权利、民事义务由被代理人享有和承担。

（2）相关术语：

① sole agency 独家代理，指委托人给予代理商在一定地区和一定期限内享有代销指定货物的专营权。

② general agency 总代理，指代理商在指定地区不仅享有独家代理的权利还代表委托人进行全面业务活动，甚至包括非商业性质的活动。

## 2.2　Financial Bond（金融债券）

**导读**

本节主要介绍金融债券概念；其次引出现代金融债券分类，简要介绍现代金融债券各种分类的依据和主要种类。

金融债券是指银行及其他金融机构所发行的债券。金融债券期限一般为3～5年，其利率略高于同期定期存款利率水平。金融债券由于其发行者为金融机构，因此资信等级相对较高，多为信用债券。

### 2.2.1　金融债券相关概念

**1. Isolation of risk　风险隔离**

Finally, the assets reorganization theory, the isolation of risk theory and the credit theory of asset securitization are studied, it produces and develops the foreshadow research for the follow-up chapter. (dict.cnki.net)

最后是对资产证券化资产重组原理、资产证券化风险隔离理论、资产证券化信用理论进行研究，最后，对资产证券化的资产重组理论、风险隔离理论和信用理论进行了研究，为后续章节的研究产生和发展做了铺垫。

注：（1）asset 资产，指因过去的交易或事项形成的、由企业拥有或控制的、预期会给企业带来经济利益的资源。（2）相关术语：① current assets：流动资产，指预计在一个正常营业周期内或一个会计年度内变现、出售或耗用的资产、现金及现金等价物。如库存现金、银行存款、交易性金融资产、应收及预付款、存货等。② non-current assets：非流动资产，指流动资产以外的资产，主要包括长期股权投资、固定资产、无形资产、长期待摊费用、在建工程、工程物资、研发支出等。（3）词义辨析：asset vs. property，二者都可以作为“资产、财产”理解，asset 主要侧重于可以动用的资源，property 主要侧重于对财产的所有权和支配权。

The isolation of risk refers to the separation or duplication of risk units, so that any risk accident does not lead to all property damage or loss.

风险隔离是指风险单位分离或重复，因此任何风险事故都不会导致所有财产的损坏或损失。

注：（1）property 财产，指拥有的金钱、物资、房屋、土地等物质财富：国家财产、私人财产，具有金钱价值、并受到法律保护的权利的总称。大体上，财产有三种，即动产、不动产和知识财产（即知识产权）。

（2）相关术语：movable property 动产，指能脱离原有位置而存在的资产；immovable property 不动产，指依照其物理性质不能移动或者移动将严重损害其经济价值的有体物；intellectual property 知识财产，指具有商业价值的知识或信息。

**2. Bond valuation　债权评估**

The purpose of this calculator is to provide calculations and details for bond valuation problems. (https://www.calculator.com/calcs/bondcalc.html)

该计算的目的是为债券评估问题提供计算和细节。

注：business calculation 业务核算，指单位在开展自身业务活动时应当履行的各种手续，以及由此而产生的各种原始记录；wage calculation 工资结算，指根据员工的基本工资信息和绩效考核信息，以及奖金、补助等，对员工应付工资、代扣款项和实发工资的计算；economic calculation 经济核算，指为提高企业生产经营成果而进行的多项经济活动及方法，是社会主义的一个客观经济范畴。它以获得最佳经济效益为目标，促进企业改善生产经营。运用会计核算、统计核算和业务核算等手段，对生产经营过程中活劳动和物资消耗以及取得的成果，用价值形式进行记录、计算、对比和分析，借以发掘增产节约的潜力和途径。

Bond valuation is the determination of the fair price of a bond. As with any security or capital investment, the theoretical fair value of a bond is the present value of the stream of cash flows it is expected to generate.

债券估值是确定债券的公允价格。与任何证券或资本投资一样，债券的理论公允价值是其预期产生的现金流的现值。

注：（1）fair price 公平价格，指某一特定时间内由要约收购者所支付的最高价，有时会要求该价格必须超过目标公司会计收益或账面价值所决定的水平。

（2）词义辨析：bond vs. debenture，均指债券，debenture 指无担保债券，或称信用债券；bond 指有担保债券

**3. Barclays Capital Aggregate Bond Index　巴克莱美国综合债券指数**

The Bloomberg Barclays US Aggregate Bond Index is a broad-based flagship benchmark that measures the investment grade, US dollar-denominated, fixed-rate taxable bond market. (https://www.bloomberg.com/quote/LBUSTRUU:IND)

巴克莱美国综合债券指数是一个基础广泛的旗舰基准，用于衡量投资级、美元计价、固定利率应税债券市场。

注：fixed interest rate 固定利率，指在整个借贷期限内，利率不随物价或其他因素的变化而调整的利率。

The Barclays Capital Aggregate Bond Index, which used to be called the Lehman Aggregate Bond Index, is a broad base index, maintained by Barclays Capital, which took over the index business of the now defunct Lehman Brothers, and is often used to represent investment grade bonds being traded in United States.

巴克莱资本综合债券指数曾被称为雷曼综合债券指数（Leclays），是由巴克莱资本（Barclays Capital）维持的一个广泛的基准指数，该公司接管现已倒闭的雷曼兄弟（Lehmanbrothers）指数业务，经常被用于代表在美交易的投资等级债券。

注：（1）investment grade bonds 投资级债券，标准普尔公司把债券的评级定为四等 12 级：AAA、AA、A、BBB、BB、B、CCC、CC、C、DDD、DD、D，BB 级和 BB 以上的是投资级债券，其债券质量相对较高。

（2）相关术语：speculative grade bond 投机级债券，BB 后面的是投机级债券，投机程度依此递增，这类债券面临大量不确定因素。

**4. Bond underwriter　债券承销商**

In acting as an intermediary between a bond issuer and a bond buyer, the investment banker serves as an underwriter for the bonds. (http://news.morningstar.com/classroom2/course.asp?docId=5458&page=3)

作为债券发行人和债券买方之间的中介人，投资银行家担任债券承销商。

注：（1）bond issuer 债券发行人，指为筹措资金而发行债券、股票等证券的政府及其机构、金融机构、公司和企业。

（2）相关术语：bond issuance 债券发行，指发行人以借贷资金为目的，依照法律规定的程序向投资人要约发行代表一定债权和兑付条件的债券的法律行为，债券发行是证券发行的重要形式之一。

A bond underwriter acts as a middleman, purchasing these securities from the bond issuer at a discount and then reselling the bonds to potential investors. Profits thus depend on the difference between the initial purchase price and the resell price of the bond. This margin is called the underwriting spread.

债券承销商充当中间人，以折扣价从债券发行人手中购买这些证券，然后将债券转卖给潜在投资者。因此，利润取决于债券初始购买价格和转售价格之间的差额。此保证金称为承销价差。

注：（1）underwriting spread 承销价差，承销商收取公开发行价格与向发行公司支付的金额之间的差额。

（2）相关术语：horizontal spread 水平价差，投资者同时买入及卖出两种同类型、行使价格相同但到期日不同的期权；credit spread 信贷息差，指卖出溢价高的期权及买入同一相关证券但溢价低的期权的期权投资策略。

**5. Basis points　基点**

In the bond market, the smallest measure used for quoting yields is a basis point. Each percentage point of yield in bonds equals 100 basis points. Basis points also are used for interest rates. (financial-dictionary.thefreedictionary.com/point, +basis)

在债券市场上，用于报价收益率的最小指标是基点。债券收益率的每一个百分点等于 100 个基点。基点也用于利率。

注：yield 收益率，指投资的收益率，一般以年度百分比表达，根据当时市场价格、面值、息票利率以及距离到期日时间计算。对公司而言，收益率指净利润占使用的平均资本的百分比。

Basis point (BPS) refers to a common unit of measure for interest rates and other percentages in finance.

基点（BPS）是指金融中利率和其他百分比的通用计量单位。

注：（1）interest rate 利率，又叫利息率，是衡量利息高低的指标，是一定时期内利息额和本金的比率。利率=利息/本金

（2）相关术语：interest rate ceiling 最高利率，一家金融机构对任何可调整的房地产抵押或贷款收取的最高利率，最高利率受到政府监管。

**6. Chicago Board of Trade　芝加哥期货交易所**

Commodities, ranging from copper on the London Metal Exchange to corn and soybean futures on the Chicago Board of Trade, also suffered heavy losses and volatile trading this week. (*China Daily*/2018-04-07)

从伦敦金属交易所的铜到芝加哥期货交易所的玉米和大豆期货，这些大宗商品本周也遭受严重损失和波动。

注：（1）volatility 波动率，指金融资产价格的波动程度，是对资产收益率不确定性的衡量，用于反映金融资产的风险水平。

（2）相关术语：volatility range 波幅，指是一种测定市场价格上下波动程度的指标。通常用同一商品市场价格波动的最高点与其最低点的差额来表示；volatile liability 易变负债，指那些受利率等经济因素影响较大的银行资金来源，这类负债受资金供求关系、市场利率、银行信誉等多种因素影响，其融资成本、规模均难以为银行所控制，是银行

最不稳定的资金来源。

The Chicago Board of Trade (CBOT), established on April 3, 1848, is one of the world's oldest futures and options exchanges. More than 50 different options and futures contracts are traded by over 3,600 CBOT members through open outcry and electronic trading.

芝加哥贸易委员会成立于 1848 年 4 月 3 日，是世界上最古老的期货和期权交易所之一。超过 3 600 名 CBOT 会员在这里通过公开喊价和电子交易，交易了 50 多种不同的期权和期货合约。

注：（1）futures 期货，指包含金融工具或未来交割实物商品销售（一般在商品交易所进行）的金融合约。

（2）词义辨析：future contract vs. forward contract，两个都是金融工具，保值的原理也很相似，最大的区别在于期货是标准化的合约，而远期是非标准化的。

**7. Collateralized mortgage obligation　抵押贷款担保证券**

The regulator's complaint against the banking giant was larded with excerpts from internal JPMorgan communications that indicated bankers sold a collateralized mortgage obligation in 2007 to ensure that it could get credit-scarred mortgage securities off its books. (*Global Times*/2011-6-23)

监管机构对这家银行业巨头的指控中充斥着摩根大通内部通信的摘录，这些摘录表明，银行家在 2007 年出售一项抵押贷款担保证券，以确保其能够将信用受损的抵押贷款证券从其账目中剥离。

注：（1）mortgage 房地产抵押，指以房地产等实物资产或有价证券、契约等作抵押，获得银行贷款并依合同分期付清本息，贷款还清后银行归还抵押物。

（2）词义辨析：mortgage vs. collateral，mortgage 是抵押，指固定资产类；collateral 指质押，多指流动资产类，最常见的是票据。

A collateralized mortgage obligation (CMO) is a type of complex debt security that repackages and directs the payments of principal and interest from a collateral pool to different types and maturities of securities, thereby meeting investor needs.

抵押贷款担保证券（CMO）是一种复杂的债务证券，它将抵押池中的本金和利息重新打包并定向到不同类型和到期日的证券，从而满足投资者的需求。

注：（1）principal 贷款本金，指借款人向贷款人借用的资金额。贷款本金不包含任何借款过程中需要花费的费用。这些费用和需要支付的利息一样，归属于贷款成本。

（2）词义辨析：principal vs. principle，词义不同。principal 有首要的、校长、本金等意思；而 principle 指作为某事基础的真理或想法依据，如信仰、行为或道德准则；公认的行为准则

**8. Market maker　做市商**（准备买卖未上市股票的经纪人/从事欧洲债券二级市场交易银行）

In the 1990s, the world mocked Microsoft when this mass market maker of relatively cheap software announced it was getting into the more sophisticated world of business applications. (www.fortunechina.com)

在20世纪90年代，当微软这个相对廉价软件的大众市场制造商宣布它将进入更复杂的商业应用领域时，全世界都在嘲笑它。

注:（1）相关术语：critical mass 关键规模，指一家公司发展非常重要或关键的阶段；mass logistics 大规模物流，指物流服务提供者对所有客户都提供同样方式、相同水平的物流服务，简化物流操作，以最小成本获得最大效益；mass customization logistics 大规模定制物流，指根据客户的不同物流需求进行市场细分，运用现代物流技术和信息技术以及先进的物流管理方法，通过物流功能的重新整合，实现以大规模物流的成本和效率为每个客户提供定制物流服务。

Market maker refers a broker who is prepared to buy or sell unlisted stocks or a bank engaged in secondary market transactions of European bonds.

做市商是指准备买卖未上市股票的经纪人或从事欧洲债券二级市场交易的银行。

注:（1）Secondary market 二级市场，也称证券流通市场，是指对已经发行的证券进行买卖，转让和流通的市场

（2）相关术语：Primary market 初级市场，投资者有机会购买新发行证券的市场

（3）词义辨析：broker vs. dealer，broker 是帮别人买卖的代理人、中间人、经纪人（或实体），不具有买卖的财产的所有权；dealer 是参与买卖的商人或交易员，买卖过程中，他的财产所有权发生变化。

**9. Market participant 市场参与者**

As a market participant you must reflect on your trades to build on strengths and work on weaknesses. (www.dictall.com)

作为一个市场参与者，你必须反思你的交易，以建立优势并克服劣势。

Market participant refers to institutions that trade in the inter bank foreign exchange market, including members and market makers.

市场参与者是指在银行间外汇市场进行交易的机构，包括会员和做市商。

注：相关术语：lending institution 借贷机构，指通过给他人贷款而获利的金融公司、银行、贷款机构或其他机构；public institution 公共机构，指全部或者部分使用财政性资金的国家机关、事业单位和团体组织；financial institution 信用机构，是专门从事信用业务活动的组织。它处于借者和贷者之间，是借贷双方的信用中介；saving institution 储蓄机构，指为家庭储蓄存款与投资提供专门服务的金融中介机构。

**10. Minimum amount 最小交易金额**

This has happened so many times in history that governments around the world now regulate banks and tell them that they have to hold a minimum amount. (www.ibm.com)

这种情况在历史上发生过很多次，以至于世界各国政府现在都在监管银行，并告诉它们必须持有最低限额。

注：相关术语：market regulation 市场规制，指国家通过制定行为规范引导、监督、管理市场主体的经济行为，也同时规范、约束政府监管机关的市场监管行为，从而保护消费主体的利益，保障市场秩序；price regulation：价格管制，指政府对处于自然垄断地位的企业的价格实行管制，以防止他们为牟取暴利而危害公共利益；incentive regulation

激励性规制，指在市场经济体制条件下，政府以治理市场失灵为目的，根据有关法律、规章和制度，干预经济主体，特别是企业活动的行为。

Minimum amount refers to the minimum amount of foreign exchange transactions allowed in the foreign exchange trading system.

最低金额是指外汇交易系统允许的最低外汇交易金额。

注：Foreign exchange transaction 外汇交易，指国际间结算债权债务关系的工具。可分为现钞、现货外汇交易、合约现货外汇交易、外汇期货交易、外汇期权交易、远期外汇交易、掉期交易等。

**11. Market manipulation　市场操纵**

Stories of fund managers and even state firms being instructed to buy particular stocks have been commonplace—as have cases of insider trading and other types of market manipulation. (www.stnn.cc)

基金经理甚至国有公司按照指示购买特定股票是司空见惯之事，内幕交易和其他性质市场操纵也是如此。

注：（1）insider trading 交易内务，指内幕人员根据内幕消息买卖证券或者帮助他人，违反了证券市场"公开、公平、公正"的原则，严重影响证券市场功能的发挥。

（2）词义辨析：fund vs. capital，capital 仅仅表示用于商业贸易以及某些经济方面的资金，而 fund 则指用于某种用途的资金，平时使用时多用在公益方面。

Market manipulation refers to affect the market price of securities, create illusions in the securities market, and induce investors to make securities investment decisions without knowing the truth by using funds, information or other advantages.

市场操纵是指影响证券市场价格，在证券市场制造幻想，通过资金、信息或者其他优势，诱导投资者在不解真相的情况下作出证券投资决策。

注：相关术语：tax illusion 税收幻觉，指根据税前考虑因素来判断价值或作出决策；在形成决策的过程中未能完全考虑税收所带来的效应；money illusion 货币幻觉，指人们只是对货币的名义价值做出反应，而忽视其实际购买力变化的一种心理错觉；fiscal illusion 财政幻觉，指政府的财政支出给人们带来了好处，但人们却因此忽略了自己付出的代价。

**12. Maker　报价方**

The notice must state that the FDM intends to cancel or adjust the order and must include documentation of the price adjustment from the maker. (blog.sina.com.cn)

这个通知必须说明交易商将要取消或调整订单，并且必须包括报价方提供的价格调整文档。

注：price adjustment 价格调整，简称调价，指对原订价格的提高或降低。

Maker refers the party in the transaction who requested the quotation。

制造商是指交易中要求报价的一方。

注：（1）quotation 报价，分为证券报价、投标报价、产品报价。证券报价，指在证券市场上交易者在某一时间内对某种证券报出的最高进价或最低出价。投标报价，是商

家竞投某项目时愿意出的价格。产品报价，指卖方通过考虑自己产品的成本、利润、市场竞争力等因素，公开报出的可行的价格。

（2）相关术语：stock quote 股票报价，指一种股票在一个交易日的价格（包括叫价及出价）清单。

（3）词义辨析：transaction vs. deal，transaction 交易，强调互换性；deal 经营/代理，强调交易具体的动作。

**13. Option value 期权价值**

Paper further uses real option theory to evaluate those three different types of real option value. (Research on the evaluation of the china inner financed bot of highway project based on the real option/2001/https://search.proquest.com/docview/1874854195/44CEEFCDCA9343 F8PQ/1?accountid=14662)

论文进一步运用实物期权理论来评估这三种不同类型的实物期权价值。

注：option 期权，是一种选择权，指一种能在未来某特定时间以特定价格买入或卖出一定数量的某种特定商品的权利。

Means that the holder of the convertible bond has the right to purchase the stock corresponding to the bond at any time before maturity.

期权价值是指可转换债券持有人有权在到期前的任何时候购买与债券相对应的股票。

注：（1）convertible bond 可转换公司债券，一种被赋予了股票转换权的公司债券，也称可转换债券。发行公司事先规定债权人可以选择有利时机，按发行时规定的条件把其债券转换成发行公司的等值股票（普通股票）。

（2）词义辨析：buy vs. purchase，均为“购买”，buy 是最普遍的用词；purchase 一般用于书面语，或者比较正式的场合以及商务文档中。

**14. Outright purchases 买断**

That means share sales are structurally higher than outright purchases. (http://www.iciba.com/)

这意味着从结构上来说，售出股票数量要超过买断数量。

注：（1）share 股票，也称 stock，股票是股份证书的简称，是股份公司为筹集资金而发行给股东作为持股凭证并借以取得股息和红利的一种有价证券。每股股票都代表股东对企业拥有一个基本单位的所有权。

（2）相关术语：golden share 黄金股，指给予持有股东对修改公司章程行使否决权的股票。

Government securities purchased outright by the authorities, with no agreement to subsequently sell them through a repurchase pact or reverse repo.

买断是当局直接购买政府证券，而没有随后的回购协议或逆回购协议。

注：reverse repo 逆回购协议，指证券持有者，即证券卖主，为与证券买主达成一笔证券交易，在签订的合约中规定卖主在卖出一笔证券后须在某个双方商定的时间以商定的价格再买回这笔证券，并以商定的利率付息。这对于买主来讲，这就是个逆回购协议。

**15. Obligatory right　债权**

Injuring obligatory right by the third party is the modern creditor's rights system and the torts system development product. (On the issues on injuring obligatory right by the third party/ 2009/https://search. proquest.com/docview/1870499457/329A8472C353450BPQ/1? Accountid = 14662)

第三方侵权责任是现代债权制度和侵权制度发展的产物。

注：tort 侵权，根据《民法通则》的规定，侵权行为一般是指行为人由于过错侵害他人的财产、人身，依法应承担民事责任的行为；行为人虽无过错，但法律特别规定应对受害人承担民事责任的其他侵害行为，也属于侵权行为。

The obligatory right means a kind of debtor-creditor relationship which results from public law or with nature of public law.

债权是指源于公法或具有公法性质的一种债权债务关系。

注：（1）public law 公法，是指调整国家与普通公民、组织之间关系以及国家机关及其组成人员之间关系的法律。

（2）相关术语：private law 私法，指调整普通公民、组织之间关系的法律。

## 2.2.2　金融债券类型

**1. Asset-backed Security (ABS)　资产支持证券**

Hunton Andrews Kurth LLP's asset-backed securitization (ABS) practice started more than 30 years ago and is still expanding today. (https://www.hunton.com/en/practices/ structured-finance-and-securitization/asset-backed-securitization.html)

Hunton Andrews Kurth LLP 的资产支持证券化（ABS）业务始于 30 多年前，至今仍在扩张。

An asset-backed security (ABS) is a financial security backed by a loan, lease or receivables against assets other than real estate and mortgage-backed securities.

资产支持证券（ABS）是一种以房地产和抵押贷款支持证券以外的资产为抵押，由贷款、租赁或应收款支持的金融证券。

注：receivables 应收账款，指客户因交付或使用但尚未付款的商品或服务而欠公司的债务。

**2. Accrual bond　应计债券**

An accrual bond is a fixed interest rate bond which is similar to a zero coupon bond with the only exception that the interest payments are accrued to the principal value and paid at maturity. (https://www.mbaskool.com/business-concepts/finance-accounting-economics-terms/ 1539-accrual-bond.html)

应计债券是一种固定利率债券，类似于零息债券，唯一例外是利息支付应计为本金并在到期时支付。

注：principal 本金，是一个有多种金融含义的术语。最常用的是指在贷款中借入的原始金额或投入投资的金额。与前者相似，它也可以指债券的面值。

Accrual bond is a bond on which interest accrues but is not paid to the investor during the time of accrual. The amount of accrued interest is added to the remaining principal of the bond and is paid at maturity.

应计债券是一种债券，在应计期间，应计利息，但不支付给投资者。应计利息数额被添加到债券剩余本金中，并在到期时支付。

**3. Accrued interest 应计利息**

Accrued Interest is added to the contract price of a bond transaction. (http://dict.youdao.com/search?q=accrued%20interest&keyfrom=hao360)

应计利息要加到债券交易合同价格中。

注：contract 合同，指两个或两个以上的人之间具有法律约束力的协议。

Accrued interest is a term used in accrual accounting that disregards cash flows and reports interest that has been earned but not collected.

应计利息是权责发生制会计中使用一个术语，它无视现金流量和报告已赚取但未收取的利息。

注：accrual accounting 权责发生制会计，这种方法在确认收入和费用时，不考虑交易发生时有没有现金流的变化。它不仅可以帮助公司节省资金还可以增加资金流动，这也是你的公司成功的关键。比如，公司购买一台机器设备，要等到好几个月之后才支付现金，但会计师却在购买当时就确认这项费用。如果不使用权责发生制会计，那么该会计系统就称作“收付制”或“现金会计”。

**4. Bunny bond 兔子债券**

Bunny bonds are an effective way to protect against reinvestment risk, which arises from the possibility that interest rates will drop in the future. With a normal bond, investors are exposed to the risk of having to reinvest their coupons at a lower interest rate. (Bunny Bond https://www.investopedia.com/terms/b/bunnybond.asp#ixzz5CHgBIrOS)

兔子债券是防范再投资风险的有效方法，这是源于未来利率可能下降。对于普通债券，投资者面临的风险是必须以较低的利率对其息票进行再投资。

注：reinvestment 再投资，是指将投资所得的股息、利息或任何其他形式的收入分配用于购买额外的股票或单位，而不是以现金形式获得分配。

Bunny bond is a type of bond that offers investors the option to reinvest coupon payments into additional bonds with the same coupon and maturity. Also known as “multiplier bond” or “guaranteed coupon reinvestment bond.”

兔子债券是为投资者提供选择，将息票支付再投资于息票和期限相同的额外债券。也被称为“乘数债券”或“担保息票再投资债券”。

**5. Bearer bond 无记名债券**

Bearer bonds, at the center of a new probe faced by UBS, have figured large in popular culture. (https://blogs.wsj.com/.../02/04/5-things-to-know-about-bearer-bonds)

作为瑞银面临的一项新调查的核心，不记名债券在流行文化中占据了重要地位。

注：probe 探查

Bearer bond is a fixed-income instrument that is owned by whoever is holding it, rather than having a registered owner. Coupons representing interest payments are likely to be physically attached to the security and it is the bondholder's responsibility to submit the coupons for payment.

无记名债券是一种固定收益债券，由持有该债券的人持有，而不是由注册所有人持有。代表利息支付的息票可能附在证券上，债券持有人有责任提交息票进行支付。

注：coupon 息票

**6. Bulldog bond　斗牛犬债券**

The term bulldog bond refers to a security issued in the United Kingdom, in British pound sterling, by a foreign bank or corporation. (https://www.money-zine.com/.../ investing-dictionary/bulldog-bonds)

猛犬债券一词是指由英国一家外国银行或公司在英国发行的证券。

注：security 债券，是发行者为筹集资金发行的、在约定时间支付一定比例的利息，并在到期时偿还本金的有价证券。其本质是债务的证明书，具有法律效力，发行者通常是政府、企业、银行等。政府债券因为有政府税收作为保障，因而风险最小，但收益也最小。公司债券风险最大，收益相应较高。债券购买者或投资者与发行者之间是一种债权债务关系，债券发行人即债务人，投资者（债券购买者）即债权人。

A type of bond purchased by buyers interested in earning a revenue stream from the British pound or sterling. A bulldog bond is traded in the United Kingdom. If the revenue is used to reduce debt also in British pounds, the exchange rate risk is decreased.

斗牛犬债券是一种由有意从英镑或英镑？中获得收入的买家购买的一种债券。牛头犬债券在英国交易。

注：revenue stream 收入流

**7. Brady bonds　布雷迪债券**

The Brady bonds themselves are coupon-bearing bonds with a variety of rate options (fixed, variable, step, etc.) with maturities of between 10 and 30 years. (www.investorwords.com/567/Brady_bond.html)

布雷迪债券本身是息票债券，具有多种利率选择（固定、可变、分步利率等），期限在 10 年至 30 年之间。

注：(1) coupon 息票，是附印于各种债券面上的利息票券，债券持有人可将其剪下，在债券付息日携至债券发行人处要求兑付当期利息。

(2) 相关术语：coupon rate 息票率，指债券的年利率，相当于债券面值的某个百分比；息票率可以是固定、浮动或零息率。

Brady bonds are dollar-denominated bonds, issued mostly by Latin American countries in the late 1980s. The bonds were named after US Treasury Secretary Nicholas Brady, who proposed a novel debt-reduction agreement for developing countries.

布雷迪债券是以美元计价的债券，主要由拉丁美洲国家在 20 世纪 80 年代末发行。这些债券是以美国财政部长尼古拉斯·布雷迪（Nicholas Brady）的名字命名的，他提出了一项新的发展中国家减债协议。

相关术语：（1）debt reduction 债务减免，指减少债务人的还债金额，债务人只需偿还部分借款；（2）debt relief 债务免除，指债权人免除债务人部分或者全部债务，合同的权利义务部分或全部终止。

**8. Bond Market Index　债券市场指数**

See Vanguard Total Bond Market Index performance, holdings, fees, risk and other data from Morningstar, S&P, and other. (https://money.usnews.com/funds/mutual-funds/intermediate-term-bond/vanguard-total-bond-market-index/vbmfx)

请从晨星、标普及其他评级机构中参阅 Vanguard 的债券市场指数的表现、持有量、费用、风险及其他数据。

注：（1）holding 持股（持有一定股份）或控股（持股达 30%）；（2）absolute holding 绝对控股（持股超过 50%）

A bond or bond market index is a method of measuring the value of a section of the bond market. It is computed from the prices of selected bonds (typically a weighted average). It is a tool used by investors and financial managers to describe the market, and to compare the return on specific investments.

债券指数或债券市场指数是衡量债券市场某一部分价值的一种方法，其根据选定的债券价格（通常是加权平均数）进行计算。它是投资者和基金经理用来描述市场和比较特定投资回报的一种工具。

注：（1）index（物价和工资等的）指数；indices [ pl.] ；indicator 指标；（2）相关术语：bond market 债券市场，是发行和买卖债券的场所，是金融市场的一个重要组成部分）；（3）债券市场的分类：① 按照债券运行过程和市场基本功能可分为 primary market / new issue market（一级市场/债券发行市场）和 parallel market（二级市场/债券流通市场）；② 根据市场组织形式可分为 market in the field（场内交易市场）和 over-the-counter market （场外交易市场）；③ 根据债券发行地点可分为 domestic bond market（国内债券市场）和 international bond market（国际债券市场）

**9. Bond fund　债券基金**

There are four types of bond funds: mutual funds, closed-end funds, unit investment trusts (UITs) and exchange-traded funds (ETFs). (www.finra.org/investors/bond-funds)

债券基金有四种类型：共同基金，封闭式基金，单位投资信托（UITs）和交易所交易基金（ETFs）。

注：（1）trust 信托，即信用委托，信托业务是由委托人依照契约或遗嘱的规定，为自己或受益人的利益，将财产上的权利转给受托人，受托人按规定条件和范围，占有、管理、使用信托财产，并处理其收益。（2）closed-end funds 与 open-end funds 的区别：closed-end funds（封闭式基金）是基金规模在发行前已确定，在发行完毕后和规定的期限内，基金规模固定不变的投资基金；open-end funds（开放式基金）不上市交易，一般通过银行申购和赎回，基金规模不固定，基金单位可随时向投资者出售，也可应投资者要求买回。

A bond fund or debt fund is a fund that invests in bonds, or other debt securities. Bond funds can be contrasted with stock funds and money funds. Bond funds typically pay periodic dividends that include interest payments on the fund's underlying securities plus periodic realized capital appreciation.

债券基金或债务基金是投资于债券或其他债务证券的基金。债券基金可以与股票基金和货币基金进行对比。债券基金通常定期支付股息，其中包括基金标的证券的利息支付及定期实现的资本增值。

相关术语：（1）capital appreciation 资本增值，指现有资产价值减除购入时之价格，所赚取或损失之价值；（2）money fund 与 bond fund 的区别：二者的区别主要在于投资对象不同，货币基金投向货币市场，以投资于债券、央行票据、回购等安全性极高的短期金融品种为主；而债券基金是专门投资于债券的基金，主要是国债、金融债和企业债。

**10. External bond　外部债券**

At the end of March, Slovenia's 10-year government bond yields had climbed to around 7%, prompting fears it would need external support to finance itself. (*Wall street Journal*/MAR 6, 2012 https://www.forbes.com/WJS/2008/0324/100.html#42c626f962)

3 月底，斯洛文尼亚的 10 年期政府债券收益率已攀升至 7%左右，这引发了该国对其自身融资将需要外部支持的担忧。

注：（1）finance [*n.*] 财政，金融；finances [*pl.*]（机构或个人的）财务状况；finance [*v.*] 提供资金；（2）yield（投资的）收益，收益率；returns 回报，收益，利润；fear 害怕，担忧；panic 经济恐慌，金融恐慌（程度比 fear 更深）；（3）相关术语：Ministry of Finance（Treasury Department）财政部；the Minister of Finance 财政部长；international finance 国际金融；corporate finance 公司金融

External bond that is sold to investors in several countries at the same time.

外部债券是同时向几个国家的投资者出售的债券。

注：（1）investor 投资者，指投入现金购买某种资产以期望获取利益或利润的自然人和法人；（2）speculator 投机者，指在金融市场上通过“买空卖空”和“卖空买空”，希望以较小的资金来博取利润的投资者；（3）investor 和 speculator 的区别：投资者的投资行为基本遵循价值规律，他们根据多种科学的经济指标进行买卖操作；而投机者只追求“利润”，甘愿冒任何风险，不会考虑价值规律的存在。

**11. Eurobond　欧元债券**

There are a few other clever eurobond plans out there (if you're interested, *Breaking Views* has a useful potted summary). (BBC/June 15, 2012/http://www.bbc.com/news/ 18463879)

还有其他一些巧妙的欧元债券计划（如果你感兴趣，*Breaking Views* 有可用的成套摘要）。

注：（1）plan 计划，投资方式；（2）相关术语：planned economy 计划经济，是根据政府计划调节经济活动的经济运行体制；market economy 市场经济，指通过市场配置社会资源的经济形式；mixed economy 混合经济，是各种不同因素在一定社会制度下混合的经济运行体制。

A eurobond is denominated in a currency other than the home currency of the country or market in which it is issued. These bonds are frequently grouped together by the currency in which they are denominated, such as eurodollar or euroyen bonds. Issuance is usually handled by an international syndicate of financial institutions on behalf of the borrower, one of which may underwrite the bond, thus guaranteeing purchase of the entire issue.

欧元债券以发行国或市场本币以外的货币计价。这些债券通常按其计价货币组合在一起，如欧洲美元或欧洲日元债券。发行通常由金融机构的一个国际财团代表借款人进行，其中一家可以承销债券，从而保证购买整个债券。

注：（1）syndicate 辛迪加，由同一生产部门的少数大企业，通过签订统一销售商品和采购原料的协定以获取垄断利润而建立的垄断组织；（2）其他垄断组织的形式：cartel 卡特尔；trust 托拉斯；konzern 康采恩

**12. Euroclear 欧元清算所**

But opening its bond market through Euroclear shows that even Putin knows the future of Russian democratic capitalism is pushing down on him. (*Forbes*/APR20,2012/https://www.forbes.com/sites/kenrapoza/2012/04/20/russias-bond-market-grows-up/#2f7bbf8666ac)

但通过欧元清算所开放其债券市场这一行为表明，甚至普京也知道，俄罗斯民主资本主义的未来正在向他施加压力。

注：（1）capitalism 资本主义，是资本属于个人所有的经济制度，以私有制为基础；（2）相关词汇：socialism 社会主义，由社会拥有和控制产品、资本、土地、资产等，其管理和分配基于公众利益；communism 共产主义，主张消灭生产资料私有制，并建立一个没有阶级制度、没有剥削、没有压迫，实现人类自我解放的社会。

Euroclear is one of two principal clearing houses for securities traded in the Euromarket. Euroclear specializes in verifying information supplied by brokers involved in a securities transaction and the settlement of securities. Euroclear is market owned and governed, and acquired London Crest, Necigef Netherlands, Sicovam Paris, and Caisse Interprofessionnelle de Dépôts et de Virements de Titres (CIK) Brussels, following a series of acquisitions that occurred from 2001 to 2007.

欧元清算所是在欧洲市场上交易证券的两家主要清算所之一，其专门核实由参与证券交易和证券结算的经纪人所提供的信息。欧元清算所是由市场拥有和管理的，在 2001 年至 2007 年进行了一系列收购之后，它又收购了 London Crest、Necigef Netherlands、Sicovam Paris 以及 Caisse Interprofessionnelle de Dépôts et de Virements de Titres (CIK) Brussels。

注：（1）acquire 获得，盘购（某企业等）；acquired enterprise 被购企业；acquirer 兼并公司，盘购公司；acquiree 被盘购公司；M&A（Mergers and Acquisitions）企业并购；（2）相关术语：clearing house 清算所，是随期货交易的发展以及标准化期货合同的出现而设立的清算结算结构；清算所是期货市场运行机制的核心，一旦期货交易达成，交易双方分别与清算所发生关系。

**13. Fixed income 固定收益**

Fixed income funds were the most consistent with about 95 percent holding their original style category. (*Forbes*/Oct,11,2012/https://www.forbes.com/sites/rickferri/2012/10/11/indexes-beat-active-funds-again-in-sp-study/#2abb577a520c /)

固定收益基金最稳定，约95%的基金保持原始风格类型。

注：（1）fund [*n.*] 基金，专款；funds [*pl.*] 资金，现款；fund [*v.*] 为……提供资金，资助；（2）相关术语：trust fund 信托基金；mutual funds 共同基金；investment funds 投资基金；money fund 货币基金；equity fund 股票基金；fund asset 基金资产

Fixed income refers to any type of investment under which the borrower or issuer is obliged to make payments of a fixed amount on a fixed schedule.

固定收益是指借款人或发行人有义务按固定时间表支付固定金额的任何投资类型。

注：（1）borrower 借款人，指在信贷活动中以自身的信用或财产作保证，或者以第三者作为担保而从贷款人处借得货币资金的企事业单位或个人。（2）相关术语：issuer of securities 证券发行人，指为筹措资金而发行债券、股票等证券的政府及其机构、公司和企业。（3）fixed-income securities 与 equity securities 的区别：fixed-income securities（固定收益证券）是指持券人可以在特定的时间内取得固定的收益并预先知道取得收益的数量和时间，如固定利率债券、优先股股票等；而 equity securities（股票）的收益是不固定和难以预料的。

**14. Floating rate notes (FRN) 浮息利率票据**

The FRN interest would be includible in gross income and the interest to Optech would be deductible or not based on how Mr. Sollberger had spent the money he received from Optech. (*Forbes*/AUG31,2012/https://www.forbes.com/sites/peterjreilly/2012/08/31/sometimes-you-should-just-pay-the-tax/#2b76597430f9)

浮动利率票据的利息可包含在总收入内，而 Sollberger 先生对 Optech 的利息是否可扣除将取决于他如何使用从 Optech 获得的钱。

注：（1）interest 利息，利益，是货币在一定时期内的使用费，指债权人因贷出货币或货币资本而从债务人手中获得的报酬；（2）相关术语：interest rate 利率；principal 本金；the term of the deposit/deposit term 存款期限；（3）income 与 earnings 的区别：earnings 表示工作所得的报酬，不包括非劳动所得，例如银行存款的利息等；income 一般看作是可靠的固定收入，而 earnings 指设法挣得的非固定收入。

Floating rate notes (FRNs) are bonds that have a variable coupon, equal to a money market reference rate, like LIBOR or federal funds rate, plus a quoted spread (also known as quoted margin).

浮动利率票据是指具有可变息票率的债券，其票面利率等于货币市场参考利率（如伦敦银行同业拆放利率或联邦基金利率）加上报价价差（也称为报价保证金）。

相关术语：（1）federal funds rate 联邦基金利率，指美国银行同业拆借市场的利率，其中最主要的为隔夜拆借利率；（2）inter-bank offered rate 同业拆借利率，指金融机构同业之间的短期资金借贷利率；overnight rate 隔夜拆借利率，各银行间进行短期的相互借

贷所适用的利率，通常是隔夜拆借或者 1～7 天内拆借；Shanghai Interbank Offered Rate（SHIBOR）上海银行间同业拆放利率；Hongkong InterBank Offered Rate（HIBOR）香港银行同业拆借利率

**15. Fixed-maturity　固定期限**

These factors make fixed maturity securities and ideal choice for insurance companies, which typically invest 50% to 70% of their total invested assets in fixed maturity securities. (*Forbes*/Sep21,2011/https://www.forbes.com/sites/greatspeculations/2011/09/21/feds-twisting-is-no-fun-for-insurance-companies-like-metlife-aig-hartford/#2544ceac388b)

这些因素使得固定期限证券成为保险公司的理想选择，保险公司通常将其总投资资产的 50%至 70%投资于固定期限证券。

注：（1）assets 资产，指由企业过去的交易或事项形成的、由企业拥有或者控制的、预期会给企业带来经济利益的资源；（2）相关词汇：liability 负债，指由企业过去的交易或者事项形成的，预期会导致经济利益流出企业的现时义务；（3）资产的分类：current assets 流动资产；long-term investments 长期投资；fixed assets 固定资产；intangible assets 无形资产

The term fixed maturity is applicable to any form of financial instrument under which the loan is due to be repaid on a fixed date. This includes fixed interest and variable rate loans or debt instruments, whatever they are called, and other forms of security such as redeemable preference shares, provided their terms of issue specify a date. It is similar in meaning to "redemption date".

固定期限适用于应在固定日期偿还贷款的任何形式的金融工具，包括固定利率和可变利率贷款或债务工具（无论其名称是什么），以及在发行条款中规定了日期其他形式的证券（如可赎回的优先股）。它的含义类似于"偿还期"。

注：（1）debt 借款，债务，负债情况；bad debt 坏账，呆账，倒账；（2）相关术语：financial instrument 金融工具，指在金融市场中可交易的金融资产，如 commercial paper 商业票据、bank deposit certificate 银行存款凭证、stock 股票、bond 债券、futures 期货等。

**16. Hedge fund　对冲基金**

Soros, on the other hand, manages a huge offshore hedge fund for wealthy individuals and institutions. (*Forbes*/May 5,2008/https://www.forbes.com/2008/05/08 /croesus-chronicles-soros-oped-cz_rl_0509croesus.html#77d7b17b2bab）

另一方面，Soros 为富人和机构管理着大量离岸对冲基金。

注：institution 机构；financial institutions 金融机构；organization 组织（指团体机构等）；hedge 防止损失（尤指金钱）的手段；offshore 设在海外（尤指税制较宽松的国家）的，投放国外的，离岸的

Hedge funds are alternative investments using pooled funds that employ numerous different strategies to earn active return, or alpha, for their investors.

对冲基金是使用集合基金的另类投资，这些基金采用多种不同策略，为投资者赚取积极回报。

注：（1）earn 挣（钱），获得（利润）；（2）return 回报，收益，利润；earnings 利润，收益，赢利；yield 利润，收益；profit 利润，收益，赢利；（3）相关术语：earned income 劳动所得；capital income 资本所得；alpha 投资积极回报（在金融中用作衡量业绩的指标）

**17. High-yield bond　高收益债券**

Even worse for investors: Some funds haven't come close to matching high-yield bond indexes. (*Wall Street Journal*/ http://online.wsj.com/article/SB10000872396390443493304578036330669954870.html/)

对投资者来说更糟糕的是有些基金收益率还没有接近高收益债券指数。

注：（1）yield 证券投资收益（率）；（2）相关术语：current yield 本期收益；dividend yield 股息收益；fixed-yield 固定收益；nominal yield 名义收益；（3）bond index 债券指数，债券指数反映的是债券市场价格总体走势的指标体系，债券指数是一个比值，其数值反映了当前市场的平均价格相对于基期市场平均价格的位置；（4）all-bond index 中国债券指数（总指数）；Shanghai (securities) composite index 上海证券综合指数；Citic securities index 中信债券指数

In finance, a high-yield bond (non-investment-grade bond, speculative-grade bond, or junk bond) is a bond that is rated below investment grade, because they are more likely to default. They have lower credit ratings than investment-grade bonds, so they must pay a higher yield than investment-grade bonds to compensate investors.

在金融领域，高收益债券（非投资级债券、投机级债券或垃圾债券）是一种评级低于投资级的债券，因为可违约，这种债券信用级别低，因此支付回报高于投资级债券以补偿投资者。

相关术语：（1）investment grade 投资等级（指对证券评定的资信等级）；（2）美国两家最著名的资信评价机构是 Moody's Investors Service（穆迪投资者服务公司）和 S&P（标准普尔公司）。标普的长期信用评级主要分为投资级和投机级，信用级别由高到低，投资级分为 AAA、AA、A 和 BBB，投机级分为 BB、B、CCC、CC、C 和 SD/D 级；穆迪长期评级等级分为 Aaa、Aa、A、Baa、Ba、B、Caa、Ca 和 C 级。

**18. Hedging　套期保值**

Hedging credit risk is not uncommon, and if done properly, reflects sound risk management. (*Forbes*/March18,2013/https://www.forbes.com/sites/francinemckenna/2013/03/18/no-accounting-for-auditor-pwc-at-levins-whale-hearing/#367739966ff9/)

对冲信用风险并不少见，如果操作得当，能反映出良好的风险管理。

注：（1）risk 风险（发生不幸事件的概率）；（2）相关术语：credit risk 信用风险；market risk 市场风险；risk assessment 风险评估；risk analysis 风险分析

Hedging means any technique designed to reduce or eliminate financial risk; for example, taking two positions that will offset each other if prices change

套期保值是指旨在降低或消除金融风险的任何技术；例如，采取两个能使价格变化所带来的盈亏相互抵消的买进与卖出两个头寸。

注：（1）offset 抵销，冲销；（2）相关术语：financial risk 金融风险，指与金融有关的风险，如金融市场风险、金融产品风险、金融机构风险等。

**19. Hongkong InterBank Offered Rate（HIBOR）香港同业拆借利率**

By October 6th, Hong Kong interbank offered rate (HIBOR) had risen to 3.85%, its highest level since last December. (*The Economist*/ http://www.economist.com/node/12370755/recommend/)

截至 10 月 6 日，香港同业拆借利率已升至 3.85%，为去年 12 月以来的最高水平。

注：（1）rise 增加，增长，上升；（2）相关词汇：increase 增加，提高；growth 增长；fall 下降，下跌，降低；decrease/decline 减少，减小

HIBOR is an interest rate stated in Hong Kong dollars on the lending and borrowing between banks in the Hong Kong interbank market. The terms of the deposits vary from overnight to one year.

香港同业拆借利率是以港元表示的在香港同业拆借市场上的银行间的借贷利率。存款期限从隔夜到一年不等。

注：（1）deposit 存款；withdrawal（从银行账户中）提款，取款；（2）相关术语：interbank market 银行同业拆借市场；interbank lending market 同业拆借市场，是除中央银行之外的金融机构之间进行短期资金融通的市场，即金融机构之间利用资金融通的地区差、时间差调剂资金头寸，由资金多余的金融机构对临时资金不足的金融机构短期放款；（3）同业拆借市场分为两类：银行同业拆借市场（银行业同业之间短期资金的拆借市场）和短期拆借市场（商业银行与如证券商之类的非银行金融机构之间的一种短期资金拆借形式）。

**20. Junk bond　垃圾债券**

In the junk bond sector, my decision was to avoid duration risk with a few exceptions. (*Forbes*/Jun14,2011/https://www.forbes.com/sites/martinsosnoff/2011/06/14/is-your-portfolio-1961-chateau-latour/#4147e11865d2)

在垃圾债券领域，除了少数例外，我的决定是避免持续期风险。

注：（1）sector（尤指一国经济的）部门，领域，行业；（2）duration 持续期（也称久期，是债券各期现金流支付所需时间的加权平均值）；（3）相关术语：the manufacturing sector 制造业；private sector（国家经济的）私营部分；public sector 公营部门；公共部门

If a company issues junk bonds, it borrows money from investors, usually at a high rate of interest, in order to finance a particular deal that is risky.

如果一家公司发行垃圾债券，它会从投资者那里借钱，通常是以很高的利率，以便为某一特定风险交易提供资金。

相关术语：（1）rate of interest /interest rate 利率，指一定时期内利息额与借贷资金额即本金的比率；（2）部分利率分类方式：① 根据计算方法不同分为 simple interest（单利）和 compound interest（复利）；② 根据与通货膨胀的关系分为 nominal interest rate（名义利率）和 real interest rate（实际利率）；③ 根据与市场利率供求关系分为 fixed interest rate（固定利率）和 floating interest rate（浮动利率）

**21. Investment grade bonds　投资等级**

Your typical diversified growth fund has an array of options, from equities to investment grade bonds, private equity, property, even emerging market sovereign debt.(*Fortune*/May4,2010/http://www.fortunechina.com/investing/c/2010-05/04/content_34898.htm)

典型的多元化增长型基金有一系列选择，从股票到投资级债券、私募股权、房地产，甚至新兴市场主权债务。

注：（1）sovereign 有主权的；完全独立的；（2）相关术语：private equity（PE）私募股权，指投资于非上市股权，或者上市公司非公开交易股权的一种投资方式；（3）著名的私募股权投资公司：Blackstone Group 黑石集团；KKR 集团；Carlyle Group 凯雷集团；Texas Pacific Group 德州太平洋集团；Goldman Sachs Group 高盛集团；Merrill Lynch 美林证券公司

An investment grade is a rating that indicates that a municipal or corporate bond has a relatively low risk of default. Bond rating firms, such as Standard & Poor's and Moody's, use different designations consisting of upper- and lower-case letters "A" and "B" to identify a bond's credit quality rating. "AAA" and "AA" (high credit quality) and "A" and "BBB" (medium credit quality) are considered investment grade. Credit ratings for bonds below these designations ("BB", "B", "CCC", etc.) are considered low credit quality, and are commonly referred to as "junk bonds."

投资等级是指市政债券或公司债券违约风险相对较低的评级。标准普尔和穆迪等债券评级公司使用不同名称以确定债券信用质量评级，这些名称由大小写字母“A”和“B”组成。“AAA”和“AA”（高信用质量）以及“A”和“BBB”（中等信用质量）被视为投资级。低于这些名称的（“BB”“B”“CCC”等）债券信用评级被认为属于低信用质量，通常被称为“垃圾债券”。

注：（1）credit 信贷；（2）default 违约，指合同当事人违反合同义务的行为；（3）根据违约行为发生的时间可将违约分为 anticipatory breach（预期违约）和 actual breach（实际违约）；实际违约又可细分为不履行（包括 fundamental breach of contract 根本违约和 repudiate 拒绝履行）、不符合约定的履行及其他违反合同义务的行为。

**22. Interest rate futures　利率期货**

The Actuarial Exchange of Chicago filed notice in January 2004 that it would begin trading interest rate futures. (*Forbes*/Dec15,2005/https://www.forbes.com/2005/12/14/gambling-derivatives-exchange-cx_lm_1215gamble.html#1a011f837aa9)

芝加哥精算交易所于 2004 年 1 月发出通知，表示将开始进行利率期货交易。

注：（1）trade 买卖，交易；（2）futures 期货，是以某种大众产品如棉花、大豆、石油等及金融资产如股票、债券等为标的标准化可交易合约；actuals/physicals 现货，指可供出货、储存和制造业使用的实物商品；（3）相关术语：balance of trade 贸易差额；favorable balance of trade 贸易顺差；trade deficit 贸易逆差；fair trade 公平贸易；free trade 自由贸易

An interest rate future is a futures contract with an underlying instrument that pays interest. An interest rate future is a contract between the buyer and seller agreeing to the future delivery of any interest-bearing asset. The interest rate future allows the buyer and seller to lock in the price of the interest-bearing asset for a future date.

利率期货是一种带有支付利息的基础工具的期货合约。利率期货是买卖双方同意未来交付任何计息资产的合同，其允许买卖双方锁定未来某个日期的计息资产价格。

相关术语：futures contract 期货合约，指买方同意在一段指定时间之后按特定价格接收某种资产，卖方同意在一段指定时间之后按特定价格交付某种资产的协议；futures market 期货市场；commodity futures 商品期货，指标的物为实物商品的期货合约；financial futures 金融期货，指交易双方在金融市场上，以约定的时间和价格，买卖某种金融工具的具有约束力的标准化合约。

**23. Mutual fund　共同基金**

Apart from small deposits, should we, in a crisis situation like this, consider extending guarantees to the money markets and mutual funds?（article.yeeyan.org）

在这样一场危机形势中，除小额存款外，我们应该考虑扩大对货币市场和共同基金的担保吗？

注：（1）crisis 危机，危急关头；guarantee 保证/担保，指当事人根据法律规定或者双方约定，为促使债务人履行债务实现债权人的权利的法律制度；（2）担保的五种方式：ensure 保证；mortgage 抵押；pledge 质押；retain 留置；earnest money/hard money 定金。

Mutual Fund is a way of collective investment with sharing profit and risk.

共同基金是一种分享利润和风险的集体投资方式。

注：（1）profit 利润；（2）loss 损失，亏损；（3）相关术语：normal profit 正常利润，是成本的一个组成部分，支付给企业家资本投资的报酬；economic profit 经济利润（总收入和总成本之间的差额）；gross profit 毛利（产品销售收入与销售时实际成本之间的差额）；net profit 净利润（即企业的税后利润）

**24. Maturity yield　到期收益率**

The maturity yield on an indexed bond is already in real terms because the coupons are indexed to inflation.(http://.dictall.com)

指数债券的到期收益率就是实际收益率，因为息票是与通货膨胀指数挂钩的。

注：（1）index 将（工资等）与（物价水平等）挂钩；使指数化；peg [usually passive] 使工资、价格等固定于某水平（或与……挂钩）；（2）相关术语：indexed bond 指数债券，指通过利率与通货膨胀率挂钩来保证债权人不至于因为物价上涨而遭受损失的公司债券；（3）inflation index bonds 通货膨胀指数化债券（IIS），指债券本金和利息的到期支付根据既定的通胀指数变化情况进行调整的债券。

Maturity yield refers to the total return on a bond investment realized if held to maturity.

到期收益率是指持有至到期日时债券投资所实现的总收益。

注：（1）realize 把（财产等）变卖，变现，以……价格卖出；（2）maturity（保险单、债券等的）到期；（3）相关术语：bond investment 债券投资，指债券购买人以购买债券的形式投放资本，到期向债券发行人收取固定的利息以及收回本金的一种投资方式。

## 2.3 Corporate Bond（公司债券）

本节主要介绍公司债券概念；其次引出现代公司制度下公司债券的分类，简要介绍现代公司债券各种分类依据和主要种类。

公司债券是指股份公司在一定时期内（如 10 年或 20 年）为追加资本而发行的借款凭证。公司债券期限较长，一般在 10 年以上，债券一旦到期，股份公司必须偿还本金，赎回债券。

### 2.3.1 公司债券类型

**1. Baklava Bond　巴克拉瓦债券**

This is the first paper to evaluate Turkish corporate bonds in local currency, coined by the author as “Baklava bonds”. (https://www.amazon.com.au/Baklava-Bonds-Evaluating-Corporate-Currency-ebook/dp/B008NOHZ0I)

这是第一份用当地货币评估土耳其公司债券的文件，作者将它命名为“巴克拉瓦债券”。

注：（1）evaluate 评估，在专业名词中，评估通常是指一种专业分析；（2）同义词辨析：assess，指对事物的数量、价值以及重要性等作出评价、评定，但谈及和“税款、税务”有关的话题时，通常会用单词 assess；evaluate，更侧重于评价事物的重要性和价值）；（3）相关术语：subject property 股价对象；real estate appraisal 房地产评估；used car evaluation 旧车评估

A Baklava bond is a bond denominated in Turkish Lira and issued by a domestic or foreign entity in Turkey. The name refers to baklava, a Turkish dessert. In October 2010, Turkish authorities allowed companies to issue bonds.

巴克拉瓦债券是一种以土耳其里拉计价的债券，由土耳其国内或外国实体发行。这个名字是指一种土耳其甜点巴克拉。2010 年 10 月，土耳其当局允许公司发行债券。

注：（1）Turkish Lira 土耳其里拉，是土耳其原先使用的货币，但由于面值太大使用不便，更一度成为世界上最不值钱的货币之一。2005 年 1 月 1 日起开始启用新土耳其里拉；（2）相关术语：Yeni Türk Lirası 新土耳其里拉；fractional currency 辅币；standard currency 主币；Kurus 库鲁（土耳其辅币）；exchange rate 兑换汇率

**2. Callable bond　可赎回债券**

For instance, on Nov 28, HongKong-listed Long For Properties Co. Ltd. informed the Hong Kong Stock Exchange that it has redeemed callable bonds of $417 million maturing in 2019.(*China Daily*/2016-12-22)

例如，11 月 28 日，香港上市龙湖置业有限公司通知香港证券交易所，它已经赎回 2019 年到期的 4.17 亿美元可赎回债券。

注：（1）HongKong Stock Exchange 香港证券交易所，简称港交所，是全球一大主要交易所集团，也是一家在香港上市的控股公司，在香港及伦敦均有营运交易所。

（2）相关术语：① New York Stock Exchange 纽约证券交易所；② Tokyo Stock Exchange 东京证券交易所；③ Nasdaq Stock Exchange 纳斯达克证券交易所；④ London Stock Exchange 伦敦证券交易所；⑤ Nyse Euronext 纽约泛欧证交所；⑥ Toronto Stock Exchange 多伦多证券交易所；⑦ Frankfurt Stock Exchange 法兰克福证券交易所；⑧ Madrid Stock Exchange 马德里证券交易所；⑨ Swiss Stock Exchange 瑞士证券交易所

A callable bond (also called redeemable bond) is a type of bond (debt security) that allows the issuer of the bond to retain the privilege of redeeming the bond at some point before the bond reaches its date of maturity.

可赎回债券亦称"可买回债券"，是指发行人有权在特定的时间按照某个价格强制从债券持有人手中将其赎回的债券，可视为是债券与看涨期权的结合体。

注：（1）date of maturity 到期日，就是期权生命中的最后一日，债券的到期日是指偿还本金的日期；（2）近义词辨析：① expiry date，指信用证的有效期，过了这个期限，信用证则作废；② maturity date，指远期信用证下的汇票的付款期限，到这一天就应付款；（3）相关术语：① futures 期货；② maturity factoring 到期保付代理业务；③ maturity yield 到期收益率

**3. Collateralized debt obligation　债务抵押债券**

Lenders in the world's second-biggest economy have issued 148.7 billion yuan ($24.2 billion) in collateralized debt obligations this year, Bloomberg data showed. (*China Daily*/ 2014-09-13)

彭博社数据显示，世界第二大经济体借款人今年已发行 1487 亿元（242 亿美元）的债务抵押债券。

注：（1）obligation 义务，职责，债务；（2）近义词辨析：① duty，指按道德和法律的标准，一个人应该要尽的义务，强调自觉性；② responsibility，指任何义务、职责、责任或职务上所应尽的本分，强调对他人的责任；③ function，指因职务或职业关系而履行某种职责；④ liability 与 assets 相对；⑤ obligation，指道义上或法律上对他人的义务，强调强制性，也指因作出承诺而被迫履行的某种义务；（3）相关术语：creditor's rights 债权；creditor 债权人；debtor 债务人

A collateralized debt obligation (CDO) is a type of structured asset-backed security (ABS). Originally developed for the corporate debt markets, over time CDOs evolved to encompass the mortgage and mortgage-backed security (MBS) markets.

债务抵押债券（CDO）是一种结构性资产支持证券（ABS）。最初是为公司债券市场开发的，随着时间的推移，CDO 逐渐演变为包括抵押贷款和抵押担保的证券（MBS）市场。

注：（1）structured asset-backed security 结构性资产支持债券，指企业通过利用特定目的的实体将拥有未来现金流的特定资产剥离开来，并以该特定资产为标的进行融资。（2）相关术语：dual-currency bonds 双货币债券；equity-index-linked notes 股指联系债券；commodity-linked bull and bear notes 商品联系债券；swap-linked notes 互换联系债券；forward contract 远期合约；principal 本金

**4. Corporate bonds　公司债券**

The Zhejiang-based Hengyi Petrochemical Co. on Monday issued 500 million yuan ($79 million) of three-year Belt and Road corporate bonds on the Shenzhen Stock Exchange.(*China Daily*/2018-03-06)

总部位于浙江的恒益石油化工股份有限公司周一在深圳证券交易所发行了三年期 5 亿元（7.9 亿美元）一带一路公司债券。

注：（1）Shenzhen Stock Exchange (SZSE)，深圳证券交易所，中国大陆有两家证券交易所，即上海证券交易所和深圳证券交易所，连同香港证券交易所和台湾证券交易所，中国一共有四家证券交易所；（2）相关术语：Shanghai Exchange Stock (SSE) 上海证券交易所；Taiwan Stock Exchange Corporation (TWSE) 台湾证券交易所

A corporate bond is a bond issued by a corporation in order to raise financing for a variety of reasons such as to ongoing operations, M&A, or to expand business.

公司债券是一种由公司发行的债券，其目的是为各种原因筹集资金，如持续经营、并购或扩大业务。

注：（1）M&A（mergers and acquisitions）合并与收购、并购，指两家或者更多的独立企业、公司合并组成一家企业，通常由一家占优势的公司吸收一家或者多家公司。

（2）近义词辨析：① merger 兼并，指一个公司对另一个公司的兼并，其多以被兼并公司的消亡形式进行，此时被兼并公司已失去其法人身份，不再是独立的商务实体；② acquisition 并购，多指一个公司以收购某公司股份的方式进行接管或达到控股的目的，结果是两个法人的实体地位在交易之后仍可同时存在，多用作收购小公司；③ consolidation 合并，常用于大公司的合并，在合并时多有新资本注入，与 M&A 的主要区别在于它是把两个或两个以上的公司合并成为一家新公司，而原有的诸公司都得宣布解散。

（3）相关术语：legal person 法人；legal representative 法定代表人；corporate restructuring 公司重组

**5. CoCo　应急可转换债**

Contingent convertible bonds, or "cocos," have been proposed as a solution to this problem. (*China Daily*/2011-10-13)

应急可转换债券，或又被称为"cocos"，已被提议作为解决这一问题的方法。

注：（1）propose 提议，建议；（2）同义词辨析：① suggest，语气较委婉，指提出一些不成熟的建议，或发表一些参考意见；② propose，常用于正式地提出建议；（3）相关术语：propose someone for 推荐某人（参加某组织），提名某人（任某职）；make a proposal 提出建议

A contingent convertible bond (CoCo), also known as an enhanced capital note (ECN), is a fixed-income instrument that is convertible into equity if a pre-specified trigger event occurs.

应急可转换债券（CoCo），也称为增强型资本票据（ECN），是一种固定收益工具，在发生预先规定的触发事件时可转换为权益。

注：（1）capital note 资本票据，是企业发行作为短期债务来源的定息工具，用于弥

补公司短期资金不足；这种票据没有担保，完全依赖公司的信用，通常评定等级较低；（2）相关术语：credit 信用；credit guarantee 信用担保；short-term debt 短期债务；fixed interest 定息

**6. Exchangeable bond 可交换债券**

The national securities watchdog on Friday announced plans to allow shareholders of listed companies to issue exchangeable bonds, in an attempt to ease oversupply in the stock market. (*China Daily*/September,96,2008/http://www.chinadaily.com.cn/cndy/2008-09/06/content_7004137.htm)

周五，国家证券监管机构宣布计划允许上市公司股东发行可交换债券，以缓解股市中的过度供应。

注：（1）the national securities watchdog 国家证券监管机构，是国家行政管理机构，由国家或政府组建的对证券市场实施监督管理的主管机构；（2）相关术语：China Securities Regulatory Commission（CSRC）中国证监会；China Banking Regulatory Commission 中国银保监会

An Exchangeable bond (or XB) is a type of hybrid security consisting of a straight bond and an embedded option to exchange the bond for the stock of a company other than the issuer (usually a subsidiary or company in which the issuer owns a stake) at some future date and under prescribed conditions.

可交换债券（或 XB）是一种混合证券，由直接债券和嵌入期权组成，用于在未来某个日期和规定条件下，将债券与发行人以外的公司（通常是发行人持有股份的子公司或公司）的股票进行交换。

注：（1）straight bond 普通公司债券，指按照既定利率，到期获得本息，不参与发行公司任何管理事项的一般公司债券，是一种典型的公司债券。通常情况下，普通公司债券的信用度比政府债券略低，但其利率比政府债券略高。（2）相关术语：special corporate bond 特殊公司债券；government bond 政府债券；financing 筹资；OMO（open-market operation）公开市场业务

**7. Eurodollar bonds 欧洲美元债券**

In the latter regard, the *Boston Globe* recently put a spotlight on a major public policy issue that has been ignored by virtually every other newspaper in the United States: the ominous financial, political and strategic implications of Moscow's incipient bid to market bonds on the Eurodollar market. (*Forbes*/ April 11, 2012 https://www.forbes.com/forbes/2012/0411/100.html#42c626f962)

在后一方面，《波士顿环球报》最近将焦点放在了一个几乎被美国所有其他报纸忽视的重大公共政策问题上：莫斯科刚刚开始竞购欧元市场债券所带来的在财政、政治和战略方面的不祥的影响。

注：（1）bid 出价，投标；（2）近义词辨析：① tender 招标书，是一种邀请供应商为提供产品或服务而进行报价的正式且结构化的邀请文件；② bid 投标，是供应商对那些招标书的报价，包括的内容有定价、有效性和交付时间表等；（3）相关术语：bid price

投标价格，买入价；bid document 投标文件；bid security 投标保证金；to bid 叫牌，申报，出价

A Eurodollar bond is a US-dollar denominated bond issued by an overseas company and held in a foreign institution outside both the U.S. and the issuer's home country. Eurodollar bonds are an important source of capital for multinational companies and foreign governments.

欧洲美元债券是由海外公司发行的以美元计价的债券，由美国和发行人母国以外的外国机构持有。欧洲美元债券是跨国公司和外国政府的重要资金来源。

注：（1）multinational company 跨国公司，主要是指发达资本主义国家的垄断企业，以本国为基地，通过对外直接投资，在世界各地设立分支机构或子公司，从事国际化生产和经营活动的垄断企业。（2）相关术语：monopoly enterprise 垄断企业；subsidiary corporation 子公司；parent company 母公司，总公司；headquarters（HQ）总部

**8. Engagement letter　审计业务约定书**

The NYSE's chairman, Marshall Carter, and its chief executive, John Thain, told members that the arrangement with Goldman (where Thain used to work, incidentally) was carefully vetted by former Chairman John Reed, who signed the engagement letter with the investment bank. (*Forbes*/MAR 6, 2008/https://www.forbes.com/forbes/2008/0324/100.html#42c626f962)

纽约证交所主席马歇尔·卡特和首席执行官约翰·塞恩告诉成员们，与高盛（顺便提一下，塞恩过去曾在高盛工作）的安排经过了前董事长约翰·里德的仔细审查，里德与高盛签署了审计业务约定书。

注：（1）investment bank 投资银行，主要从事证券发行、承销、交易、企业重组、兼并与收购、投资分析、风险投资、项目融资等业务的非银行金融机构，是资本市场上的主要金融中介；（2）投资银行的组织形态主要有四种：① 独立型的专业性投资银行，比如美国的高盛、摩根士丹利；② 商业银行拥有的投资银行，在英德等国非常典型，比如汇丰集团、瑞银集团；③ 全能型银行，直接经营投资银行业务，主要出现在欧洲，既从事投资银行业务又从事商业银行业务；④ 跨国财务公司。（3）相关术语：Goldman-Sachs 高盛；Morgan Stanley 摩根士丹利；HSBC Group 汇丰集团；UBS group 瑞银集团

An engagement letter defines the legal relationship (or engagement) between a professional firm.

业务约定书定义了专业公司之间的法律关系（或约定）。

注：（1）professional firm 专业公司，由同一行业，生产同类产品或同类零件，或工艺相同的企业联合组成的公司，它主要是工业生产中横向联合而形成的。（2）相关术语：part 零部件；combination 联合；professionalization 专业化

### 2.3.2　公司债券相关概念

**1. Credit spread　信贷息差**

Domestic companies had troubles in raising funds through bond sales as credit spread turned upward in the corporate debt market amid concerns over the earlier-than-expected end of the US quantitative easing. (*Global Times*/2013-07-08)

由于对美国量化宽松政策提前结束的担忧，企业债务市场的信用利差上升，国内企业在通过债券销售筹集资金方面遇到了困难。

注：（1）quantitative easing 量化宽松，主要指中央银行在实行零利率或近似零利率政策后，通过购买国债等中长期债券，增加基础货币供给，向市场注入大量流动性资金的干预方式，以鼓励开支和借贷，也被简化地形容为间接增印钞票。（2）相关术语：quantitative tightening 量化紧缩

Credit spread is (in finance) a credit spread, or net credit spread is an options strategy that involves a purchase of one option and a sale of another option in the same class and expiration but different strike prices.

在金融中，信用利差（Credit spread）或净信用利差是一种期权策略，涉及购买一种期权，出售同一类别、到期日相同但执行价格不同的另一种期权。

注：（1）option 期权，指一种合约，源于 18 世纪后期的美国和欧洲市场，该合约赋予持有人在某一特定日期或该日之前的任何时间以固定价格购进或售出一种资产的权利。（2）相关术语：① put option 看跌期权；② call option 看涨期权；③ exotic option 奇异期权；④ binary option 二元期权

**2. Debenture　债券**

As viewed from the five-year debenture bonds that are comparatively important in the market, the interest spread has dropped from a peak of 1.8 percentage points to around 0.6 percentage points currently. (*China Daily*/2015-07-23)

从市场上相对重要的五年期债券来看，息差已从 1.8 个百分点的峰值下降到目前的 0.6 个百分点左右。

注：（1）debenture 无担保债券，或称信用债券，也指海关退税凭单（海关发给进口商，对其进口后又出口的货物予以降低或减免关税的凭单）；（2）区分：bond，指有担保债券，二者区别在于有无担保。

Debenture is a medium to long-term debt instrument used by large companies to borrow money, at a fixed rate of interest.

债券是大公司以固定利率借钱的一种中长期债务工具。

注：（1）long-term debt 长期债务；（2）相关术语：long-term debt rate 长期负债比率；subordinated long-term debt 次级长期债务

**3. Coupon payment　债券票息支付**

The Hong Kong branch of mainland brokerage firm Guosen Securities has defaulted on its “dim sum” bonds traded in the city, putting a coupon payment of 38 million yuan ($5.9 million) at risk. (*Global Times*/2016-3-31)

中国内地券商国信证券香港分行在其“点心”债券上违约，支付 3 800 万元（590 万美元）利息。

注：（1）trade vs transact：transaction 交易，强调互换性，在形容商品和业务之间的

交易时用。trade 贸易，泛指行业，货物的进出口买卖等使用。（2）Guosen Securities 国信证券，成立于 1994 年，AA 级券商，在全国 38 个城市有 54 家营业网点；（3）2018 年中国 TOP5 证券公司（按市场份额）排名：HTSC 华泰证券、Guotai J&A Securities 国泰君安证券、CITICS 中信证券、Galaxy Securities 银河证券及 Haitong Securities 海通证券。

A coupon payment is a payment made to the holder of a bond for the interest that bond accrues while it is maturing.

债券息票支付是向债券持有人支付债券到期时产生的利息。

注：bondholder 债券持有人，是在采用发行债券的方式筹措长期资金时，资金贷方即为债券持有人，为购买债券之人，在债券法律关系中处于债权人地位。债券持有人主要有个人和机构投资者，如私人银行、保险公司、投资信托公司、退休金基金、中央银行、商业银行、公司法人等。各类债券持有人购买债券的共同目的是为了获取利息和资本收益。

**4. Company Limited　有限责任公司**

Last year the Maldives Airport Company Limited (MACL) decided to hand over the development of the Seaplane Facilities at the Maldives Velana International Airport to BUCG. (*Global Times*/2018/2/14)

去年，马尔代夫机场有限公司（MACL）决定将马尔代夫 Velana 国际机场水上飞机设施开发移交给 BUCG。

注：BUCG 北京城建集团有限公司，是以工程总承包、房地产开发、设计咨询、经营生产和资本运作相结合的大型综合性建筑企业集团，具有房屋建筑工程、公路工程施工总承包特级资质和市政公用工程、机电安装、地基与基础、钢结构、公路路面、城市轨道交通工程等具有房屋建筑工程、公路工程施工总承包特级资质和市政公用工程、机电安装、地基与基础、钢结构、公路路面、城市轨道交通工程等总承包一级资质。

Company Limited is a company in which the liability of its members or subscribers is limited to what they have invested or guaranteed to the company. Limited companies may be limited by shares or by guarantee.

在有限责任公司，公司成员或认购人的责任仅限于他们向公司投资或担保的内容。有限公司可以是股份有限公司或担保有限公司。

注：（1）Company Limited 有限责任公司，指根据《中华人民共和国公司登记管理条例》规定登记注册，由 50 个以下的股东出资设立，每个股东以其所认缴的出资额为限对公司承担有限责任，公司法人以其全部资产对公司债务承担全部责任的经济组织；（2）区分：Stock Corporation 股份有限公司；二者区别在于股份有限公司可以公开募股集资，且发起人数应有 2 人以上 200 人以下，股东以其出资额为限承担有限责任。

**5. Follow-on offering　后续发行**

Tesla this morning said it plans a follow-on stock offering of 5.3 million shares, all to be sold by the company. (*Forbes*/MAY 25, 2011/https://www.forbes.com/sites/ericsavitz/2011/05/25/telsa-jumps-plans-stock-offer-musk-daimler-to-boost-stakes/#66be6ff3770e)

特斯拉今天上午表示，计划后续发行 530 万股股票，全部由该公司出售。

注：（1）share 股份，代表对公司的部分拥有权；（2）相关术语：initial public offerings (IPO) 首次公开募股；share price 股价；share capital 股本；lion's share 最大的份额；on shares 共同担负盈亏

Follow-on offering (FPO) is an issuance of stock shares following a company's initial public offering (IPO). There are two types of follow-on offerings, diluted and non-diluted. A diluted follow-on offering results in the company issuing new shares which cause the lowering a company's earnings per share (EPS). During a non-diluted follow-on offering, shares coming into the market already existed and the EPS remains unchanged. Companies offering additional shares must register the FPO offering and provide a prospectus to regulators.

后续发行（FPO）是在公司首次公开发行（IPO）之后发行股票。有两种后续产品，稀释和非稀释。公司发行新股后续发行业绩被稀释，导致公司每股收益（EPS）下降。在非稀释后续发行期间，入市股票已经存在，EPS 保持不变。发行额外股份的公司必须登记 FPO 发行，并向监管机构提供招股说明书。

注：earnings per share (EPS) 每股收益

**6. Market capitalization 市值**

The index is weighted by the firm' market capitalization and the share of their revenues they get from China.(article.yeeyan.org)

这些指数是根据企业总市值和他们在中国收入份额进行加权平均计算而得。

注：（1） weighted 加权，即由测量值精度的不同在平差计算中所取的权重不同。精度越高，权越大。"加权"的意思就是"乘以权重"，即"乘以系数"的意思。（2）相关术语：diffusion-weighted 弥散加权；weighted sum of square 加权平方和

Market capitalization is the total value of stocks calculated from the market price of a listed company's issued shares.

市值是根据上市公司已发行股票的市场价格计算的股票总价值。

注：（1）issued shares 已发行股票，公司通过发行股票收到现金，则这些股票就成为已发行股票。股份有限公司的资本划分为股份，每一股的金额相等。公司通过出售这些股份筹集资本，成为发行股份。因此，股份是公司资本最基本的构成单位，每个股份不可再分；（2）相关术语：issued and outstanding shares 总发行股数

**7. Net financing of corporate bonds 企业债券**

Only a few net financings of corporate bonds have been going through lately, and most have been through the government, which has agreed to guarantee financial institutions' bond sales.

最近只有少数企业债券有所交易，而且绝大部分是通过政府来实现，美国政府已同意担保金融机构债券销售。

注：（1）financial institution 金融机构，指从事金融业有关的金融中介机构，为金融体系的一部分；（2）金融机构包括：bank 银行，securities company 证券公司，insurance company 保险公司，trust and investment company 信托投资公司，SAIF Partners 基金管理

公司等。

Net financing of corporate bonds is a kind of bond that is issued by an enterprise in accordance with legal procedures and agreed to repay the principal and interest within a specified period of time.

公司债券净融资是指企业按照法律程序发行公司债券净融资是指企业按照法定程序发行并约定在一定期限内偿还本息的债券。

注：principal and interest 本金及利息

**8. Netting settlement　净额清算**

Netting settlement is a common way for multinational corporations to manage cash. (www.treasurer.org.cn)

净额清算是跨国公司现金管理的一种常用方式。

注：（1）multinational corporations 跨国公司，主要是指发达资本主义国家的垄断企业，以本国为基地，通过对外直接投资，在世界各地设立分支机构或子公司，从事国际化生产和经营活动的垄断企业；（2）跨国公司又称 multi-national enterprise（多国公司）、international firm（国际公司）、supranational enterprise（超国家公司）和 cosmo-corporation（宇宙公司）等。

Netting settlement means that within a certain period of time, the parent company of a multinational company and its subsidiaries and between the subsidiaries do not follow the amount of the transaction, but pay the net amount after the gap.

净额结算是指在一定时期内，跨国公司的母公司与子公司之间以及子公司之间不按照交易金额进行结算，而是按照差额后的净额进行支付。

注：近义词辨析：transaction 交易，强调互换性，在形容商品和业务之间的交易时使用；trade 贸易，泛指行业货物的进出口买卖等使用 trade；deal 经营、代理，强调交易具体的动作。

**9. Offering price　发行价格**

The theory unifies previous explanations of the underpricing phenomenon while yielding a closed-form solution for the optimal offering price for underwritten securities. (The optimal offering price for underwritten securities/1993/https://search.proquest.com/docview/304076815/8F2D4C9F0F0948DBPQ/2?accountid=14662)

该理论统一先前对低估现象的解释，同时为包销证券最优发行价格提供封闭形式的解决方案。

注：（1）underpricing phenomenon 抑价现象，指首次公开发行定价明显低于上市初始的市场价格。当抑价发生时，由于发行方以低于股票自身价值的价格进行销售，现有股东可能会遭受损失，而新股东则能够从他们购买的股份中获得更高的报酬率。（2）相关术语：IPO（Initial Public Offerings）首次公开募股

Offering price is the price at which someone offers a share or bond for sale.

发行价格是指某人出售股票或债券的价格。

**10. Option value　期权价值**

Paper further uses real option theory to evaluate those three different types of real option value. (Research on the evaluation of the china inner financed bot of highway project based on the real option/2001/https://search.proquest.com/docview/1874854195/44CEEFCDCA9343 F8PQ/1?accountid=14662)

论文进一步运用实物期权理论来评估这三种不同类型的实物期权价值。

注：（1）real option 实物期权，是一种期权，其底层证券是既非股票又非期货的实物商品，又叫 equity option 股票期权和 index option 指数期权，是管理者对所拥有的实物资产进行决策时所具有的柔性投资策略。（2）分类：option to delay investment 延迟投资期权；option to expand 扩张期权；option to contract 收缩期权；option to stop 中止期权；option to switch use 转换期权；corporate growth option 企业增长期权

Option value means that the holder of the convertible bond has the right to purchase the stock corresponding to the bond at any time before maturity.

期权价值是指可转换债券持有人有权在到期前的任何时间购买与债券对应的股票。

注：bond maturity 债券到期，指偿还本金的日期。债券一般都要规定到期日，以便到期归还本金。

**11. Outright purchases　买断**

That means share sales are structurally higher than outright purchases.(http://www.iciba.com/)

这意味着从结构上来说，售出股票数量要超过买断数量。

Outright Purchases is government securities purchased outright by the authorities, with no agreement to subsequently sell them through a repurchase pact or reverse repo.

买断是当局直接购买政府证券，随后没有通过回购协议或逆回购协议出售。

注：repurchase pact 回购协议，是卖出一种证券，并约定于未来某一时间以约定的价格再购回该证券的交易协议。根据该协议所进行的交易称回购交易。

**12. Obligatory right　债权**

Injuring obligatory right by the third party is the modern creditor's rights system and the torts system development product. (On the issues on injuring obligatory right by the third party/2009/https://search. proquest.com/docview/1870499457/329A8472C353450BPQ/1?accountid=14662)

第三方侵权责任是现代债权制度和侵权制度发展的产物。

注：（1）tort system 侵权，是一种侵害他人权益的行为，因此侵权行为也可以称为一种侵害行为。（2）相关术语：civil tort 民事侵权；（3）infringement vs. tort：infringement 表示主观上不要求有过错的侵权行为类型，即为无过错责任侵权行为；tort 表示主观上要求有过错的侵权行为类型，即过错责任侵权行为类型。在英美法系，infringement 一词专用于知识产权侵权，tort 一词泛指一切类型的侵权行为。

The obligatory right means a kind of debtor-creditor relationship which results from public law or with nature of public law.

债权指源于公法或具有公法性质的一种债权债务关系。

注：（1）public law 公法，主要是指调整国家与普通公民、组织之间关系以及国家机关及其组成人员之间关系的法律，私法主要是调整普通公民、组织之间关系的法律。（2）我国公法有 Constitution of the People's Republic of China 宪法、Criminal Law of the People's Republic of China 刑法、Administrative Law 行政法等。

**13. Price bidding　竞价**

It was also discussed how to collect useful compete information for bidding strategy and made them available for enterprises' bidding price strategy. (Study on strategies of bidding price in projects/2010/https://search.proquest.com/ docview/1868353367/A70BF0EE5F694425PQ/1?accountid=14662)

如何为竞价策略收集有用的竞争信息并使之适用于企业竞价策略也在讨论之列。

The price bidding is marked by the interest rate or price, which aims to find the real interest rate of the interbank market and the expectation of the commercial bank to the interest rate.

价格竞价是以利率或价格为标的，目的是找出银行间市场实际利率和商业银行对利率的预期。

注：（1）commercial bank 商业银行，英文缩写为 CB，是银行的一种类型，职责是通过存款、贷款、汇兑、储蓄等业务承担信用中介的金融机构；（2）中国六大商业银行，是指六个全国性股份制商业银行：CMBC（China Merchants Bank）招商银行、HXB（Hua Xia Bank）华夏银行、CCB（China CITIC Bank）中信银行、CIB（China Industrial Bank）兴业银行、SPDB（Shanghai Pudong Development Bank）浦发银行、CMBC（China Minsheng Banking Corp）民生银行。

# Chapter 3

# Terminologies of Trust
# （信托篇）

## 3.1 Trust（信托）

### 3.1.1 信托

**1. Trust 信托**

信托是一种理财方式，是一种特殊的财产管理制度和法律行为，同时又是一种金融制度。信托机构的首要职能和唯一服务宗旨是为财产所有者提供广泛有效的服务，并把管理、运用、处分、经营财产的作用体现在业务中。信托已成为现代金融业的一个重要组成部分，与银行业、保险业、证券业既有联系又有区别。

Trusts have many potential advantages, but they can be complicated and expensive. In many cases, there are better ways to achieve results. So when can trusts usefully play a role and how can their users avoid becoming ensnared in costs and complexity? (*Financial Times* /2 February 2018/https://www.ft.com/content/8a260fe4-e1c7-11e7-8f9f- de1c2175f5ce)

信托机构有很多潜在优势，但机构复杂并且昂贵，在很多情况下有更好方法达到目的。因此信托机构何时能够真正发挥作用，其用户如何才能避免陷入成本和复杂性陷阱？

注：cost 成本，成本价格（产品价值中属于投入的生产要素价值的那一部分）

A trust is a fiduciary relationship in which one party, known as a trustor, gives another party, the trustee, the right to hold title to property or assets for the benefit of a third party, the beneficiary.

信托是一种受信关系，在这种关系中一方作为委托人以第三方（受益人）利益为目的，将财产或资产所有权授予另一方（受托人）。

注：（1）asset 资产，指由企业过去交易或事项所形成，由企业拥有或者控制，预期会给企业带来经济利益的资源；（2）property 财产，指所拥有金钱、物资、房屋、土地等物质财富，是具有金钱价值并受到法律保护的权利总称，大体上财产分为三种，即动产、不动产和知识财产；（3）相关术语：owners' equity 所有者权益，会计主体所有者对

于该主体净资产的索取权；liabilities 负债，会计主体所承担由过去经济活动形成的以货币计量的经济责任

**2. Handling of the trust　处理信托**

处理信托是指改变信托财产的性质、原状以实现财产增值的信托业务。在处理信托中，信托财产具有物上代位性，即财产可以变换形式，如将财产变卖转为资金，或购买有价证券等。若以房屋为对象设立处理信托，受托人就可以将房屋出售，换取其他形式的财产。若以动产为对象设立处理信托，受托人就可以将动产出售。

The debts incurred from the trustee's handling of the trust and the creditor requires the debts to be paid off. (http://dict.youdao.com/search)

受托人处理信托所产生债务，债权人要求清偿该债务（这种情形下，对信托财产不得强制执行）。

注：（1）trustee 受托人，信托关系中依信托意图管理被授予信托财产并承担信托义务的当事人；（2）creditor 债权，主要是指预付款者，有权请求他方为特定行为的权利主体，是指那些对企业提供需偿还的融资的机构和个人，包括给企业提供贷款的机构或个人（贷款债权人）和以出售货物或劳务形式提供短期融资的机构或个人（商业债权人）。

Handling of the trust is the act of changing the nature of the trust property to realize the appreciation of the property.

信托处理是指改变信托财产性质、原状以实现财产增值的信托业务。

相关术语：（1）appreciation of the property 财产增值；（2）impairment of property 财产减值

**3. Management buyout (MBO)　管理层收购**

管理层收购，意为管理层利用杠杆融资对目标企业进行收购。目标公司的管理者或经营层利用借贷所融资本或股权交易收购本公司的股份的行为，从而改变公司所有者结构、控制权结构和资产结构，进而达到重组公司的目的，并获取预期收益。

As a hot operating technology of stock equity in Chinese enterprises, management buyout (MBO) trust has many deficiencies in practical operation in recent years. (http://www.youdao.com/example/blng/eng/mbo)

管理层收购信托作为中国企业热衷的股权经营机制，近年来在实际操作中存在诸多不足。

注：stock 股票，是一种有价证券，是股份公司在筹集资本时向出资人发行的股份凭证；equity 股权，是有限责任公司或者股份有限公司的股东对公司享有的人身和财产权益的一种综合性权利。

A management buyout is a transaction where a company's management team purchases the assets and operations of the business they manage.

管理层收购是一项交易，即公司的管理层购买他们所管理的资产和业务。

相关术语：（1）transaction 交易；（2）deal 交易

## 3.1.2 信托财产

**信托财产**，指受托人依据信托意图管理和支配的财产，是信托的构成要素之一。依信托法规则，信托财产须为特定化的和现实存在的财产；受托人因信托财产的管理运用、处分或者其他情形而取得的财产，也归入信托财产；它可由不动产、股票、公债、抵押契据、保险单、银行存款等构成，但非财产性合同权利不能作为信托财产。

**1. Value-at-risk 风险值**

风险值，照字面解释就是风险价值，确切来讲，是指在一定概率水平（置信度）下，某一金融资产或证券组合价值在未来特定时期内的最大可能损失。

But value-at-risk is a crude way to measure how much the banks are gambling, in part because it does not specify how big possible losses are on the remaining trading days in a year. (cn.reuters.com)

但风险值只是评估银行承担风险程度的粗略指标，部分原因是该数值并未具体显示一年中其他交易日的最大可能损失规模。

注：trade，指买卖或交易行为，通常指以货币为媒介的一切交换活动或行为。

Value at risk (VaR) is a measure of the risk of loss for investments. It estimates how much a set of investments might lose (with a given probability), given normal market conditions, in a set time period such as a day.

风险价值是衡量投资损失风险的指标。用来估计在正常市场条件下，在一天这样固定的时间段内，一组投资在给定概率下可能会损失多少。

注：（1）investment 投资，货币转化为资本的过程，是指国家或企业以及个人，为了特定目的，与对方签订协议，促进社会发展，实现互惠互利，输送资金的过程。又是特定经济主体为了在未来可预见的时期内获得收益或资金增值，在一定时期内向一定领域投放足够数额的资金或实物的货币等价物的经济行为。（2）分类：real investment 实物投资；capital investment 资本投资；securities investment 证券投资

**2. Working capital 营运资金，营运资本**

营运资金是企业流动资产和流动负债的总称，流动资产减去流动负债的余额称为净营运资金。营运资金周转时间短，可以通过短期筹资方式加以解决。非现金形态的营运资金如存货、应收账款、短期有价证券容易变现，这一点对企业应付临时性的资金需求有重要意义。营运数量具有波动性，流动资产或流动负债容易受内外条件的影响，数量的波动往往很大。营运资金来源具有多样性，既可通过长期筹资方式解决，也可通过短期筹资方式解决，短期筹资方式有：银行短期借款、短期融资、商业信用、票据贴现等多种方式。

It means you have been profitable for a while but need working capital because of fast growth. Most banks like to fund these.（article.yeeyan.org）

这意味着你已经盈利一段时间，但因为迅速发展而需要营运资金。大多数银行愿意为这些项目提供资金。

注：营运资金分为广义的营运资金和狭义的营运资金，前者是指毛营运资金，即公

司流动资产的总额；后者是指净营运资金，即流动资产减去流动负债以后的余额。

Working capital (abbreviated WC) is a financial metric which represents operating liquidity available to a business, organisation or other entity, including governmental entities. Along with fixed assets such as plant and equipment, working capital is considered a part of operating capital. Gross working capital is equal to current assets.

营运资金（缩写 WC）是一种财务指标，表示企业、组织或包括政府实体在内的其他实体可获得的操作流动性。与厂房、设备等固定资产一样，营运资金被认为是运营资本的一部分。总营运资本等于流动资产。

注：current assets 流动资产，指企业可以在一年或者超过一年的一个营业周期内变现或者运用的资产，是企业资产中必不可少的组成部分。

**3. Trust property　信托财产**

信托财产是指受托人依据信托意图而管理和支配的财产，是信托的构成要素之一。

The trustee is required to manage the trust property in accordance with the trustor's wishes and in the beneficiary's best interests. (Investopedia/https://www.investopedia.com/terms/t/trust-property.asp)

受托人应当按照委托人的意愿和受益人的最大利益管理信托财产。

Trust property refers to assets that have been placed into a fiduciary relationship between a trustor and trustee for a designated beneficiary. Trust property may include any type of asset such as cash, securities, real estate or life insurance policies.

信托财产是指委托人与受托人之间为指定受益人而建立信托关系的财产。信托财产可能包括任何类型的资产，如现金、证券、房地产或人寿保险政策。

相关术语：property 财产；material property 有形财产（capital, resources, products, equipment）；intangible property 无形财产（creditor's rights, intellectual property rights, virtual property rights）

**4. Principal　本金**

本金即贷款、存款或投资在计算利息之前的原始金额。企业本金（包括固定资金和流动资金）作为整体，是同时地、在空间上并列地处在它的各个不同阶段上，以不同的本金占用形态表现。本金的每一种占用形态又都不断地依次由上一阶段过渡到下一阶段，由一种形态转化为另一种形态。

Your success as a trustee lies mainly in your ability to determine what's principal and what's income. (Dummies/http://www.dummies.com/personal-finance/estate-planning/what-are-a-trusts-principal-and-income/)

作为受托人，你的成功取决于你判断本金和收入的能力。

注：income 收入，指企业在日常活动中形成的、会导致所有者权益增加的、与所有者投入资本无关的经济利益的总流入。

The principal is all the property that's available to produce ordinary income like dividends, interest, or rents. As you make payments, some may come from principal and some from income, depending on what you, as trustee, decide. Others, such as beneficiary payments, come only from the income.

本金是所有可以产生普通收入的财产，如股息、利息或租金。当你支付款项时，有些可能来自本金，有些可能来自收入，这取决于你作为受托人的决定。其他的，如受益人的付款，则只来自收入。

注：（1）interest 利息，是货币在一定时期内的使用费，指货币持有者（债权人）因贷出货币或货币资本而从借款人（债务人）手中获得的报酬，interest=principle×interest rate；（2）相关术语：deposit interest 存款利息；loan interest 贷款利息

### 3.1.3 信托目的

**Value investment　价值投资**

价值投资就是实业投资思维在股市上的应用，以获取企业发展、扩大促使股票上涨所产生的收益。凡是买股票时把自己当成长期股东的都是价值投资者，这里的长期是指5～10 年的股票持有期。价值投资要求回到初心，强调股票投资和实业投资的一致性。股票投资、股权投资、风险投资、天使投资等投资方式的内核都是一致的。

To be a value investor, you must buy at a discount from underlying value. Analyzing each potential value investment opportunity therefore begins with an assessment of business value.（szjxhy.blog.163.com）

要成为一名价值投资者，你必须以低于内在价值的价格买入（股票）。因此，分析每个潜在的价值投资机会首先要评估业务价值。

注：（1）assessment 公司估值，指着眼于上市或非上市公司本身，对其内在价值进行评估；（2）business value 企业价值，指企业本身的价值，是对企业有形资产和无形资产价值资产的市场评价。企业价值不是指企业账面资产的总价值，由于企业商誉的存在，通常企业的实际市场价值远远超过账面资产的价值；（3）相关术语：goodwill 商誉；impairment 减值

Value investment is an investment paradigm which generally involves buying securities that appear underpriced by some form of fundamental analysis, though it has taken many forms since its inception.

价值投资是一种投资模式，它通常涉及购买那些被某些基本分析方法低估的证券，虽然它从一开始就采取了多种形式。

注：基于分析方法的几种形式：① relative valuation or comparative valuation 相对估值法：price-earnings ratio 市盈率；enterprise multiple 企业倍数；price-to-book ratio 股价与账面价值比率；② absolute valuation 绝对估值法：自由现金流（FCFF）、股权自由现金流（FECE）和股利贴现模型（DDM）

### 3.1.4 收益凭证

**收益凭证**，指由证券公司以自身信用发行，约定本金和收益的偿付与特定标的相关联的有价证券；特定标的包括但不限于货币利率、基础商品、证券的价格，或者指数。

**1. Trust agreement　信托协议**

信托协议（主要指信托合同及其附件）是信托行为的依据，即信托关系的成立必经由相关的信托关系文件作保证。信托行为的发生必须由委托人和受托人进行约定。

Trust agreements can be great tools, but they're complex；it's important to understand how they work and how to get started. (Financial resource center/28 November 2005/http://resourcecenter.cuna.org/21654/article/ 1143/html)

信托约定可能是很好的工具，但它们太复杂；理解它们怎么运作、怎么开始是很重要的。

Formal agreement through which a trustor vests the ownership rights (title) to one or more assets to one or more trustees for conservation and protection on behalf of one or more beneficiaries of the trust.

委托人将所有权授予一个或多个受托人，以代表信托一个或多个受益人进行保护的正式协议（trust agreement）。

注：（1）ownership rights 所有权，所有权是所有人依法对自己财产所享有的占有、使用、收益和处分的权利。是对生产劳动的目的、对象、手段、方法和结果的支配力量，它是一种财产权，所以又称财产所有权。（2）特点：imperium 绝对权；exclusiveness 排他性；property right 物权

**2. Declaration of trust　信托声明**

A declaration of trust outlines who the trust is in benefit of, who can amend or revoke the trust (if it can be amended at all), who will serve as trustee and what powers the trustee holds.（Investopedia/https://www.investopedia.com/terms/d/declaration-of-trust.asp）

信托声明概述谁是信托的受益人，谁可以修改或撤销信托（如果可以修改的话），谁将担任受托人以及受托人拥有什么权力。

注：powers the trustee holds：They have the right to manage the trust property as they wish；The right to choose the appropriate opportunity to sell the trust property and invest；Shall be entitled to remuneration as prescribed. 受托人拥有的权力：有权按照自己的意愿管理信托财产；有权选择适当的机会出售信托财产并进行投资；有权按照规定获得报酬。

A declaration of trust defines a trust's beneficiaries, the trustee and certain guidelines the trustee must abide by.

信托声明规定了信托受益人、受托人以及受托人必须遵守某些准则。

注：受托人的义务主要体现在：按规定将信托财产的收益交给收益人，并以公正态度对待各受益人；定期向受益人提供充分的收支账目报告；除非得到委托人或法院认可，不得将自己的职权委托他人行使；不得从所经营的信托财产中牟利，不得购买信托财产；必须像管理自己的财产一样管理信托财产，始终善意地为受益人的利益进行管理。

**3. Grantor trust rules　委托人信托规则**

委托人信托规则允许委托人控制信托中的资产和投资。它产生的收入按照其税率向委托人征税，而不是信托本身。在这方面，委托人信托规则为个人提供一定程度的税收

保护，因为税率通常对个人而言比对信托更有利。

The grantor trust rules allow grantors to control the assets and investments in a trust.（Investopedia/https://www.investopedia.com/terms/g/grantortrustrules.asp）

委托人信托规则允许委托人控制信托中的资产和投资。

注：grantor 委托人，是收取出售期权的保费的看涨期权或看跌期权的卖方。期权通过交易所出售给负责支付保费的期权持有人。

The grantor trust rules are guidelines within the Internal Revenue Code, which outline certain tax implications of a grantor trust.

委托人信托规则是《国内税收法典》内的准则，它概述了委托人信托的某些税务影响。

注：tax 税：commodity turnover tax 流转税；income tax 所得税；property tax 财产税；added-value tax 增值税；consumption tax 消费税

### 3.1.5 信托报酬

信托报酬指受托人根据信托契约经营信托业务所得的收益。获取信托报酬是受托人经营信托业务的主要目的。受托人一般采取计提手续费的方式，手续费按信托资财或信托收益的一定百分比计算。

**1. Rate of return 回报率**

回报率科技简单理解为效益的百分比，即指投入成本后所得到的收益比上之前的成本。如果资产在某个时间点购买并在未来的某个时间点产生现金流，则可以对任何投资工具（从房地产到债券、股票和艺术品）应用回报率。投资的评估部分基于过去的回报率，可以与同类型的资产进行比较，以确定最具吸引力的投资。

**2. Return on investment 投资回报率**

投资回报率（ROI）是指通过投资而应返回的价值，即企业从一项投资活动中得到的经济回报。投资回报率是一种绩效衡量指标，用于评估投资效率或比较多种不同投资的效率。投资回报率试图直接衡量特定投资的回报金额，相对于投资成本。计算投资回报率等于投资的收益（或收益）除以投资成本，结果表示为百分比或比率。

A rate of return can be applied to any investment vehicle, from real estate to bonds, stocks and fine art, provided the asset is purchased at one point in time and produces cash flow at some point in the future. (www.investopedia.com/term)

只要在某时间点买进资产并在未来某个时间点产生现金流，投资回报率可用于从房地产到债券、股票和艺术品等任何投资工具。

注：（1）cash flow 现金流量，是投资项目在其整个寿命期内所发生的现金流出和现金流入的全部资金收付数量。（2）相关术语：cash inflow 现金流入；cash outflow 现金流出；cash flow statement 现金流量表

Rate of return is a profit on an investment over a period of time, expressed as a proportion of the original investment.

回报率是一段时间内投资利润，以原始投资比例表示。

注：总回报率 $r$ =（收入/最初投资 + 价格变动/最初投资）×100% =（收入+价格变动）/最初投资×100%

**3. Valuable consideration 有价对价**

Compensation means payment of any valuable consideration for services in excess of reasonable medical and ancillary costs.（yulane.com）

报酬是指对超出合理的医疗和辅助成本服务后因提供服务而获得的人有价值的支付。

注：（1）ancillary costs 辅助成本，工业企业的辅助生产，指主要为基本生产车间、企业行政管理部门等单位提供服务而进行的产品生产和劳务供应；为生产和提供一定种类和一定数量的产品或劳务所耗费的辅助生产费用之和，构成该种产品或劳务的辅助生产成本。（2）相关术语：financial compensation 经济补偿，指为某人提供金钱或其他具有经济价值的东西，以换取其商品、劳动力，或补偿其所遭受的伤害；compensation shall 补偿款赔偿；advance compensation 预付补偿金

Valuable consideration is a kind of return equaling to the benefit value.

对价是一种与利益价值相等的回报。

相关术语：benefit value 效益价值；benefit-value method 效益价值法；benefit present value method 收益现值法；benefit current value 效益现值；benefit value theory 收益价值论

**4. Yield 收益（率）**

收益率是指在特定时间段内投资产生和实现的收益，并以基于投资额或当前市场价值或证券面值的百分比表示。它包括从持有特定证券所获得的利息或股息。根据证券的性质和估值（固定/波动），收益率可分为已知或预期。

**5. Loss ratio 损失率**

一般而言，损失率是损失与收益的比率。它最常用于保险业，指付费保险索赔（包括调整费用）与所赚保费之比。

A yield is the amount of money or profit produced by an investment.

收益率是指投资所产生的金钱或利润。

注：（1）profit 利润，指企业在一定会计期间的经营成果；（2）investment 投资，货币转化为资本的过程，是为了在未来获得一些收益而分配资金。在金融领域，投资的收益被称为回报。（3）相关术语：value investment 价值投资；intermediaries and collective investments 中介人及集体投资；traditional investments 传统投资；alternative investment 另类投资

In finance, the yield on a security is the amount of cash (in percentage terms) that returns to the owners of the security, in the form of interest or dividends received from it. Normally, it does not include the price variations, distinguishing it from the total return.

在金融学中，证券收益（率）是以利息或股息的形式返还给证券所有者的现金（以百分比计算）。通常情况下，它不包括价格变化，将其与总回报区分开来。

相关术语：（1）dividends 分红，股息；（2）payout ratio 股息支付；（3）constant dividend payout ratio 固定股利支付率政；（4）constant payout ratio policy 固定比例股利政策；（5）target payout ratio 目标股利发放率

### 3.1.6 信托责任

信托责任是指受托人对委托人/受益人负有的、严格按委托人的意愿（而不是受托人）进行财产管理的责任。一旦委托人和受托人之间的信托关系成立，受托人就负有信托责任。信托责任，是一种对社会成员有约束作用的内在制度。内在制度被定义为群体内随经验而演化的规则，在构建社会交往、沟通自我中心的个人和实现社会整合上有着重要的作用，它作为行为规则的约束作用是通过内化于人们的意识并贯彻于日常活动的，而且一旦形成后就成为共同的价值观，因而是一种长期的、而且是非常有效的行为规则。

**1. Duty of loyalty 忠诚义务**

忠诚义务是公司董事履行的两项主要信托义务之一，它要求指董事在执行公司业务时所承担的以公司利益作为行为和行动的最高准则，不得追求自己和他人利益的义务。它还规定了避免可能的利益冲突的责任，从而阻止董事自我交易或利用公司机会谋取私利。违反忠诚义务可能会使董事受到法院命令，要求赔偿和罚款。

**2. Duty of care 注意义务**

对于公司董事来说，注意义务是一种信托责任，要求他们以诚信和合理谨慎的方式做出决策。注意义务要求董事在考虑所有可用信息后做出业务决策，然后以明智的方式行事，以促进公司的最佳利益。董事必须在做出业务决策时尽最大努力履行其信托义务。

The duty of loyalty imposes a number of additional responsibilities upon directors of a company. They are required to keep confidential, and not disclose or use, any information that they come across in their official capacity as directors.（Investopedia/https://www. investopedia. com/terms/d/duty-loyalty.asp）

忠诚义务强加给公司董事一些额外的义务。他们需要对作为董事所接触到的任何信息保密，不得披露和使用这些信息。

注：（1）official capacity 公职权力，官方权力，法定资格；（2）相关术语：capacity 能力（法律），采取法律行动的能力和权威

Duty of loyalty is a director's responsibility to act at all times in the best interests of their company.

忠诚责任是指董事在任何时候都有责任以公司的最佳利益为目的行事。

注：director 管理者，董事，理事；managing director 总经理，常务董事；executive director 执行董事；company director 公司董事；finance director 财务总监

**3. Trustee sale 受托人出售**

A trustee's sale is one option that a lender has if you get behind on your mortgage and default on your payments. (Chron/http://smallbusiness.chron.com/trustees-sales-work- 36571. html)

受托人出售是贷款者没有及时还贷款时的一个选择。

注：（1）morgage 按揭贷款，指以房地产等实物资产或有价证券、契约等作抵押，获得银行贷款并依合同分期付清本息，贷款还清后银行归还抵押物。（2）相关术语：property ownership 财产所有权；certificate mortgage loan 房产证抵押贷款；a second mortgage on a home 房屋二次抵押贷款；loan portfolio 组合贷款；turn mortgage 转按揭

A trustee sale is a sale by a property in foreclosure due to default in the loan made from the lender, who holds a trustee deed on the property.

受托人出售是由持有财产受托契据的贷款人所持有贷款中的违约所导致的止赎财产的出售。

注：（1）foreclosure 丧失抵押品赎回权，指借款人因还款违约而失去赎回抵押品的权利。贷款机构根据规定的法律程序获得相关房产抵押品所有权或将房产抵押品出售以抵消借款人欠债。（2）相关术语：lenders 借贷方；the redemption 赎回

### 3.1.7 信托主体

**信托主体**，又称信托关系人，指信托行为中的当事人，包括委托人、受托人、受益人等。

**1. Beneficiary of trust　信托受益人**

受益人是在信托中享有信托受益权的人，可以是自然人、法人、或依法成立的其他组织。

**2. Trustee　受托人**

受托人是为第三方的利益持有和管理财产或资产的个人或公司。受托人可被指定用于各种目的，例如在破产的情况下，为慈善机构，信托基金或某些类型的退休计划或退休金。信托受托人可以根据受益人的最佳利益做出决策，并且通常对信托受益人负有信托责任。

Beneficiaries of an irrevocable trust generally can't be changed and trust terms usually can't be amended without the beneficiaries' permission. (Investopedia/https://www.investopedia.com/terms/b/beneficiary-of-trust.asp)

不可撤销信托受益人一般不得变更，信托条款在未经受益人同意的情况下也不得修改。

注：（1）irrevocable trust 不可撤销信托，是一种未经设保人指定受益人的许可，不得修改或终止其条款的信托。（2）相关术语：irrevocable letter of credit /irrevocable credit 不可撤销信用证；credit market 信贷市场

A beneficiary of trust is the individual or group of individuals for whom a trust is created for.

信托受益人指为其建立信托的个人或个人群体。

注：（1）individual 个人（微观经济学的重要主体）；（2）economic man 经济人；（3）microeconomics 微观经济学

**3. Fund manager　基金经理**

基金经理负责实施基金的投资策略并管理其投资组合交易活动。基金可以由一个人

管理，两个人作为共同管理者，或由三个或更多人的团队管理。

**4. Hedge Fund manager　对冲基金经理**

对冲基金经理是决策和监督对冲基金运作的个人。管理对冲基金可能是一个有吸引力的职业选择，因为它有可能是非常有利可图的。要获得成功，对冲基金经理必须考虑如何获得竞争优势、明确定义的投资策略、充足的资本化、营销和销售计划以及风险管理策略。

ARK is the only fund manager to offer an ETF with Bitcoin exposure, ARKW.（*Forbes*/June 29, 2016/https://www.forbes.com/sites/laurashin/2016/06/29/getting-closer-to-a-bitcoin-etf-winklevoss-trust-chooses-new-exchange/#1ccd0abb194d）

ARK 是唯一一家提供比特币敞口交易基金 ARKW 的基金管理公司。

注:（1）exposure 敞口，指在金融活动中存在金融风险的部分以及受金融风险影响的程度。敞口是金融风险中的一个重要概念，但是与金融风险并不等同。（2）相关术语：transaction exposure 交易敞口；economic exposure 经济风险；risk exposure 风险敞口；credit risk exposure 信用风险敞口；risk exposure fee 风险承担费用

A fund manager someone paid to be responsible for implementing a fund's investing strategy and managing its portfolio trading activities.

基金经理是负责实施基金投资策略和管理投资组合交易活动的人员。

注：portfolio 证券投资组合；risk appetite 风险偏好；indifference curve 无差异曲线；feasible set 可行集；efficient set 有效集；optimal portfolio 最优投资组合；risk-free lending 无风险借贷

**5. Income beneficiary　收益受益人**

受益人是从某事物中获得优势或利润的任何人。在金融界，受益人通常指有资格接受信托、遗嘱或人寿保险单分配的人。受益人要么在这些文件中具体命名，要么符合指定分配条件的规定。

This may be preferable if the income beneficiary doesn't need cash every year, but it can lead to bickering among beneficiaries. ( *Forbes*: New Cash From Old Trusts)

如果收益受益人每年不需要现金可能会更好，但可能会导致受益人之间的争端。

注:（1）beneficiary 受益人（资金或其他福利的接受者）;（2）相关术语：beneficiary living 现存受益人；trust beneficiary 信托受益人；contingent Beneficiary 第二受益人；beneficiary interest 受益人的权益；beneficiary payee 受款人

A trust arrangement whereby a designated beneficiary is to receive income generated from the trust's principal without access to the principal itself.

收益受益人是一种信托安排，根据这种安排，指定受益人无需接触信托本金，仅接受本金产生的收入。

注：principal 本金；principal balance 本金；principal and interest 本利，本金及利息；repayment of principal 偿还本金；principal value 本金值；average capital plus interest 等额本息

**6. Judicial trustee　司法受托人**

司法受托人是基于法院判令指定而产生的信托受托人。司法受托人可以是有行为能力的自然人，也可是法人。司法受托人除负有一般信托义务外，还有义务向法院报告信托管理情况，公开管理账目，接受法院监督。

When a judicial trustee is appointed, a separate account for receipts and payments on behalf of the trust shall be kept in the name of the trustees at some bank approved by the court. (http://dict.youdao.com/example/blng/eng/trustee_bank/)

委任司法受托人时，须以受托人的名义，在经法院核准的银行设立单独的用以收支的账户。

注：（1）receipts 收据，是企事业单位在经济活动中使用的原始凭证，主要指财政部门印制的盖有财政票据监制章的收付款凭证。（2）相关术语：temporary receipts 暂收款项；suspense receipts 暂收款；advance receipts 预收账；bank receipts 银行收益；payment receipts 付款收据，支付凭据；receipts and disbursements 收支

A judicial trustee is an individual or a company who manages assets in a trust on behalf of the beneficiary.

司法受托人是代表受益人管理信托资产的个人或公司。

注：assets 资产；current assets 流动资产；long-term investment 长期投资；fixed assets 固定资产；intangible assets 无形资产；deferred assets 递延资产

### 3.1.8　信托客体

信托客体，指信托关系的标的物，是委托人通过信托行为转移给受托人并由受托人按照一定的信托目的进行管理或处置的财产，信托财产通常具有转让性、独立性、有限性、有效性等特征。

**1. Trust property　信托财产**

信托财产是指通过信托行为从委托人手中转移到受托者手里的财产。依信托法规则，信托财产须为特定化的和现实存在的财产；它可由不动产、股票、公债、抵押契据、保险单、银行存款等构成，但非财产性合同权利不能作为信托财产。信托财产具有物上代位性，它不因财产形态的变化而改变自身的同一性；受托人基于对信托财产的管理、改良、处分或毁损而取得的财产也属于信托财产。信托财产具有法律独立性；受托人对信托财产与其自有财产须分别管理，受托人死亡时，其信托财产不得作为遗产继承。

**2. Trust fund　信托基金**

信托是“一项协议，描述了如何为另一个人的利益管理和持有资产”。合法建立的信托通常被称为信托基金。信托基金是代表另一个人或实体持有和管理资产的法人实体。

The trustee is required to manage the trust property in accordance with the trustor’s wishes and in the beneficiary’s best interests. (Investopedia/https://www.investopedia.com/terms/t/trust-property.asp)

受托人被要求按照托管人的意愿和受益人的最大利益，管理信托财产。

注：（1）property 财产，是土地、资源、改善或其他有形物体或知识产权的所有权。（2）相关术语：property right 产权；intellectual property 知识产权；physical property 实物财产；property market 地产市场；real property 不动产；private property 私有财产；public property 公共财产；property insurance 财产保险

Trust property refers to assets that have been placed into a fiduciary relationship between a trustor and trustee for a designated beneficiary. Trust property may include any type of asset such as cash, securities, real estate or life insurance policies.

信托财产是指委托人与受托人之间为指定受益人而建立信托关系的财产。信托财产可包括现金、证券、房地产或人寿保险等任何类型资产。

注：（1）fiduciary 信托的，受托的，指与一个或多个其他当事人（个人或团体）保持法律或道德上的信任关系的人。（2）相关术语：fiduciary duties 信托责任；standard of care 谨慎程度

### 3.1.9 二手信托

**二手信托**，即信托收益权的转让，这个流程必须通过信托公司，且信托收益权的转让只能是机构客户转让给机构客户。

**Principal beneficiary 主要受益人**

Can spouse still migrate when principal beneficiary dies? (*Asian Journal*/http://asianjournalusa.com/can-spouse-still-migrate-when-principal-beneficiary- dies-p11344-156.htm)

当主要收益人去世后，配偶还能移民吗？

注：（1）principal 本金，即贷款、存款或投资在计算利息之前的原始金额；migrate vs. immigrate vs. emigrate：migrate 常指随季节而移居，（鸟类的）迁徙；immigrate 指移居入境；emigrate 指移居出境，也就是通常说的移民；（2）相关术语：principal balance 本金余额；principal sum 本金，本金总额；principal sum insured 主要保额

The person who is to receive a portion of the estate after all smaller gifts and valuables are distributed.

（本金受益人是）在较小礼物和贵重物品分配后，将获得一部分遗产的人。

注：（1）valuables 贵重物品，指拥有的价值不菲的物品，尤其是像珠宝这样的小物品；词义辨析：distribute vs. dispense：都指“分发，把东西分给其他人”，后者多用在药品上；（2）相关术语：jewellery 珠宝首饰；gold 黄金；rare metals 稀有金属；gem 宝石；policy beneficiary 政策受益者；trust beneficiary 信托受益人；contingent beneficiary 第二受益人；beneficiary country 受惠国；beneficiary interest 受益人权益；beneficiary living 现存受益人

## 3.2 The Main Types of Trust（信托的主要类型）

**导读**

本节主要介绍现代信托制度下主要信托业务的分类，并简要介绍现代信托业务各种分类依据和主要业务种类。

## 3.2.1 关系划分

### 3.2.1.1 任意信托

**1. Purpose trust 目的信托**

英美法上所谓的目的信托是指不存在受益人或者受益人不能确定的信托。它也被称为不完全义务信托（imperfect obligation trust）或者名誉信托（honorary trust），是因为设立这种信托并不能给受托人设定法律上可以强制执行的义务，而只能依靠受托人的道德和名誉感来实施。

**2. Special purpose trust (SPT) 特殊目的信托**

特殊目的信托，是将金融资产信托给受托机构——可以从事信托营业的机构来解决不良资产的证券化问题；而特殊目的公司，则是拥有不良资产的银行将资产直接出售给一个特定目的公司，并由该公司来解决不良资产的证券化。特殊目的信托的核心内容是信托法律关系，即发起人将基础资产委托给受托机构，成立信托关系，再由受托机构作为证券的发行人，发行代表对基础资产享有按份权利的信托收益证书。根据信托的法律关系，发起人将基础资产信托于受托机构之后，这一资产的权利就转移到受托机构，发起人的债权人就不能对这部分资产主张权利，从而实现了证券化资产与发起人的破产风险相隔离的要求。

Purpose Trusts have become an increasingly important part of the Trusts (Jersey) Law 1984, as amended (the “Trusts Law”). (Carey Olsen/23 March 2017/https://www.careyolsen.com/briefings/non-charitable- purpose-trusts-jersey)

目的信托已成为1984修订后的《信托法》日益重要的一部分。

A purpose trust is a type of trust which has no beneficiaries, but instead exists for advancing some non-charitable purpose of some kind.

目的信托是一种没有受益人的信托，是为推进某种非慈善目的而存在的信托。

注：non-charitable 非慈善的；for-profit 营利性的；the charity 慈善的；public welfare nature 公益性质的

### 3.2.1.2 法定信托

**1. Resulting trust 法定信托**

法定信托的成立不依赖于财产所有人的明示或默示意图，也不取决于法律推定意图；只要发生了符合法定条件的法律事实，即在特定当事人之间形成信托关系。

A resulting trust arises when one party provides the consideration for a transfer of title, but the title to the property is transferred to a different party. (KOMDR/10 September 2014/https://www.komdr.com/resulting-trusts/)

当一方为转换所有权提供对价，但财产所有权又转到另一方，这就是法定信托。

注：resulting trust 法定信托，指在某些特殊情况下，委托人未明示要设立信托，但法院为实施法律或依据委托人未予明示的假定意图而施加的一种信托。

A resulting trust (from the Latin "resalire" meaning "to jump back") is the creation of an implied trust by operation of law, where property is transferred to someone who pays nothing for it, and then is implied to have held the property for benefit of another person.

法定信托（源于拉丁语"resalire"，意思是"跳回"）是通过法律运作建立的默示信托，财产被转让给不为其支付任何费用的人；然后默认为他人的利益持有该财产。

注：（1）implied trust 默示信托，是信托法的一个组成部分，指没有"由委托人明确创设"的信托。（2）相关术语：constructive trust 法定信托

**2. Arbitrary trust　任意信托**

任意信托是指根据当事人之间的自由意愿表示而成立的信托，主要指委托人、受托人、受益人自由自愿形成信托关系，而且这种自由自愿意思在信托契约中明确地表示出来，大部分信托业务都属于任意信托。信托条款中除必要事项外仅指明信托意图，而使受托人的信托财产权内容具有一定任意性。根据现代信托法的"酌定信托原则"，受托人的信托财产权内容以信托意图为主要根据，他具有为实现信托意图所必需的或适合于当时需要的基本财产权。

## 3.2.2 财产划分

### 3.2.2.1 金钱信托

**Money trust 金钱信托**

金钱信托亦称 "货币资产信托"或"资金信托"。信托设立时，信托财产为货币（包括现金和存款）形态，并规定信托结束时仍以货币形态交付受益人的信托。在信托期间，信托财产的形态可以变化，但开始和结束时都必须是货币形态。金钱信托以货币增值为目的。

Proper planning with money trust can help people achieve the purpose of property transfer and legal tax saving in a more efficient and safe way. Customer-tailored trust products, such as the children's Education Trust for young couples, the high-asset person's care trust, or the insurance trust.（https://baike.baidu.com/item/%E9%87%91%E9%92%B1%E4%BF%A1%E6%89%98/6872525?fr=aladdin）

合理的金钱信托可以帮助人们更有效、更安全的达到财产移转和合法节税的目的。可依客户需求定制不同信托产品，如年轻夫妇的子女教育信托、高资产者安养抚育信托，或保险信托等。

注：tax saving 节税；flexibility of tax-saving ability 节税能力弹性；tax saving effect 节税效果；tax saving lease 节税租赁；dot of tax saving 节税点；tax saving behavior 节税行为；tax saving design 纳税方案设计；profit form tax saving 节税收益

Money trust is also called "money asset trust" or "fund trust". When a trust is established, the trust property is in the form of currency (including cash and deposits), and it is stipulated that the trust shall be delivered to the beneficiary in the form of currency at the end of the trust. During the period of trust, the form of trust property can be changed, but it must be monetary form at the beginning and at the end.

金钱信托亦称“货币资产信托”或“资金信托”。信托设立时，信托财产为货币（包括现金和存款）形态，并规定信托结束时仍以货币形态交付给受益人。在信托期间，信托财产形态可以变化，但开始和结束时都必须是货币形态。

注：monetary 货币的；currency 货币；mutilated currency 残损货币；complementary currency 补充货币；paper money 纸币；virtual currency 虚拟货币；scrip content 代币物；general equivalent 一般等价物

### 3.2.2.2 有价证券信托

**Negotiable securities trust　可转让证券信托**

Negotiable securities trust aims to achieve rising income and long-term capital growth through investment in a balanced portfolio of global equities. (www.securitiestrust.com)

可转让证券信托旨在通过均衡的全球股票组合的投资，来实现收入增长和长期资本增值。

注：（1）long-term capital 长期资本，指企业需用期限在一年以上的资本。企业的长期资本通常包括各种股权资本和长期借款、应付债券等债权资本。这是广义的长期资本。长期资本就是股东权益加上长期负债的总和。（2）相关术语：long-term capital gain 长期资本收益；long-term capital flows 长期资本流动；long-term capital movements 长期资本流动；long-term capital market 长期资本市场；long-term capital transaction 长期资本交易；long-term capital account 长期资本项目

Negotiable securities trust is a form of trust where the trust property is securities.

可转让证券信托是以证券为信托财产的一种信托形式。

注：security 证券，一种可交易的金融资产，包括一些接近股票和固定收益的工具，例如股票权证；debt securities 债券，包括 banknotes 钞票，bonds 债券，debentures 信用债券；equity securities 股票；derivatives 衍生性金融商品，包括 forwards 远期合约，futures 期货，options 期权，swaps 互惠信贷

### 3.2.2.3 不动产信托

不动产信托（real estate investment trust）又称“房地产信托”，信托机构受托代办与房屋、土地等不动产有关的经济事项的业务。内容包括房地产的买卖、租赁、租金支付、保险金支付、登记、转让过户和纳税等。有的还受理其他的代理业务，如土地的丈量、建筑工程的承包、房地产的鉴定单价和建筑物的设计等。

**1. Leasehold land　租赁土地**

土地租赁是某一土地的所有者的所有权与土地使用者使用权在一定时期内相分离，土地使用者在使用土地期间向土地所有者支付租金，期满后，土地使用者归还土地的一种经济活动。

Absolute title also exists to leasehold land, giving the proprietor a guaranteed valid lease. (https://cn.bing.com/dict/search)

租赁土地也存在绝对所有权，它给予物主有担保的有效租借权。

注（1）proprietor 所有人，指对某事具有合法权利或专有权的人。（2）相关术语：estate proprietor 房地产权利人；peasant proprietor 占有土地的农民；subsidiary proprietor 附属业主；capital proprietor 资本所有者；partial proprietor 部分所有人；sole proprietor 独资企业

A leasehold land refers to the real property held by a lessee under a lease for a fixed term, after which it returns to the lessor.

租赁土地指承租人根据定期租赁持有不动产，租期后需返还给出租人。

注：lessor 出租人，指在租赁合同中，将租赁物交付承租人使用、收益的人；lessee 承租人，指租赁合同中使用租赁财产并按约向对方支付租金的当事人；house lease 房屋租赁；operating lease 经营租赁；financing lease 融资租赁

**2. Real estate investment trust (REIT) 房地产投资信托**

房地产投资信托是一种以发行收益凭证的方式汇集特定多数投资者的资金，由专门投资机构进行房地产投资经营管理，并将投资综合收益按比例分配给投资者的一种信托基金。

Compared with other investment approaches, REITs possesses of advantages such as strong liquidity, good stability, high level of benefits, and diversified risks, etc. (http://dict.youdao.com/search)

与其他投资方式相比，房地产投资信托具有流动性强、稳定性好、收益水平高、风险分散等优点。

注：（1）liquidity 流动性，指一项资产或证券在市场上能够以反映其内在价值的价格迅速买卖的程度。（2）相关术语：liquidity risk 流动性风险；market liquidity 市场流动性；excess liquidity 过剩流动性；liquidity crisis 流动性危机，清偿危机；liquidity ratio 流动比率；liquidity squeeze 头寸紧张，流动性短缺；liquidity support 流动性支持 bank liquidity 银行清偿能力；liquidity preference 流动性偏好

A real estate investment trust, or REIT, is a company that owns, operates or finances income-producing real estate. For a company to qualify as a REIT, it must meet certain regulatory guidelines. REITs often trades on major exchanges like other securities and provide investors with a liquid stake in real estate.

房地产投资信托（REIT）是一家拥有、经营或资助创收房地产公司。一家公司要获得房地产投资信托资格，就必须符合一定的监管准则。房地产投资信托通常像其他证券一样在主要交易所交易，并为投资者提供房地产流动性股权。

#### 3.2.2.4 动产信托

动产信托是指以各种动产作为信托财产而设定的信托。动产信托的标的物，通常是价格昂贵、资金需求量大的产品。动产信托不论是对于这类产品的生产者和销售者

（通常是动产信托的委托者）还是其用户都有方便之处。动产信托的意义在于为设备的生产和购买企业提供长期资金融通。动产信托的目的是管理或处理这些财产，能够进行受托的种类包括车辆及其他运输工具、机械设备、贵金属。

**1. Bare trust　简易信托，无担保信托**

简易信托受益人只要年满 18 岁，就拥有信托中资本、资产和收入的绝对权利。简易信托为设立信托的个人提供税收优惠，而受益人按现行税率征税，或者如果他们的收入低，可能会受到例外情况的限制。

Bare trust rules allow beneficiaries to decide when they want to recover the trust's assets as long as they are at least 18 years of age in the United Kingdom. (Investopedia/https://www.investopedia.com/terms/b/bare-trust.asp)

在英国，简易信托规则允许受益人在年满 18 岁的情况下，决定何时收回信托资产。

注：（1）asset 资产，是企业、自然人、国家拥有或者控制的能以货币来计量收支的经济资源，包括各种收入、债权。（2）相关术语：asset allocation 资产分配；current asset 流动资产；fixed asset 固定资产；financial asset 金融资产；asset stripping 拆卖资产；net asset 资产净额；deferred asset 递延资产；asset revaluation 资产重估

A bare trust is a trust in which the beneficiary has a right to both income and capital and may call for both to be remitted into his own name.

简易信托是指受益人对收入和资本都有权利，并可要求将二者汇入自己名下的信托。

注：remit 汇款；bank card remittance 银行卡汇款；general remittance 普通汇款；online banking transfer 网银转账；roaming the remittance 漫游汇款；traveler's checks 旅行支票；foreign currencies collected 外币票汇；western union 西联汇款

**2. Credit shelter trust　信用庇护信托**

信用庇护信托旨在让富裕的夫妇在将资产转移给继承人（通常是夫妇的子女）时减少或完全避免遗产税。这种不可撤销的信托的结构使得信托的创建者或定居者去世后，信托协议中规定的资产及其产生的收入将转移给委托人的配偶。

### 3.2.2.5　金钱债权信托

金钱债权信托（debt of money claim trust）指委托人以金钱债权移转给受托人。在此项债权给付清算后再交委托人或受益人管理、使用或支配，即是金钱债权信托。

**Voting trust　表决权信托**

表决权信托通常是股份公司的股东将自己在股东大会的表决权委托某人或某机构行使的一种信托。信托设立时，委托人与受托人签订表决权信托契约，并将股票过户给受托人，使受托人成为记录在公司股东名册中的股东，但须注明“表决权信托”字样。委托人凭信托证书证明自己对股票的实际所有权，受托人行使表决权和接受公司股利，在扣除信托手续费后将股利转交给委托人。

A voting trust becomes effective on the date the first shares subject to the trust are registered in the trustee's name. (translation168.lingdi.net)

表决权信托于信托的第一批股份登记在受托人名下之日起生效。

注：（1）shares 股票，是股份公司发行的所有权凭证，是股份公司为筹集资金而发行给各个股东作为持股凭证并借以取得股息和红利的一种有价证券。（2）相关术语：share price 股票价格；share repurchase 股份回购；share registrar 股票过户登记处；golden share 黄金股；share placement 批股

A voting trust is an arrangement whereby the shares in a company of one or more shareholders and the voting rights attached thereto are legally transferred to a trustee, usually for a specified period of time (the "trust period").

表决权信托是指一种安排，根据这种安排，一个或多个股东的股份及其所附表决权在规定的时间内（即"信托期"）依法转让给受托人。

注：trust period 信托期，信托公司设立的集合类信托期限不得少于一年，而单一类的项目没有该限制，目前市场上的信托产品期限一般在1～3年。

## 3.2.3 目的分类

### 3.2.3.1 担保信托

担保信托，是指以确保信托财产的安全，保护受托人的合法权益为目的而设立的信托。保证方式加重了债权危机，抵押是债权人以在他人物上所享有之抵押权保证自己债权实现的一种担保，质押虽以转移占有为特征，克服了抵押不转移占有的弊端，但也有问题。担保信托有利于改善法院审判人员的工作作风，有利于彻底解决纠纷，有利于为社会创造就业的机会。

**Testamentary trust** (or **trust under will**) **遗嘱信托**

遗嘱信托包括交付信托后遗产的管理、分配、运用及给付等，详订于遗嘱中。等到遗嘱生效时，再将信托财产转移给受托人，由受托人依据信托的内容，也就是委托人遗嘱所交办的事项，管理处分信托财产。与金钱、不动产或有价证券等个人信托业务比较，遗嘱信托最大的不同点在于，遗嘱信托是在委托人死亡后契约才生效。

Testamentary trusts are created by a will to provide a greater level of control over the distribution of assets to beneficiaries. (Dixonadvisory/https://www.dixon.com.au/estate-planning/why-use-a-testamentary-trust)

遗嘱信托是根据遗嘱设立，目的是在受益人分配资产时提供更大程度的控制权。

注：（1）asset 资产，指由企业过去的交易或事项形成的、由企业拥有或者控制的、预期会给企业带来经济利益的资源。（2）相关术语：current assets 流动资产；long-term asset 长期资产；fixed assets 固定资产；intangible assets 无形资产；financial assets 金融资产

A testamentary trust (sometimes referred to as a will trust or trust under will) is a trust which arises upon the death of the testator, and which is specified in his or her will. A will may contain more than one testamentary trust, and may address all or any portion of the estate.

遗嘱信托（有时称为遗嘱下的信托或信托），是立遗嘱人去世后并在遗嘱中明确

规定而产生的信托。一份遗嘱可包含一个以上的遗嘱信托，并且可处理全部或任何部分遗产。

注：2019 年我国信托公司综合实力前五位排名：Citic Trust 中信信托；Chongqing Trust 重庆信托；Huaneng Trust 华能信托；ZRT 中融信托；Jiangsu Trust 江苏信托。

### 3.2.3.2 管理信托

管理信托（management trust）是以对财产的管理和运用为目的而设立的信托，包括单纯的以财产管理为目的的狭义财产管理信托和以财产的运用和处分为目的而设立的处分信托。管理信托适用的范围极其广泛，既可用于对未成年人和禁治产人财产的管理和对遗产的管理与分配，也可用于信任投资。

**Generation-skipping trust　隔代信托**

Because a generation-skipping trust effectively transfers assets from the grantor's estate to his grandchildren, the children of the grantor never take title to the assets.（Investopedia/ https://www.investopedia.com/terms/g/generation-skippingtrust.asp）

由于隔代信托有效地将资产从委托人遗产转移给他的孙辈，委托人的子女永远不会获得资产所有权。

注：（1）grantor 让与人，法律术语，指权利的接收方，出让人将自己的全部或者部分权利通过合同或者协议、赠予的方式转让给受让人。（2）相关术语：grantor trust 委托人信托；credit grantor 授信方；the grantor 全押

A generation-skipping trust is a type of legally binding trust agreement in which the contributed assets are passed down to the grantor's grandchildren, not the grantor's children.

隔代信托是一种具有法律约束力的信托协议，在这种协议中，捐赠的资产将转移给委托人的孙辈，而不是委托人的子女。

### 3.2.3.3 处理信托

处理信托，是指改变信托财产的性质、原状以实现财产增值的信托业务。在处理信托中，信托财产具有物上代位性，即财产可以变换形式，如将财产变卖转为资金，或购买有价证券等等。

**Trust fund　信托基金**

信托基金（trust fund）也叫投资基金，是一种“利益共享、风险共担”的集合投资方式。指通过契约或公司的形式，借助发行基金券的方式，将社会上不确定的多数投资者不等额的资金集中起来，形成一定规模的信托资产，交由专门的投资机构按资产组合原理进行分散投资，获得的收益由投资者按出资比例分享，并承担相应风险的一种集合投资信托制度。

Trust funds are a great way to build wealth for future generations, but many new investors tend to shy away from them because they think they are only for the rich. (The balance/05 November 2017/https://www.thebalance.com/what-is-a-trust-fund-357254)

信托基金是为后代积累财富的好方法，但是许多投资者认为信托基金是为了富人而存在的，倾向于回避这类基金。

注：（1）investor 投资者，指投入现金购买某种资产以期望获取利益或利润的自然人和法人。在金融市场中，所谓投资者是指在金融交易中购入金融工具融出资金的所有个人和机构，包括存款人，出资人在验资时称为投资者；词义辨析：build wealth vs. accumulate wealth：前者偏向创造财富，后者偏向积累财富；（2）相关术语：equity investor 股权投资者；outward investor 对外投资者；institutional investor 机构投资者

A trust fund is a fund comprised of a variety of assets intended to provide benefits to an individual or organization.

信托基金是指由旨在向个人或组织提供利益的各种资产组成的基金。

注：证券投资基金种类：（1）根据基金单位是否可增加或赎回可分为 open-ended fund 开放式基金,closed-end fund 封闭式基金；（2）根据不同的组织形态可分为 corporate type fund 公司型基金，constractual type funds 契约型基金；（3）根据不同的投资风险和收益可分为 growth funds 成长型，income funds 收入型，balanced funds 平衡型基金；（4）根据不同的投资对象可分为 equity fund 股票基金，bond funds 债券基金等。

#### 3.2.3.4 管理和处理信托

**Common trust fund　共同信托基金**

The part 3 compares the ILI with the common trust fund through three respects: investment and risk, ensure, tax and expenses.（CNKI/http://dict.cnki.net/dict_result.aspx?searchword=common%20trust%20fund）

第三部分通过投资与风险、保障、税收与费用三个方面对 ILI 和共同信托基金进行比较。

注：（1）expense 费用，是企业在日常活动中发生的会导致所有者权益减少的、与向所有者分配利润无关的经济利益的总流出。（2）相关术语：finance expense 财政费用；funds finance ratio 基金开支比率

Common trust funds are unregistered bank investment products that pool fiduciary client assets to invest in a diversified portfolio of stocks, bonds, or other securities.

共同信托基金指未注册银行投资产品，将信托客户的资产集中起来，投资于股票、债券或其他证券的多样化投资组合。

相关术语：legal common trust fund 法定普通信托基金；trust fund plan 信托基金计划；trust fund ledger 信托基金分类账；trust fund program 信托基金方案

### 3.2.4 事项划分

#### 3.2.4.1 民事信托

民事信托（civil trust）指信托事项所涉及的法律依据在民事法律范围之内的信托。民事法律范围主要包括民法、继承法、婚姻法、劳动法等法律，信托事项涉及的法律依

据在此范围之内的为民事信托。由于民事信托在承办期间会涉及人与人之间的财产关系，各国都要求必须在一定法律允许的范围内承办。由于民事信托不以营利为目的，又称为“非营业信托”，如上文所讲的遗嘱信托。

#### 3.2.4.2　商事信托

商事信托（business trust）指具有私益性质、由具有商人身份的主体担任受托人的信托。从法律立场讲，凡属于“社会经济交往”引起诉讼的范围之内，称为商事信托。亦有称凡涉及“商事法”（商法）的信托事项，称为商事信托。因为这类信托事项与调整商业活动的法律规范关系十分密切。它通常包括公司法、票据法、保险法和海商法等方面的法律规范，如上文所讲的表决权信托。

### 3.2.5　委托划分

#### 3.2.5.1　个人信托

个人信托（personal trust）是以各种财产权为中心，将自己名下包含金钱、有价证券、不动产等资产，交由受托人（信托机构）依照信托契约执行各项管理运用，以期达到预定的信托目的。由于个人信托的内容具有高度的弹性及隐秘性，委托人对信托的财产亦能保有控制权，透过适当的规划，信托财产将不受委托人死亡或破产等因素影响，同时更可以享有信托机构专业的投资控管，种种优点是其他单一金融商品或服务所难以企及的。

相对概念：法人信托

法人信托，是指由公司、社团等法人委托信托机构办理的各种信托业务。法人信托又称“机构信托”“公司信托”“团体信托”，是“个人信托”的相对概念。法人信托的委托人是公司、社团等法人组织；受托人只能由法人机构承担，任何个人都没有受理法人信托的资格；与社会经济的发展有密切关系等特点。法人信托的范围包括公司债务的信托和公司创设、改组、合并、撤销和清算的信托，具有公司理财、融资服务等作用。

**Living trust　生前信托**

委托人与受托人建立信托关系，并在委托人生前具有法律效力的信托。属个人信托。无论生前信托和身后信托，都是委托人生前与受托人设定的，但遗嘱信托和遗产管理信托等身后信托的法律效力要在委托人去世后才发生，而生前信托在委托人在世时即发生法律效力。生前信托生效时由于委托人在世，可根据委托人的意愿变更信托约款；身后信托生效时委托人已去世，其信托约款是不可变更的。（相对概念是遗嘱信托）

One of the first benefits of a living trust is that it avoids probate. (With a valid will, the estate under the will go through probate, the court proceedings through which the assets are distributed according to your wishes by the executor.) (https://www.legalzoom.com/articles/top-three-benefits-of-a-living-trust)

生前信托首要益处之一是避免遗嘱检验。（有效遗嘱下财产需通过认证，并根据遗嘱撰写人的意愿来分配）

注：（1）probate 遗嘱认证，遗嘱是一份法律文件，概述了一个人最后的决定或者死后的指示，遗嘱认证是指负责发放和管理的遗产的过程。（2）相关术语：probate jurisdiction 遗嘱检验裁判权；probate courts 遗嘱检验法院；probate tribunal 遗嘱检验法院

A living trust is a written legal document through which your assets are placed into a trust for your benefit during your lifetime.

生前信托是一种书面法律文件，通过该文件，你可以将资产存入信托造福你的一生。

注：Wellcome Trust 维康信托基金会，成立于 1936 年，它托管了美国制药业巨子亨利 • 维康爵士的遗赠财产，资助提高人类和动物健康水平的研究，是英国最大的非政府资助生物医学研究的基金会。

#### 3.2.5.2 个人与法人通用信托业务

**Management trust 管理信托**

Under the management trust, the trustee assumes the obligation to manage the trust property for the benefit of the beneficiary. ( https://translate.google.cn/)

在管理信托下，受托人为受益人的利益承担管理信托财产的义务。

注：（1）management trust 管理信托，与 guarantee trust（担保信托）相对，是以对财产的管理和运用为目的而设立的信托；（2）相关术语：cash management trust 现金管理型信托；management of trust assets 委托资产管理

A management trust is the trust established for the purpose of the management and use of property.

管理信托是为了管理和使用财产而设立的信托。

相关术语：common property 共同财产；property market 房地产市场；Industrial Property Digital Library 工业产权数字图书馆

### 3.2.6 受托划分

#### 3.2.6.1 营业信托

营业信托与“非营业信托”相对的概念，是受托人以营利为目的而承办的业务。营业信托具体有两种方式：（1）受托人不分享信托资财本身的利益以及信托资财所孳生的利益，仅通过收取手续费的方式营利。特约信托业务多属于这种情况。（2）受托人不分享信托资财本身的利益，但分享信托资财所滋生的利益。普通信托业务多属于这种情况。

#### 3.2.6.2 非营业信托

非营业信托是与“营业信托”相对的概念，指受托人不收取报酬无偿承办的信托业

务。此种信托分为个人承办与法人承办两种。个人承办是金融信托发展过程中的初期形式，主要发生在英国，已不多见。法人承办的金融信托主要指非营利性财团法人举办的公益信托。非营利性的财团法人是指拥有一定的财产，根据捐助人的目的从事特定事业（一般为公益事业或慈善事业）的法人团体。此类团体的宗旨要根据捐助人的意愿而定。

**Charitable remainder trust　慈善性剩余信托**

慈善性剩余信托是指由捐款人设立的一种慈善信托，捐款人可将一部分信托收益用于自己及家庭的生活，而将剩余部分转给慈善机构。这种信托的前提是：捐款人有一大笔财产，只需要其中一小部分就可以满足自身及其家庭的生活开支，希望将其余部分捐献给慈善事业，但因为本人无力经营这笔资金，所以需要委托一家慈善机构代为管理。

Combined with charitable giving, various trusts can be used to reduce or eliminate estate assets, such as charitable remainder trusts and charitable lead trusts. (*Forbes*/February 04, 2012/https://www.forbes.com/forbes/1999/0920/6407180a_2.html)

与慈善捐赠相结合，各种信托基金可用于减少或消除房地产资产，如剩余财产慈善信托和慈善信托基金。

注：（1）charitable lead trust 剩余财产慈善信托，仅以实现社会慈善事业为目的，并以全社会或部分社会公众为受益人的信托。（2）相关术语：Pew Charitable Trusts 皮尤慈善信托

Charitable remainder trusts allows a donor to make an arrangement to provide an income interest to a non-charitable beneficiary with the remainder of the trust going to a charitable organization. Let's take a look at the two types: the CRAT and the CRUT.

慈善剩余信托允许捐助者做出安排，向非慈善受益人提供收入利息，而剩余部分将捐给慈善组织。让我们来看看 CRAT 和 CRUT 这两种类型。

注：慈善剩余信托分类：charitable residual annuity trust 慈善性剩余年金信托；charitable residual single trust 慈善性剩余单一信托；common income fund 共同收入基金

## 3.2.7　受益划分

### 3.2.7.1　自益信托

自益信托是指委托人要求设定的信托，其目的是为了本身的收益。在信托关系中，委托人与受益人从理论上讲，都是信托行为的人的要素。在自益信托中，委托人与受益人虽同为一人，但从理论上看，仍是各自独立的两方。某些信托事项还存在自益与他益兼有的情况，难以区分是纯粹的自益信托还是纯粹的他益信托。

**1. (Irrevocable) life insurance trust (ILIT)　寿险信托**

保险信托是一种不可撤销的信托，其中设有人寿保险单作为资产，允许保单的设保人将资产从其应税财产中豁免。一旦人寿保险单被置于信托中，被保险人就不再拥有该保险单，保险人在被保险人去世时将代表保险受益人管理保单。

ILITs wipe away the messy problems that can stain the estate planning effort and protect the trustee's estate. ( https://www.investopedia.com/advisor-network/articles)

寿险信托可解决扰乱房产计划的问题，保护受托人的房产。

注：（1）insurance 保险，本意是稳妥可靠的保障；后延伸成一种保障机制，是一种用来规划人生财务的工具，是市场经济条件下风险管理的基本手段，是金融体系和社会保障体系的重要支柱。（2）相关术语：unemployment insurance 待业保险，失业保险；title insurance 产权保险；insurance coverage 保险责任范围

A life insurance trust is an irrevocable, non-amendable trust which is both the owner and beneficiary of one or more life insurance policies.

寿险信托是一种不可撤销、不可修改的信托，同时是一项或者多项寿险保单的所有人和受益人。

注：我国排名前五的人寿保险公司：China Life Insurance Company 中国人寿；Ping'an Life Insurance Company 平安人寿；Pacific Life Insurance Company 太平洋人寿；Huaxia Life Insurance 华夏人寿；Taiping Life Insurance Company 太平人寿。

**2. Protective trust 保护信托**

保护信托的核心在于，委托人将财产赋予信托受托人，并且指示受托人将信托收益支付给委托人的子女。然而，一旦委托人的子女破产或遭遇其他特定事件，子女则不再享受原有的受益权，但同时会产生一项自由裁量信托，以委托人的及其家人为信托受益人。

Protective trusts (or spendthrift trusts, as they are sometimes known) share the characteristics of a life interest trust and a discretionary trust. (Cornerstonewills/https://cornerstonewills.co.uk/service/trusts-asset-protection/protective- trusts/)

保护信托（有时被称为挥霍无度信托）具有生命利益信托和自由裁量信托的特征。

注：discretionary trust 自由裁量信托，指信托文件本身并不确定受益人可享受的信托利益，而授权受托人根据实际情况加以分配。在分配决定作出之前，受益人是否能获得信托利益以及可以获得多少信托利益都处于不确定状态。

The Protective Trust is a form of settlement found in England and Wales and several Commonwealth countries. It has marked similarities to asset-protection trusts found in several offshore jurisdictions and US Spendthrift trusts. In such a trust assets are ordinarily held to pay an income to the beneficiary. The beneficiary may also have access to capital of the trust with the trustee's permission.

保护信托是一种流行于英格兰、威尔士以及几个英联邦国家的和解形式。它与几个离岸司法管辖区资产保护信托和美国保护信托基金信托资产有明显相似之处。在这种信托中，资产通常是为了向受益人支付收入而持有的。受益人也可以在受托人允许的情况下获得信托资本。

注：美国保护信托基金（US Spendthrift Trusts）是一种规定受益人不得自由处理信托资产的信托。

#### 3.2.7.2 他益信托

**他益信托**是与自益信托相对的概念，指受益人为委托人以外的他人的信托。

**Charitable trust 慈善信托**

CNBC's Jim Cramer said Monday that his charitable trust recently sold shares of Facebook due to a slew of bad headlines ahead of the tech giant's latest controversy over the use of its social media data. (CNBC/March 19, 2018/https://www.cnbc.com/2018/03/19/cramer-trust-sells-some-facebook- shares-after-social-data-controversy.html)

CNBC 的吉姆·克莱姆（Jim Cramer）于周一表示，他的慈善信托基金最近已经出售了 Facebook 的股份，原因是这家科技巨头使用社交媒体数据引起争议后，产生了一系列负面新闻。

注：（1）shares 股份，代表对公司的部分拥有权，分为普通股、优先股、未完全兑付的股权。（2）相关术语：ordinary shares 普通股；institutional shares 法人股；public shares 社会公众股

A charitable trust is an irrevocable trust established for charitable purposes and, in some jurisdictions, a more specific term than "charitable organization".

慈善信托是以慈善为目的而设立的不可撤销信托。在某些司法管辖区中，这是一个比"慈善组织"更加具体的术语。

注：2016 年 9 月 1 日，《中华人民共和国慈善法》正式施行，对关心慈善的金融人来说，《慈善法》中专门有一个章节陈述和"慈善信托"相关的法律条文。

#### 3.2.7.3 私益信托

私益信托（private trust）是指出于私益目的，即为信托人所指定的、特定的某人的利益而设立的信托。目前各国中各种各样的商业信托，以及采用英美系国家中常见的民事信托，都属于私益信托。私益信托的调整适用信托法的一般规定；公益信托的调整则不仅适用信托法的一般规定，还适用该法关于这类信托的专门规定。

公益信托（charitable trust），为学术、技艺、慈善、宗教以及其他公共福利事业而办理的信托，也指个人以自己的资金委托给信托部门办理的公共福利事业的信托业务。此类信托中的受益人为社会公众中符合特定条件的人士或团体。

**1. Employee trust 员工信托**

The most common forms of employee trusts are employee stock ownership plans (ESOP) and employee pension plans. With an ESOP, a company contributes to a trust fund and the trustee purchases stock on behalf of the employee or beneficiaries. (Investopedia/ https://www.investopedia.com/terms/e/employee-trust.asp)

最常见的员工信托形式是员工持股计划（ESOP）和员工养老金计划。员工持股计划是指公司向信托基金捐款，受托人代表员工或者受益人购买股票。

注：purchase vs. buy：前者一般用于书面语，或者比较正式的场合，以及商务文档中；后者则在日常用语中常用。

Employee Trust is a trust fund established by an employer on behalf of its employees in which the company is the grantor and its employees are the beneficiaries.

员工信托是由雇主代表其雇员设立的信托，其中公司是委托人，雇员是受益人。

相关术语：员工持股计划（ESOP）是员工所有权的一种实现形式。员工通过购买企业部分股票（或股权）而拥有企业的部分产权，并获得相应的管理权，实施员工持股计划的目的是使员工成为公司的股东。

**2. Employee share ownership trust (ESOT) 员工持股信托**

员工持股信托是信托账户，公司可以通过该账户向员工出售股票。员工持股可以提高员工士气，激励员工努力工作，并做出符合公司最佳利益的决策。因此，这种安排有助于使公司员工的利益与其他股东的利益保持一致。

An employee share ownership trust is comparable to, but differs from, an employee stock ownership plan, which often serves as a form of retirement benefit to employees. (Investopedia/https://www.investopedia.com/terms/e/employeeshareownershiptrust.asp)

员工持股信托与员工持股计划类似但又有所不同，后者通常作为员工退休福利的一种形式。

注：compare vs. contrast：前者意为“与……相比”，侧重于找到两个或多个事物的异同；后者意为“明显不同的是……”，侧重于事物的差异。

An employee share ownership trust is a program that facilitates the acquisition and distribution of a company’s shares to its employees.

员工持股信托是一项促进公司股份收购和分配给员工的计划。

相关术语：merge & acquisition 并购，指两家或者更多的独立企业、公司合并组成一家企业，通常由一家占优势的公司吸收一家或者多家公司。

**3. Unit trust 单位信托**

单位信托是投资工具之一，通过汇集许多个人投资者的资金，基金经理能够管理大型、有效、并拥有多元化投资的组合。单位信托的单位凭证总数固定，一般投资于债券，其债券组合不会发生活跃交易，且有固定到期。单位信托一旦由发起人组合（通常为经纪公司或债券承销商）并交给受托人后，直到发行人赎回债券，受托人将一直持有所有债券。

This is a fund constituted in the form of a unit trust under the laws of Mauritius. (www02.etwealth.com)

这是根据毛里求斯法律以单位信托形式设立的基金。

注：constitute vs. institute：前者的基本意思是“组成”，主要用于机构的组成或规章制度的制定，引申则可指组成人员的选定或任命；后者的基本意思是“建立，制定”，指通过权威部门的授权而建立机构、制度或法律等抽象的东西。

A unit trust is a form of collective investment constituted under a trust deed. A unit trust pools investors’ money into a single fund, which is managed by a fund manager.

单位信托是根据信托契约构成集体投资的一种形式。单位信托将投资者的资金汇集到一个由基金经理管理的基金中。

相关术语：trust deed 信托契约，亦称“信托财产”或“信托资产”。委托人转给受托人并由受托人按照信托契约进行经营管理和处置的货币资金或实物财产。

## 3.2.8 区域划分

### 3.2.8.1 国内信托

国内信托，“国际信托”的相对概念，是指业务范围限于本国境内的信托。我国经办信托业务的机构是各专业银行所属的信托公司和经批准成立的地方信托投资公司。

**Domestic trust 国内信托**

At the beginning of 2013, Ping An Trust issued the first family trust in the Mainland — Ping An Fortune Hongcheng Family Series Single All-Capital Trust. The trust product is raised on a scale of 50 million yuan and has a contract period of 50 years. The client is an entrepreneur over 40 years old. According to the agreement, the trustee and Ping An Trust jointly manage the assets. The principal can realize the inheritance of property by appointing the heir as the beneficiary. Protecting family wealth inheritance is one of the functions of Hongcheng family products, which were not specially designed for family trust at the beginning of the design. (http://ucwap.ifeng.com/finance/money/xintuo/news?aid=88883274)

2013 年年初，平安信托发行内地首个家族信托——平安财富 • 鸿承世家系列单一全资金信托。此信托产品募集资金规模为 5000 万元，合同期为 50 年，客户是一位年过 40 岁的企业家。根据协议，信托受托人与平安信托共同管理这笔资产。委托人可通过制定继承人为受益人方式来实现财产继承。保护家族财富传承是“鸿承世家”系列产品的功能之一，但在设计之初并不是专门为家族信托而设计的。

注：（1）词义辨析：issue vs. release：前者作动词时，常意为“使书等出版、发行”；后者作“发布，发行”解时，一般指发布消息，新闻等；（2）相关术语：family trust 家族信托；vested remainder 遗产继承权；legal heir 法定继承人；testamentary successor 遗嘱继承人

Domestic trust is the symmetry of “international trust”, and its business scope is limited to the trust in its own country. Trust companies affiliated to professional banks and approved local trust and investment companies are the institutions that handle trust business in China. The main contents include: trust investment and trust loan business for projects specified by the principal; financing leasing business; agency business, RMB debt guarantee and witness business, consulting business, securities issuance business, etc.

国内信托是“国际信托”的相对概念，业务范围限于本国境内的信托。中国经办信托业务的机构是各专业银行所属的信托公司和经批准成立的地方信托投资公司。其业务主要包括：委托人指定项目的信托投资和信托贷款业务、融资租赁业务、代理业务、人民币债务担保及见证业务、咨询业务、证券发行业务等。

相关术语：international trust 国际信托；国际信托是指国际交往中接受他人信任与

委托，代为经管财物或代办事务为指定的人谋利益的经济行为。信托业务主要有short-term fund trust 短期资金信托、investment trust 投资信托和 financing trust 筹资信托。

### 3.2.8.2 国际信托

国际信托指国际交往中接受他人信任与委托，代为经管财物或代办事务为指定的人谋利益的经济行为。分为信托和代理两类基本业务。其业务主有短期资金信托、投资信托、筹资信托。

**1. Active index fund 活跃指数基金**

An active index fund attempts to take a version of an index fund like the Standard & Poor's 500 Index (S&P 500) and periodically rebalance all the stocks to match the proportions found in the actual S&P 500. (Investopedia/April 02, 2018/https://www.investopedia.com/sponsored/?prx_t=ansDAAAAAA4rcDA&EXCMPGN=EX:PC:FAS:Sustaining)

活跃指数基金试图采用标准普尔 500 指数（S&P 500）等指数基金版本，并定期重新平衡所有股票以使其符合实际标准普尔 500 指数。

注：match vs. fit vs. suit: match 指在能力、水平上"与……相配"；fit 往往强调尺寸、大小或形状上的吻合；suit 侧重于符合某人的口味，或服装颜色、款式等的相配或适合。

An active index fund is a basket of assets which the fund manager constructs the initial investment with holdings from a benchmark index and then adds securities unrelated to the underlying index that can drive performance higher.

活跃指数基金是一篮子资产，基金经理用基准指数中的持股构建初始投资，然后添加与基础指数无关的证券，从而推动业绩走高。

相关术语：（1）benchmark index 基准指数：基准指数是反映某证券交易所交易状况最基本、最大众化的指数，如纽约股票交易所的 Dow Jones Industrial Average 和道琼斯工业平均指数，香港联交所的 Hang Seng Index 恒生指数。（2）Standard & Poor's 标准普尔：标准普尔由亨利·瓦纳姆·普尔先生创立于 1860 年，是普尔出版公司和标准统计公司（Standard & Poor's）1941 年合并而成的世界权威金融分析机构，总部位于美国纽约市。

**2. Active trust 积极信托**

积极信托是指受托人在信托执行中负有履行积极措施义务的信托。例如，根据信托条款受托人在取得信托财产后有义务处分该项财产，并将财产收益在财产受益人之间分配的情况即属此类。在积极信托中，受托人必定享有"法律上的所有权"，他有权为实现信托意图自主地对信托财产从事支配行为。积极信托体现了信托制度的基本要求，受到法律的充分保护。

An active trust is in contrast to a passive trust in which the trustee performs no active duties. (Investopedia/https://www.investopedia.com/terms/a/active-trust.asp)

积极信托与受托人不履行主动义务的消极信托形成对比。

注：perform vs. carry out vs. implement：perform 意为"执行"，尤指复杂的任务或行动；carry out 意为"实行"；implement 一般指"有计划下的实施，执行"。

An active trust is a trust wherein the trustee has to take additional actions beyond passively dealing with property for the benefit of the beneficiary.

积极信托是指受托人为了受益人的利益，在消极处理财产之外，还必须采取其他行动的信托。

相关术语：beneficiary 受益人，是在保险合同中由被保险人或投保人指定，在被保险人死亡后有权领取保险金的人，一般见于人身保险合同。如果投保人或被保险人未指定受益人，则他的法定继承人即为受益人。

**3. Passive trust　消极信托**

消极信托是指受托人在信托执行中不负有任何积极作为义务的信托。在此类信托中，受托人实质上对信托财产不具有对物权；“法律上的所有权”和“衡平法上的所有权”实际上已合而为一并归于信托受益人，受益人已经从财产利益享用人转变为法律上的所有人；因此法院有权在消极信托依信托条款终止前对其加以解除。

**4. Clifford trust　克利福德信托**

Clifford Trusts allow grantors to transfer assets that produce income into the trust and then reclaim them when the trust expires.

克利福德信托基金允许委托人将产生收入的资产转移到信托基金，然后在信托到期后收回这些资产。

注：transfer vs. transform：前者意为“转移”，一般指空间的转移；后者往往表达“改变、改观、变换”的意思，指本身发生了变化。

**5. Constructive trust　推定信托**

推定信托规则旨在禁止占有他人财产的当事人不公正地取得他人财产利益的状况；此类财产占有人依法只能以推定信托受托人的身份管理财产，不得谋取财产上的利益；衡平法理论上又称之为“财产受托人不享有受益权原则”。

Constructive trusts, implied as a matter of law, have become an essential device for avoiding unjust enrichment in cases of fraud and mistake. (DictAll/http://www.dictall.com/dictall/result_sentence.jsp?cd=UTF-8&keyword=constructive+trusts)

推定信托，作为普通法默认制度，已成为避免欺诈和错误案件中不当得利的重要手段。

注：fraud vs. cheat vs. deceive vs. trick：fraud 指诈欺的行为，不正当的手段；cheat 指为达目的，以不正当的手段欺骗对方；deceive 指以隐瞒或歪曲事实的方式欺骗对方；trick 指运用计谋骗人

A constructive trust is an equitable remedy resembling a trust (implied trust) imposed by a court to benefit a party that has been wrongfully deprived of its rights due to either a person obtaining or holding a legal property right which they should not possess due to unjust enrichment or interference, or due to a breach of fiduciary duty, which is intercausative with unjust enrichment and/or property interference.

推定信托是一种由法院施加的公平的补救办法信托（默示信托），以使因获得或持有因不当得利或干涉而不应拥有的合法财产权的人或因违反信托义务而被错误剥夺其权利的一方受益，这与不当得利和财产干涉是相互关联的。

相关术语：fiduciary duty 信托责任，指受托人对委托人/受益人负有的、严格按委托

人的意愿（而不是受托人）进行财产管理的责任。一旦委托人和受托人之间的信托关系成立，受托人就负有信托责任。

**6. Express trust 明示信托**

明示信托指财产授予人以明示声明方式而直接订立的信托。其形式包括遗嘱、契据文件、非盖印文件和口头方式四种。依据英联邦国家的法律，凡地产信托必须通过书面方式设立，其中又包括契据文件、非盖印文书和书面三种摘记方式；凡以遗嘱方式设立信托的，须采取书面形式并须符合遗嘱证明和签署的程序。

Law generally requires only a simple formality to create an express trust. (Wikipedia/August 2014/https://en.wikipedia.org/wiki/Express_trust)

在法律上建立一个明示信托通常只需要简单的手续。

注：create vs. produce：前者主要意思是“创造”，即产生新的东西，其对象往往是精神上的，如艺术、文学作品中的人物以及新的科学领域等，也可指创造出新的具体事物；后者是“制造，生产或创造某事物”，是自然地生产、制造。

An express trust is a trust created “in express terms, and usually in writing, as distinguished from one inferred by the law from the conduct or dealings of the parties.”

明示信托是“以明确调侃，通常以书面形式，区别于根据当事人的行为或交易由法律推断的信托”的信托。

注：term 的基本意思是“期，期限”，引申可表示“学期”“开庭期，会期”“终止期”等；term 也可作“术语，行话”解，指有特定意义的词或专门名词，通常用复数形式。

## 3.2.9 业务划分

### 3.2.9.1 信托的特点

**1. Separation of ownership and interest 所有权与收益权相分离**

Family trust is characterized by the separation of ownership and income rights. Once the property is put into the family trust structure, it will not involve the trust property because of the client’s death, divorce or bankruptcy, and will not have to pay inheritance tax in the future, so as to reduce the cost of inheritance. (http://trust.jrj.com.cn/2016/06/23072621103019.shtml)

家族信托的特点在于所有权与收益权的分离。财产一旦被纳入家族信托架构，就不会因为委托人身故、离异或破产而牵连信托财产，日后也不用缴纳遗产税，从而降低继承成本。

注：family trust 家族信托，是一种信托机构受个人或家族的委托，代为管理、处置家庭财产的财产管理方式，以实现富人的财富规划及传承目标。

That is to say, the trustee enjoys the ownership of the trust property, while the beneficiary enjoys the benefits arising from the trustee’s operation of the trust property.

所有权与收益权相分离即受托人享有信托财产的所有权，而受益人享有受托人经营信托财产所产生的利益。

注：trustee 信托受托人，指信托关系中依信托意图管理被授予的信托财产并承担受

托义务的当事人。受托人可以是有行为能力的自然人，也可是具有受托经营能力的法人；可以为一人，也可为数人。

**2. Independence of property　独立运作财产**

After the establishment of the trust, the trustor no longer has the ownership of the trust property, but only has the right to supervise the trust. (http://finance.sina.com.cn/trust/xthydt/2018-10-11/doc-ihmhafiq8692921.shtml)

信托设立后，委托人对信托财产不再享有所有权，仅享有对信托的监督权。

注：相关术语：movable property 动产，指能脱离原有位置而存在的资产，如各种流动资产、各项长期投资和除不动产以外的各项固定资产；immovable property 不动产，指依照其物理性质不能移动或者移动将严重损害其经济价值的有形物体；intellectual property 知识财产，具有商业价值的知识或信息。一般分为艺术财产（如艺术品、文学作品、音乐作品等）和工业财产（如发明、商标、商业秘密等）。

Once the trust is established effectively, the trust property is separated from the proprietary property of the principal, the trustee and the beneficiary, and becomes an independent property.

信托有效设立后，信托财产与委托人、受托人和受益人的专有财产分离，成为独立的财产。

独立财产是指法人的财产不仅独立于其他社会组织的财产，而且独立于自己成员的其他个人财产，同时也独立于创立人国家的其他财产。拥有独立的财产，是法人参加民事法律关系和担负物质责任的前提和根据。

注：ownership 所有权，是所有人依法对自己财产所享有的占有、使用、收益和处分的权利，是对生产劳动的目的、对象、手段、方法和结果的支配力量，它是一种财产权，所以又称财产所有权。

### 3.2.9.2　代理

**1. Agency　委托代理**

The act of agency is the act of an agent. That is to say, the acts of the agent in the name of the principal to the third party are of legal significance. It includes civil legal acts, litigation acts and other acts of legal significance.(https://baike.baidu.com/item/%E4%BB%A3%E7%90%86%E5%95%86/849539?fr=aladdin)

代理行为是代理人的行为，即代理人以被代理人名义对第三人进行具有法律意义的行为，包括民事法律行为、诉讼行为和其他具有法律意义的行为。

注：（1）civil legal acts 民事法律行为，指民事主体通过意思表示设立、变更、终止民事法律关系的行为。民事法律行为可以采用书面形式、口头形式或者其他形式。法律规定用特定形式的，应当依照法律规定。（2）词义辨析：agent 是一个独立主体，负责完成任务但不负责执行任务，具有一定的自主决策能力；broker 是一个独立主体，但没有自主决策能力，只负责订约过程。

Principal-agent refers to the legal acts between the agent and the third party within the scope of authorization in the name of the principal-agent. The legal consequences of such acts are directly borne by the principal-agent.

委托代理是指代理人以被委托代理人名义，在授权范围内与第三者发生法律行为，这种行为的法律后果直接由被委托代理人承担。

注：authorization 授权，是组织运作的关键，它是以人为对象，将完成某项工作所必需的权力授给部属人员。即主管将处理用人、用钱、做事、交涉、协调等决策权移转给部属，只授予权力，不可托付完成该项工作的必要责任，这是授权的绝对原则性。

**2. Differences between agency and trust 代理与信托的区别**

Principal-agent refers to the legal acts between the agent and the third party within the scope of authorization in the name of the principal-agent. The legal consequences of such acts are directly borne by the principal-agent. The so-called trust refers to the act that the trustee transfers his property rights to the trustee on the basis of trust in the trustee, and the trustee manages or disposes of the property in his own name for the benefit of the beneficiary according to the wishes of the trustee. (https://baike.baidu.com/item/%E4%BF%A1%E6%89%98/221065?fr=aladdin)

委托代理是指受托人以被委托代理的名义，在授权范围内与第三者发生法律行为，这种行为的法律后果直接由被委托代理人承担。所谓信托，是指委托人基于对受托人的信任，将其财产权转移给受托人，受托人按委托人之意愿，以自己的名义为受益人的利益而管理或处分财产的行为。

注：principal agent theory 委托代理理论。20 世纪 30 年代，美国经济学家伯利和米恩斯因为洞悉企业所有者兼具经营者的做法存在着极大的弊端，于是提出“委托代理理论”，倡导所有权和经营权分离，企业所有者保留剩余索取权，而将经营权利让渡。

One of the main differences between trust system and agency in common law countries is: in the agency, the agent must conduct legal acts in the name of the principal. Under the trust system, the trustee is the right subject of the trust property, and manages or disposes of the trust property on behalf of the principal in his own name.

英美法系国家信托制度与代理制度的主要区别之一是：在代理制度中，代理人须以被代理人的名义对外进行法律行为；而在信托制度下，受托人是信托财产的权利主体，是以自己的名义代委托人管理或处分信托财产。

注：common law 英美法系；普通法系，指英国从 11 世纪起主要以源于日耳曼习惯法的普通法为基础而逐渐形成的一种独特的法律制度以及仿效英国的其他一些国家和地区的法律制度。注重法典的延续性，以传统、判例和习惯为判案依据。

# Chapter 4

# Terminologies of Bank
# （银行篇）

## 4.1 Central Bank（中央银行）

本章主要介绍现代金融制度下中央银行的业务，并简要介绍中央银行资产负债表。在此基础上，本章进一步区分中央银行业务与其他金融机构业务的根本不同。

中央银行国家中居主导地位的金融中心机构，是国家干预和调控国民经济发展的重要工具。负责制定并执行国家货币信用政策，独具货币发行权，实行金融监管。

中国的中央银行为中国人民银行，简称央行。

中央银行的业务主要有货币发行、集中存款准备金、再贷款、再贴现、证券、黄金外汇占款、为商业银行和其他金融机构办理资金划拨清算和资金转移业务等。

中央银行所从事的业务与其他金融机构所从事的业务根本区别在于，中央银行所从事的业务不是为营利，而是为实现国家宏观经济目标服务，这是由中央银行所处的地位和性质决定的。

### 4.1.1 中央银行业务

**Anti-money laundering　反洗钱**

Consummating the anti-money laundering supervision system construction, promoting the anti-money laundering cooperation and fighting against as well as controlling the crime of money laundering have important practical significance for our country's economic development and social stability to strike and control money laundering. (https://en.wikipedia.org/)

完善反洗钱监管体系建设，推动反洗钱合作，深入有效打击和控制洗钱犯罪活动，对我国经济发展和社会稳定有重要现实意义。

注：money laundering 洗钱，是一种将非法所得合法化的行为。主要指将违法所得及其产生的收益，通过各种手段掩饰、隐瞒其来源和性质，使其在形式上合法化。

Anti-money laundering refers to laws, regulations, and procedures intended to prevent disguising, concealing drug crimes, organizing crimes of the underworld, crimes of terrorist activities, smuggling, corruption and bribery, and the crime of destroying financial management order.

反洗钱指为防止伪装罪、隐瞒毒品犯罪、组织黑社会犯罪、恐怖活动犯罪、走私、腐败、贿赂、破坏金融管理秩序而制定的法律，法规和制度。

注：crime：指严重的违法行为或罪行；sin：主要指违反道德原则或违反宗教戒律的过失或罪过行为；guilt：多用于指违反道德或社会标准的不法行为，含应惩办之意，这种惩办是以证据为依据的。

### 4.1.2 中央银行资产负债表

**1. Balance sheet 资产负债表**

The preparation of the statement of cash flows is different from the balance sheet and the income statement. (*The Economist*/The Great Divide in China)

现金流量表的编制不同于资产负债表和损益表。

注：财务报表的三个基本报告为：balance sheet 资产负债表；statement of cash flow 现金流量表，指在一个固定期间（通常是每月或每季）内，一家机构的现金的增减变动情况；income statement 利润表（反映企业在一定会计期间的经营成果）。

A balance sheet is a written statement of the amount of money and property that a company or person has, including amounts of money that are owed or are owing. Balance sheet is also used to refer to the general financial state of a company.

资产负债表是反应一个公司或个人拥有的资本和财产的会计报表，包括负债和应付账款。资产负债表也用来表示公司的一般财务状况。

注：balance sheet 资产负债表，根据“资产 assets=负债 liabilities+所有者权益 equity”这一平衡公式，依照一定的分类标准和一定的次序，将某一特定日期的资产、负债、所有者权益的具体项目予以适当的排列编制而成。

**2. Bank statement 银行对账单**

Most audit work on cash is done working from the bank statement. (www.ftchinese.com)

大部分现金审计工作都是根据银行对账单进行的。

注：（1）四大会计师事务所：普华永道（PwC）；德勤（DTT）；毕马威（KPMG）；安永（EY）；（2）audit 审计，指由专设机关依照法律对国家各级政府及金融机构、企业事业组织的重大项目和财务收支进行事前和事后的审查的独立性经济监督活动。

A bank statement is a printed document showing all the money paid into and taken out of a bank account. Bank statements are usually sent by a bank to a customer at regular intervals.

银行对账单是一份打印文件，显示从银行账户中支付和取出的所有款项。银行对账单通常由银行定期发送给客户。

注：银行对账单的作用：有助于企业防范操作风险；有助于企业防范管理风险；有助于企业防范外部风险；有助于企业编制现金收支计划；有助于企业检查其财务制度的有效性。

## 4.2 Policy Bank（政策性银行）

本节首先介绍政策性银行概念，其次介绍政策性金融工具和相关机构，并进一步分析相关机构职能和作用。

政策性金融，指在一国政府支持下，以国家信用为基础，运用各种特殊融资手段，严格按照国家法规限定业务范围、经营对象，以优惠性存贷利率，直接或间接为贯彻、配合国家特定经济和社会发展政策，而进行的一种特殊性资金融通行为。它是一切规范意义上的政策性贷款，是一切带有特定政策性意向的存款、投资、担保、贴现、信用保险、存款保险、利息补贴等一系列特殊性资金融通行为的总称。

### 4.2.1 政策性金融工具

**1. Draft 汇票**

At present, the non-cash payment tools in China are made up of bills (draft, promissory notes and checks), bank cards and network payments, but does it mean that every business should agree with every kind of legal payment? (www.ftchinese.com/story/001077011?full=y)

当下中国的非现金支付工具主要由票据（汇票、本票和支票）、银行卡、网络支付等构成，但这是否意味着每一个商家都应当同意（使用）每一种合法支付方式呢？

注：汇票 draft、本票 promissory notes 与支票 checks 的区别：支票的出票人与付款人之间必须先有资金关系，才能签发支票；汇票的出票人与付款人之间不必先有资金关系；本票的出票人与付款人为同一个人，不存在所谓的资金关系。

Draft is defined as an unconditional order in writing, addressed by one person to another, signed by the person giving it, requiring the person to whom it is addressed to pay on demand, or at a fixed or determinable future time, a sum certain in money to or to the order of a specified person, or to bearer.

汇票，指出票人签发的，委托付款人在见票时，或者在指定日期无条件支付确定的金额给收款人或者持票人的票据。

注：汇票 draft、本票 promissory notes 与支票 checks 的相同点：都是设权有价证券；都是格式证券；都是文字证券；都是可以流通转让的证券；都是无因证券。

**2. Exposure 风险敞口**

Stock market risk exposure is different from economic exposure, and there are great differences between different emerging markets. (www.ftchinese.com/story/001076859?archive)

股市风险敞口不同于经济风险敞口，且不同新兴市场间差异很大。

注：emerging market 新兴市场，是市场经济体制逐步完善、经济发展速度较高、市场发展潜力较大的市场。

Exposure is financial positions exposed to market risk.

风险敞口是指暴露于市场风险的财务状况。

注：financial performance 财务业绩（财务运作取得的绩效）；financial position 财务状况（盈利还是亏损）

**3. Deposit account　存款账户**

Social Finance Inc. said it will start offering deposit accounts and debit cards to some customers next month, the first major new product under Chief Executive Officer Anthony Noto. (www.finance.yahoo.com/news/sofi-plans-start-rolling-checking-222815799.html)

社会金融公司表示将于下个月开始向部分客户提供存款账户和借记卡，这是首席执行官安东尼・诺托旗下的首个重要新产品。

注：（1）debit card 借记卡，指发卡银行向持卡人签发的，没有信用额度，持卡人先存款、后使用的银行卡；（2）credit card 贷记卡、信用卡，是由商业银行或信用卡公司对信用合格的消费者发行的信用证明，持卡人可以在规定额度内透支。

A deposit account is a savings account, current account or any other type of bank account that allows money to be deposited and withdrawn by the account holder.

存款账户是储蓄账户、活期账户或任何其他类型的银行账户，允许账户持有人存取资金。

注：bank holder 银行账户持有人；account number 银行账号；current balance 当前余额；available balance 可用余额

**4. Endorsement　背书**

When a signature or endorsement is required to be on a document consisting of more than one page, and the credit or the document itself does not indicate where a signature or endorsement is to appear, the signature or endorsement may appear anywhere on that document. (ISBP745, Para A25)

当要求多页单据载有签字或背书，而信用证或单据自身未规定签字或背书位置时，签字或背书可以出现在任何位置。

注：brand endorsement 品牌背书，指某一品牌要素以某种方式出现在包装、标号或者产品外观上，但不直接作为品牌名称的一部分。通常，这一特殊的品牌要素是公司的品牌或标识。

An endorsement is a signature on a negotiable instrument such as a check (cheque), indicating a person's intent to become a party to the instrument.

背书是可转让票据上的签字，如汇票（支票），表明某人有意成为票据一方。

注：背书有三种方式：限定背书，有些限定背书规定汇票只交付一次，受让人只能自行使用汇票而无再次转让的权利；特定背书，又称记名背书，此种背书既有出让人签名，又指明了受让人是谁，但无“仅付”“不得转让”等字样；空白背书，又称不记名背书，即背书人在汇票上只有签名，不写付给某人，即没有被背书人。

**5. D/P　付款交单**

Our payment term usually is to accept document against payment in 60 days, which we hope can satisfy you. (www.dyebbs.cn)

我方支付条件通常是 60 天付款交单，希望这能令贵方满意。

注：payment term 付款条件也叫现金折扣，是指企业为了鼓励客户偿还贷款而允诺在一定期限内给予的规定的折扣优待。通常可表示为 5/10，2/20，n/30；price term 价格条款，指国际贸易合同中表明价格条件的款项，是对外经济贸易合同中的重要条款之一。

D/P is document against payment. It is an arrangement under which an exporter instructs the presenting bank to hand over shipping and title documents (see document of title) to the importer only if the importer fully pays the accompanying bill of exchange or draft.

付款交单（D/P）指代收行必须在进口商付清货款后，才可将商业（货运）单据（所有权单据）交给进口方的一种结算方式。

注：2019 年上半年我国对外进口前十的国家和地区中总额较大的有韩国、日本、美国等，这些经济发达国家和地区又呈现出低增长率、甚至负增长率的状况。而受"一带一路"影响，我国对沿线国家的进口增速大大提高，特别是沙特阿拉伯，增速达到 30.4%。

**6. D/A 承兑交单**

The international factoring business has received increasing attention from various parties and has been widely used because it meets the needs of the development of trade methods such as credit sales and acceptance of acceptance. (Sina Finance/5 July, 2001/http://finance.sina.com.cn/d/79589.html)

国际保理业务由于迎合诸如赊销、承兑交单等贸易方式发展的需要，越来越受到各方重视并得到广泛运用。

注：international factoring 国际保理、承购应收账款，指在以商业信用出口货物时，出口商交货后把应收账款的发票和装运单据转让给保理商，即可取得应收取的大部分贷款，日后一旦发生进口商不付或逾期付款，则由保理商承担付款责任，在保理业务中，保理商承担第一付款责任。

D/A is document against acceptance. It is an arrangement in which an exporter instructs a bank to hand over shipping and title documents (see document of title) to an importer only if the importer accepts the accompanying bill of exchange or draft by signing it.

D/A 是承兑交单，指出口商只有在进口商接受所附的汇票或汇票并签字后，才指示银行将装船单据和所有权单据（见所有权单据）交给进口商的一种结算方式。

注：bill of exchange 汇票，由出票人签发的，要求付款人在见票时或在一定期限内，向收款人或持票人无条件支付一定款项的票据。汇票是国际结算中使用最广泛的一种信用工具。

**7. D/D 即期汇票**

Inward and outward remittances are usually carried out by a mail transfer, demand draft(DD), or telegraphic transfer(TT). (www.examw.com)

汇进和汇出通常是通过信汇、即期汇票（DD）或电汇（TT）来完成。

注：remittance 汇款，国际结算支付方式之一。付款方通过第三者（一般是银行）使用各种结算工具，主动将款项汇付给收款方的一种业务处理方式。

D/D is demand draft. It is a demand draft is a negotiable instrument similar to a bill of exchange. A bank issues a demand draft to a client (drawer), directing another bank (drawee) or one of its own branches to pay a certain sum to the specified party (payee).

D/D 是即期汇票。它是一种与汇票类似的可转让票据。银行向客户（出票人）发出需求汇票，指示另一家银行（付款人）或其自己的分支机构之一向指定方（收款人）支付一定金额。

注：（1）drawer 出票人，是开立票据并将其交付给他人的法人、其他组织或者个人。出票人对持票人及正当持票人承担票据在提示付款或承兑时必须付款或者承兑的保证责任；（2）drawee/payer 受票人，又叫“付款人”，指受出票人委托支付票据金额的人、接受支付命令的人；（3）payee 收款人，是凭汇票向付款人请求支付票据金额的人。是汇票的债权人，一般是卖方，是收钱的人。

**8. Dishonor　拒付**

Since the nature of Teleingreso is a real-time transfer of online banking, it is generally operated only by the consumer. So once the payment is successful, there will not be dishonored. (www.ibtimes.com.cn/press-release/-4648.htm)

由于远程登录（Teleingreso）的本质是在线银行的实时转帐，它通常只由消费者操作。所以一旦付款操作成功，不会产生拒付。

注：transfer of account 转账，指不直接使用现金，而是通过银行将款项从付款账户划转到收款账户完成货币收付的一种银行货币结算方式。

Teleingreso：西班牙当地其中一种安全便捷的现金支付方式，消费者凭借网上生成的代金券可以通过分布在境内的数千个取款机、邮局、零售店等终端完成交易。

The action of refusing to fulfill contractual obligations or pay a charge. Dishonoring a transaction can occur if a seller does not deliver the goods or when the buyer does not provide payment. In contracts, a party may dishonor the agreement by altering the specifications, delivering late payment or goods, or failing to act on their required duties.

拒付是拒绝履行合同义务或支付费用的行为。如果卖方不交付货物或买方不提供付款，则可能发生拒付。在合同中，一方当事人可能会改变规格，交付滞纳金或货物，或者不履行所要求的职责，从而拒绝履约。

注：汇票的持票人向付款人提示时，拒付可能遭到拒绝付款（dishonor by non-payment）或拒绝承兑（dishonor by non-acceptance）两种情形。根据我国的票据法，持票人提示承兑或提示付款被拒绝的，承兑人或付款人必须出具拒绝证明，或出具退票理由。

**9. Discount　贴现**

However, the actual situation is that before the repurchase expires, the bank notes were taken out by a bill institution from Chongqing in advance and the institution repurchased and discounted with another bank. The funds entered into the stock market illegally but not return to the accounts of the Beijing branch of Agricultural Bank of China. (*International Business Times*/8, April, 2016/http://www.ibtimes.com.cn/articles/48264/20160408/113209.htm)

但实际情况是，银行券在回购到期前就被一家重庆的票据机构提前取出，将它与另外一家银行进行回购贴现交易。这笔资金并未退回到中国农业银行北京分行账上，而是非法地进入股市。

注：bank notes 银行券，指由银行发行的、用以代替商业票据的，由银行票据表征的货币，主要包括银行本票、银行汇票、银行签发的支票等。

Discount is a financial mechanism in which a debtor obtains the right to delay payments to a creditor, for a defined period of time, in exchange for a charge or fee.

贴现是一种金融机制，在这种机制下，债务人用支付一定的费用或收费获得向债权人延迟支付一定期限的权利。

注：（1）贴现的期限：贴现的期限从其贴现之日起至汇票到期日止，最长不超过 6 个月；实付贴现金额按照票面金额扣除贴现日至汇票到期前一日的利息计算；（2）贴现的利率：贴现利率按人民银行的规定执行，按商业银行同档次流动资金贷款利率下浮 3 个百分点执行。

**10. Debenture 公司债券**

After the treasury bills were sold in November, the prices of debentures continued to decline. The difference between the yields of 5-year AAA corporate bonds and the equivalent treasury bonds had reached the highest point in three years. (www.ftchinese.com/story/001075504?archive)

自 11 月份国库券被抛售后，公司债券价格持续走低。五年期 AAA 公司债券和等值国债收益率之差已达到三年以来的最高点。

注：treasury bill/short-term government bond/treasury bond/treasury government bond/treasury bond/short term bill 短期国债，指一国政府为满足先支后收所产生的临时性资金需要而发行的短期债券；短期国债最早发行于英国，在英美被称为国库券。

Debenture is a promissory note or a corporate bond which (in the US) is backed generally only by the reputation and integrity of the borrower and (in the UK) by the borrower's specific assets. When unsecured, it is called a bare debenture or naked debenture；when secured by a charge on a specific property, it is called a mortgage debenture.

公司债券是一种本票或企业债券，在美国通常仅由借款人的声誉和信用担保，在英国由借款人的特定资产担保。 当公司债券无担保时，称作裸债权证；以特定财产作抵押时，称为抵押债权证。注：mortgage 抵押，指抵押人和债权人以书面形式订立约定，不转移抵押财产的占有，而是将该财产作为债权的担保。当债务人到期不履行债务时，债权人有权依法以该财产折价或者以拍卖、变卖该财产的价款优先受偿。

**11. Default 违约**

The time between defaulting on storage payments and going to auction is usually a few months at best, depending on the place. (www.ibtimes.com/man-arrested-after-child-porn-found-storage-locker-sold-auction-2669785)

通常仓储支付违约和拍卖之间的时间间隔最多是几个月，具体取决于发生的地点。

注：auction 拍卖，指专门从事拍卖业务的拍卖行接受货主的委托，在规定的时间与场所，按照一定的章程和规则，将要拍卖的货物向买主展示，公开叫价竞购，最后由拍卖人把货物卖给出价最高的买主的一种现货交易方式。

Default is the failure to pay interest or principal on a loan or security when due. Default occurs when a debtor is unable to meet the legal obligation of debt repayment, and it also refers to cases in which one party fails to perform on a futures contract as required by an exchange.

违约是指未能在到期时支付贷款或证券的利息或本金。违约是指债务人无法履行清偿债务的法律义务，也指一方未按交易所要求履行期货合约的情况。

注：large/massive/long-term/short-term/interest-free/low-interest/secured/unsecured loan 大额贷款/巨额贷款/长期贷款/短期贷款/免息贷款/低息贷款/担保贷款/无担保贷款；apply for/ask for/request/arrange/get/raise/take out/receive/pay off/repay loan 申请贷款/安排贷款/获得贷款/筹集贷款/抵充贷款/接受贷款/还清贷款/偿还贷款

**12. Disclosure 披露**

Sessions had said Andrew "made an unauthorized disclosure to the news media and lacked candor—including under oath—on multiple occasions." (*International Business Times*/4, March, 2018/http://www.ibtimes.com/jill-mccabe-facts-ex-fbi-deputy-directors-wife-attacks-trump-fiery-op-ed-2668454)

塞申斯曾表示安德鲁"未经授权多次向新闻媒体披露信息，并且在包括宣誓在内的许多场合中缺乏坦率精神"。

The act of releasing all relevant information pertaining to a company that may influence an investment decision. To make investing as fair as possible for everyone, companies must disclose both good and bad information.

企业应该披露所有与公司相关、可能影响公司投资决策的信息，包括好消息和坏消息，使得每个投资者能公平地投资。

**13. Emergency fund　紧急备用金**

Being prepared with an emergency fund gives you confidence that you can tackle any of life's unexpected events without adding money worries to your list. (https://investor.vanguard.com/emergency-fund/)

准备好紧急备用金，将使你有信心解决生活中任何突发事件且不会增加金钱方面的担忧。

An emergency fund is an account for funds set aside in case of the event of a personal financial dilemma, such as the loss of a job, a debilitating illness or a major repair to your home. The purpose of the fund is to improve financial security by creating a safety net of funds that can be used to meet emergency expenses as well as reduce the need to draw from high interest debt options, such as credit cards or unsecured loans.

紧急备用金是为预防个人经济困境发生而预留的资金账户，如失业、重大疾病或房屋大修。该基金的目的是通过建立可用于支付紧急开支的资金安全网，提高财务安全，并减少个人从信用卡或无担保贷款等高息债务中提取资金的需要。

**14. Electronic check　电子支票**

This smart card application system can verify customers and has the function of electronic check. Combined with POS payment, it ensures many transactions. (dict.cnki.net)

这种智能卡应用系统可以鉴别用户，同时具有电子票据的功能，结合 POS 支付功能，该系统可以支持多类交易服务。

An electronic check, also referred to as an e-check, is a form of payment made via the internet, or other data network, designed to perform the same function as a conventional paper check. Since the check is in an electronic format, it can be processed in fewer steps. Additionally, it has more security features than standard paper checks including authentication, public key cryptography, digital signatures and encryption, among others.

电子支票也称 e-支票，是一种通过互联网或其他数据网络进行的支付形式，旨在履行与传统纸质支票相同的功能。由于支票是电子格式，因此使用时需要的步骤更少。此外，比起标准纸质支票，电子支票可以提供更多安全功能，包括身份验证、公钥加密、数字签名和加密等。

**15. Digital currency 数字货币**

Fortunately, one of the solutions being considered by central bank officials in the absence of cryptocurrency bubbles or fraud is to introduce a kind of digital currency. (*Financial Times*/20 March,2018/http://www.ftchinese.com/story/001076792)

幸运的是，在没有加密货币泡沫或欺诈时，央行官员们考虑的解决方案之一就是引入一种数字货币。

Digital currency (digital money or electronic money or electronic currency) is a type of currency available only in digital form, not in physical (such as banknotes and coins). It exhibits properties similar to physical currencies, but allows for instantaneous transactions and borderless transfer-of-ownership. Examples include virtual currencies and cryptocurrencies or even central bank issued “digital base money”.

数字货币（或电子货币）是一种只能以数字形式存在的货币，而不是实物货币（如纸币和硬币）。它具有与实物货币类似的属性，允许即时交易和无国界的所有权转让。类似的包括虚拟货币和加密货币，以及中央银行发行的“数字基础货币”。

**16. Electronic Funds Transfer (EFT) 电子资金转账**

Petra: I don’t have any checks. In this day and age, I should be able to use one of the many electronic funds transfer options. (www.niuyingyu.cn)

佩特拉：我不使用支票，在这个时代，我可以选择使用哪种电子资金转账形式。

Electronic Funds Transfer (EFT) is the electronic transfer of money from one bank account to another, either within a single financial institution or across multiple institutions, via computer-based systems, without the direct intervention of bank staff. EFT transactions are known by a number of names. In the United States, they may be referred to as electronic checks or e-checks.

电子资金转账（EFT）指在没有银行工作人员直接干预的情况下，通过计算机系统，在一个金融机构内或跨多个机构，将资金从一个银行账户电子转账到另一个银行账户。EFT 交易有许多别名，比如在美国被称为电子支票或 e-支票。

**17. Fractional reserve banking　部分准备金银行制度**

In the 1930s, scientists suggested repealing "fractional reserve banking". The capital condition of the banking industry remains worrying. (*Financial Times*/28 September, 2017/ http://www.ftchinese.com/story/001074498)

科学家们在 20 世纪 30 年代建议废除"部分准备金银行制度"。银行业资本金状况仍然令人忧虑。

Fractional reserve banking is a banking system in which only a fraction of bank deposits are backed by actual cash on hand and are available for withdrawal. This is done to expand the economy by freeing up capital that can be loaned out to other parties.

部分准备金银行制度是一种银行系统，指的是只有一小部分银行存款有实际库存现金作后盾，可供用户随时提取，这样做可以腾出资本借给其他方来扩大经济。

**18. Factoring　保理**

The red wine dealer and debt factoring company plunged by 40% yesterday and the market value evaporated 12 billion US dollars. 10 billion dollars market value evaporation happened within two days. What should regulators do? (*Financial Times*/22 May,2015/http:// www.ftchinese.com/story/001062160?archive)

这家红酒经销商和债务保理公司昨日股价暴跌 40%，市值蒸发 120 亿美元。两天之内发生百亿美元市值蒸发事件。对此监管机构应该做些什么呢？

Factoring is a financial transaction and a type of debtor finance in which a business sells its accounts receivable (i.e., invoices) to a third party (called a factor) at a discount. A business will sometimes factor its receivable assets to meet its present and immediate cash needs.

保理是一种金融交易，也是一种债务人融资，企业以折扣价将应收账款（即发票）出售给第三方（称为保理人）。企业有时会对其应收账款资产进行保理，以满足当前和即时的现金需求。

**19. Ethical banking　道德银行**

She says: "Ethical banking is complex, encompassing the decisions made by fund managers for institutions to the direct experience of customers with a retail bank." (Independent/22Feburay, 2017/https://www.independent.co.uk/money/where-now-for-ethical-banking-a7593421.html)

她说："道德银行业务很复杂，包括基金经理为机构做出的决定，以及客户在零售银行的直接体验。"

An ethical bank, also known as a social, alternative, civic, or sustainable bank, is a bank concerned with the social and environmental impacts of its investments and loans. The ethical banking movement includes: ethical investment, impact investment, socially responsible investment, corporate social responsibility, and is also related to such movements as the fair trade movement, ethical consumerism, and social enterprise.

道德银行，也被称为社会银行、替代银行、公民银行或可持续银行，是一家关注其投资和贷款的社会、环境影响的银行。合乎道德银行的活动包括：道德投资、影响力投资、社会责任投资、企业社会责任，以及与公平贸易、道德消费主义和社会企业等有关的活动。

**20. Gearing ratio 资产负债率**

One banker said the government had also raised numerous demands regarding the structure of debt for the buy-out and the company's post-acquisition gearing ratio.

一位银行工作人员指出，政府还就此次收购债务的结构和公司收购后资产负债率提出大量要求。

Gearing ratio refers to the fundamental analysis ratio of a company's level of long-term debt compared to its equity capital. The point when processing what amount of debt an organization is undertaking as contrasted with its equity, the debt to equity ratio is generally utilized. Debt to equity ratio is the sum contract taken by the organization divided by the equity of the organization at the point where the ratio is computed.

资产负债率指公司长期负债水平与其股权资本的基本分析比率。在处理一个组织与其股权相比所承担的债务数额时，一般都会使用债务与股权比率，由组织所采取的总合同额除以该组织在计算比率时的权益得出。

**21. Sale and leaseback 售后回租**

In a sale and leaseback, the government would sell public buildings to an investor and enter into a long-term agreement to rent the space in the building. (www.dictall.com)

在售后回租交易中，政府可向投资者出售国有房产，再签订长期协议租回房产。

Sale-and-leaseback is a financial transaction in which one sells an asset and leases it back for the long term.

售后回租是一种金融交易，通过人们出售资产并将其长期租回实现。

**22. Structured deposit 结构性存款**

In addition, there is a significant difference between investment in gold directly and investment in gold-linked structured deposit. (www.dictall.com)

此外，直接投资黄金和投资与黄金挂钩的结构性存款，两者存在显著差异。

The term structured deposit refers to a type of financial account with funds placed into conventional fixed deposits with an investment on a derivative instrument on assets such as currencies, commodities, equities or bonds.

结构性存款是指将资金存入常规定期存款，并投资于货币、商品、股票或债券等资产的衍生工具的一种金融账户。

**23. SIBOR (Singapore interbank offered rate) 新加坡银行同业拆放利率**

Most banks in Singapore offer SIBOR-based home loan packages. It is considered the most widely used reference rate for home loan packages in Singapore and the most popular amongst consumers. (www.fabiao.net)

在新加坡，大部分银行提供以 SIBOR 为基础的家庭贷款，它被认为是新加坡住房贷款中最广泛使用的参考利率，也是最受消费者欢迎的利率。

SIBOR stands for Singapore Interbank Offered Rate and is a daily reference rate based on the interest rates at which banks offer to lend unsecured funds

新加坡银行同业拆放利率（SIBOR）是基于银行提供的无担保资金贷款利率的每日参考利率产生的。

**24. Signature loan　无担保贷款**

The cash or scrip would be offered as part of a pro rata return of capital to shareholders. (www.ebigear.com)

现金或票据将作为按比例向股东返还资本的一种方式。

Signature loan is a type of personal loan offered by banks and other finance companies that uses only the borrower's signature and promise to pay as collateral.

无担保贷款是一种由银行和其他金融公司提供的个人贷款，它只使用借款人签名和承诺作为抵押。

**25. Senior loan　优先备款**

"There has been a lot of technical demand for high-yielding loan assets this summer," said Dan Norman, managing director of the ING Investment Management senior loan group in the US. (www.ftchinese.com)

荷兰国际集团投资管理公司（ING Investment Management）美国优先贷款部门董事总经理丹•诺曼表示："今年夏天，市场对高收益贷款资产的技术需求很旺盛。"

Senior debt, loan debt for which claims on the assets of the borrower rank ahead of other debts in case of liquidation.

优先债务，是指在清算时，借款人的资产债权排在其他债务之前的贷款债务。

## 4.2.2　政策性金融相关机构

**1. SAFE (The State Administration of Foreign Exchange)　中国国家外汇管理局**

The State Administration of Foreign Exchange, an agency under the central bank, did not acknowledge any role in guiding the currency. (www.ftchinese.com)

中国央行下属的中国国家外汇管理局不承认它在引导汇率走势方面发挥了作用。

注：政策性金融相关机构：

（1）基本定义：政策性金融机构是由政府或政府机构发起或出资，以某种特定政策性金融业务为其基本业务活动的金融机构。

（2）类别：政策性金融相关机构包括政策性银行机构和政策性非银行金融机构。

（3）目标：政策性金融相关机构不以利润最大化为经营目标，它是专门为贯彻和配合政府特定的社会经济政策和意图而设立的。

（4）作用：政策性金融相关机构充当政府发展经济、促进社会发展和稳定、进行宏观经济调节管理的工具。

**2. Acknowledge a role in...　承担……职责**

The State Administration of Foreign Exchange (SAFE) of the People's Republic of China is an administrative agency tasked with drafting rules and regulations governing foreign exchange market activities, and managing the state foreign-exchange reserves.

中华人民共和国国家外汇管理局（SAFE）是负责起草外汇市场活动规章制度、管理国家外汇储备的行政机关。

相关术语：foreign exchange reserve: 外汇储备，根据外汇来源不同可分为以下几类：financial foreign exchange 金融外汇；trade foreign exchange 贸易外汇；travelling foreign exchange 旅游外汇；private foreign exchange 私人外汇

**2. Ex-Im Bank　进出口银行**

"Ex-Im is a key competitive issue for our U.S. workforce and the 1.5 million American workers in our supply chain nationwide," the company said in a statement. "Ex-Im bank plays an important role in supporting American competitiveness and U.S. manufacturing by leveling the playing field for manufacturers and their suppliers." (CNBC/10 Feburay, 2017/https://www.cnbc.com/2017/02/10/ex-im-bank-trump-likes-it-conservatives-hate-it.html)

该公司在一份声明中表示："进出口对于我们美国的劳动力和全国供应链中 150 万美国工人来说，是一个关键的竞争问题。进出口银行通过为制造商及其供应商提供公平的竞争平台，在支持美国竞争力和美国制造业方面发挥着重要作用。"

注：（1）manufacturer vs. producer: ① 释义：manufacturer: 生产商；② manufacturer 更偏重加工、制造等第二产业的生产；producer 包括种植培养、制造、供给，包括第一产业和第二产业的生产；（2）根据释义，manufacturer 用于个人、企业；producer 除此之外还可用于描述国家；（3）level 使公平；playing field 竞技场，平台

Also known as Export-Import Bank of the United States. A federal agency responsible for facilitating international trade by financing the purchase of domestic exports and providing guarantees or insurance for foreign lines of credit.

进出口银行也被称为美国进出口银行，它是一个通过为购买国内的出口产品提供资金和为外国的信贷额度提供担保或保险来促进国际贸易的联邦机构。注：进出口银行属于政策性银行。

**3. Policy bank　政策性银行**

The bank system consists of Bank of China, Commercial Bank, and policy bank in China. (word.hcbus.com)

我国的银行体系由中央银行、商业银行、政策性银行组成。

注：bank system 银行体系

Policy bank refers to an institution that is funded by the government to carry out financing and credit activities for the implementation and coordination of specific economic policies and intentions of the government.

政策性银行指由政府出资，为执行和协调政府具体经济政策和意图而开展融资和信贷活动的机构。

注：商业银行与政策性银行的差异：（1）资本来源不同，政策性银行多由政府出资建立，业务上由政府相应部门领导；商业银行多采取股份制的形式，业务上自主经营、独立核算；（2）资金来源不同，政策性银行一般不接受存款，也不从民间借款；而商业银行以存款作为其主要的资金来源；（3）经营目的不同，政策性银行是为了支持某些部

门的发展而专门成立的，不以营利为目的，与相应的产业部门关系密切；而商业银行以利润最大化为经营目的，业务范围广泛。

**4. SDBC (State Development Bank of China)　中国国家发展银行**

There are three State Policy Banks in China: the State Development Bank, the Export and Import Bank of China and the Agriculture Development Bank of China. (*The Economist*: The opening up of China's economy goes into reverse)

中国有三家国家政策性银行，即国家开发银行、中国进出口银行和中国农业发展银行。

注：go into reverse 倒退

## 4.3　Commercial Bank（商业性银行）

本节首先介绍商业性银行的概念，其次追溯商业性银行的渊源，最后引出现代金融制度下的商业性金融票据，简要介绍现代商业性金融票据各种分类依据和主要票据种类。

商业性金融，指在国家产业政策指导下，运用市场法则，引导资源合理配置和货币资金合理流动等经济行为而产生一系列货币商业性金融活动总称。商业性金融的主要特点有：（1）决策主体是各国有商业银行而非国家政府；（2）追逐利润最大化；（3）活动是在国家产业政策引导下，通过自主决策来实现；（4）充当信用中介，实行有偿借贷是其基本原则；（5）以资金营利性、安全性和流动性为主要经营原则。

### 4.3.1　商业银行产生与发展

商业银行，英文缩写为 CB，是银行的一种类型，是通过存款、贷款、汇兑、储蓄等业务，承担信用中介的金融机构。主要的业务范围是吸收公众存款、发放贷款以及办理票据贴现等。一般的商业银行没有货币的发行权，它的传统业务主要集中在经营存款和贷款业务。

**1. Banking syndicate　银团**

He assured the parliament that in future only banks with sufficient foreign cash reserves could be part of the banking syndicate that finances fuel imports. (Newstex Finance & Accounting Blogs/Mar 31, 2015/https://search.proquest.com/ docview/1667734903?accountid=14662)

他向议会保证，将来只有那些拥有充足外币现金储备的银行，才有资格加入向石油进口提供资金的银团。

注：foreign cash reserve 外汇储备；finance 融资，资助

A banking syndicate is an association of banks that is formed for business purposes or to carry out a project.

银团是为商业目的或执行项目而成立的银行协会。

注：银团贷款：（1）银团贷款亦称“辛迪加贷款”，是一种由一个特定的银行集团采用同一贷款协议，按照商定的期限和条件向同一借款人提供融资的贷款方式，这个银行

集团由获准经营贷款业务的一家或数家银行牵头，多家银行与非银行金融机构参加组成；（2）服务对象：有巨额资金需求的大中型企业、企业集团和国家重点建设项目；（3）当借款者寻求的资金数额太大，以至于任何一个单一的银行都无法承受该借款者的信用风险时，就产生了对银行团体的需求。

**2. Confirming bank　保兑行**

Such undertakings shall neither be amended nor cancelled without the agreement of the issuing bank, the confirming bank and the beneficiary. (Business Wire/Jun 11, 2008/https://search.proquest.com/docview/444581457?accountid= 14662)

未经开证行、保兑行和受益人同意，该项承诺既不能修改，也不能取消。

注：undertaking 承诺；amend 修改；issuing bank 发行银行；beneficiary 受益人

Confirming bank refers to the bank that adds its confirmation to a credit upon the issuing bank's authorization or request.

保兑行是根据开证行授权或请求，对信用证添加证明的银行。

相关术语：confirmation 证明

**3. Clearing bank　清算银行**

London plans to underline its credentials by designating China Construction Bank as a clearing bank for the currency. (http://www.bbc.com/news/uk-scotland-42515932)

伦敦想通过指定中国建设银行（CCB）为人民币清算银行来凸显自己的资质。

注：credential 资格，资质

Clearing bank refers to a bank that uses a clearing house when dealing with other banks.

清算银行指作为结算所与其他银行打交道的银行。

相关术语：Bank for International Settlements, BIS 国际清算银行

## 4.3.2　商业银行票据

**1. Certificate of origin　原产地证书**

In addition to the ordinary shipping document, please also submit certificate of origin of each shipment. (http://www.bbc.com/news/world-latin-america-23906661)

除一般装运所需的文件外，还应提交每批货物的原产地证明书。

注：shipping document 装运文件；origin 原产地

The certificate of origin is used to prove the origin or the place of manufacture of the goods, which is the basis for the customs of the importing country to collect the tax rate.

原产地证书用于证明货物的原产地或制造地，这是进口国海关征收税率的基础。

注：（1）相关术语：customs 海关；collect 征收（税）；（2）Shipping documents basically include invoice, packing list and bill of lading. 装运单据主要包括发票、装箱单和提单。

**2. Confirmed letter of credit　保兑信用证**

Under a confirmed letter of credit, the beneficiary is given double assurance of payment since the confirming bank has added its own undertaking to that of the opening bank.

(http://news.bbc.co.uk/2/hi/programmes/moneybox/9710162.stm)

在保兑信用证中，受益人得到双重付款保证，因为保兑银行在开证行承担付款义务基础上又加上自己的承诺。

注：assurance 保险；保证

A confirmed letter of credit is a letter of credit drawn from another bank, which guarantees payment to the documents that meet the stipulations of the letter of credit, and guarantees the payment of the letter of credit.

保兑信用证指从另一家银行提取信用证，保证向符合信用证规定的单据付款，并保证信用证付款。

注：信用证分为：documentary credit 跟单信用证；clean credit 光票信用证；irrevocable L/C 不可撤销信用证；revocable L/C 可撤销信用证；confirmed L/C 保兑信用证；unconfirmed L/C 不保兑信用证；sight L/C 即期信用证，usance L/C 远期信用证；usance credit payable at sight 假远期信用证

**3. Check for transfer　转账支票**

Generally, the business payment adopts check for transfer, and the time varies from several days to several months. (https://www.thetimes.co.uk/edition/sport/antonio-conte-safe-for-now-as-eden-hazard-vows-to-bring-home-fa-cup-for-chelsea-tg95hqf50)

一般业务付款方式采用转账支票的形式，付款时间从几天到几个月不等。

注：adopt 采用某种支付方式

A check for transfer is a bill issued by a drawer, and the bank that is entrusted with the check deposit business unconditionally pays determined amount to the payee or the holder at the time of seeing the ticket. The transfer check can only be used for transfer.

转账支票是由出票人出具的票据，委托办理支票存款业务的银行在看到支票时无条件向受款人或者持票人支付确定金额，转账支票只能用于转账。

相关术语：drawer 出票人；payee 持票人，收款人

**4. Bearer check　不记名支票**

Bearer checks are widely circulated all over the world. (www.ftchinese.com)

不记名支票在国际社会上广泛流通。

注：circulate（货币、支票、使用权）流通

例：It is regulated that right to use collective land should not circulate and then it is a limited property right. And the subject of circulation is not clear.

法律规定集体土地使用权不能流转，这是一种限制物权，而且流转的主体不明确。

Bearer check refers to the check that the name of the payee is not recorded on the check.

不记名支票指的是支票上不记录收款人姓名的支票。

注：不记名支票可以不背书转让。

**5. Blank check　空白支票**

We are not prepared to write a blank check for companies that have run into trouble.（《柯林斯高阶英汉双解学习词典》）

我们不打算给那些陷入困境的公司开空白支票。

Blank check refers to a check that has been signed but with the amount payable left blank.

空白支票指已签署但应付金额为空白的支票。

注：blank cheque 美式英语中表示“自由处理权”，例：He has been given a blank cheque to negotiate the new South Africa. 他已被允许全权洽谈新南非问题。

**6. Clean collection 光票托收**

Based on whether commercial documents are involved, collection can be classified as clean collection and documentary collection. (www.ftchinese.com)

依据是否附有商业单据，托收可以分为光票托收和跟单托收。

注：involved=companied=attached 附有……

Clean collection means the collection of financial documents only by draft or simple financial documents and not accompanied by any collection of commercial documents.

光票托收指只通过汇票或简单的金融单据进行托收，而不附带任何商业文件。

注：跟单托收可分为付款交单（D/P）和承兑交单（D/A）。

**7. Crossed check 划线支票**

The provisions of this Ordinance relating to crossed checks shall apply to a warrant for payment of dividend. (www.dictall.com)

本条例有关划线支票的条文，适用于支付股息的凭单。

相关术语：warrant 担保，证书；dividend 股；bonus 红利

A crossed check refers to a special check that the payer or the obligee carries out two parallel lines on the front of a check, or a financial institution, such as a specific bank in parallel lines, that the payer has to pay the amount of the bill only to the particular bank or financial institution.

划线支票指的是一种特殊的支票，即付款人或债权人在支票的正面划两条平行线，或者是金融机构（例如特定银行）划两条平行线，要求付款人支付其金额。划线支票仅向特定银行或金融机构开票。

注：划线支票可分为一般划线支票（generally-crossed check）和特殊划线支票（specially-crossed check）。

**8. Assignable letter of credit 可转让信用证**

Unless otherwise agreed to by seller, payment is to be made against sight draft drawn under a confirmed, irrevocable, divisible and assignable letter of credit without recourse for the full amount, established through a first class bank acceptable to the sellers. (http://www.ftchinese.com/)

除得到卖方同意者外，买方应通过卖方所能接受的第一流银行开立的保兑、不可撤销、可分割、可转让的无追索权信用证即期汇票支付全额款项。

注：recourse 追索权，例：The investor had no recourse as his money left the country with the entrepreneur. 投资者没有追索权，因为他的钱已经和创业者一起离开了中国。

An assignable letter of credit means that a bank authorized by the issuing bank (the Bank of the letter of credit) may transfer the whole or part of the letter of credit to a letter of credit of the second beneficiary at the request of the beneficiary.

可转让信用证指的是经开证行（信用证银行）授权的银行，可以应受益人请求，将信用证全部或部分转入第二受益人的信用证。

注：（1）本信用证只能转让一次，即第一受益人只能转让给第二受益人；（2）第二受益人不得要求将信用证转让给其后的第三受益人，但可再转让给第一受益人。

**9. Bill of lading　提单**

"The plane's cargo was documented in detail on the bill of lading and the plane did not carry any illegal material or any weapons," the ministry said according to Sana state news agency. (http://www.bbc.com/news/world-europe-19912534)

根据萨那州通讯社报道："该架飞机上的货物详细记录在提单上，并且飞机上没有携带任何非法材料或武器。"

注：（1）bill 清单，是一种计价方法，它没有消耗量的标准，同时规范了清单列项的标准，统一了一个列项报价的标准，方便以后报价的一致性和比较，同时清单计价也是一个综合的报价方式，它可以包含一个定额或包含 N 个定额。（2）词义辨析：cargo & goods：cargo 多用于国际贸易中，指（船或飞机装载的）货物；goods 是一个统称，意思是"商品、货物"，还可以引申为"动产，私人财产"。（3）相关术语：negotiable bill of lading 可转让提单；original bill of lading 正本提单；dirty bill of lading 不洁提单；foul bill of lading 有不良批注提单

Bill of lading refers to a receipt given by the carrier to the shipper acknowledging receipt of the goods being shipped and specifying the terms of delivery.

提单指承运人向托运人发出的收据，用于确认收到所装运货物并具体说明交货条件。

注：（1）提单是一份具有法律约束力的文件，它为承运人和托运人提供了准确处理货物的所有必要细节。它有三个主要功能，首先，它是提单中所描述货物的所有权凭证；其次，它是装运产品的收据；最后，提单代表货物运输的约定条款和条件。（2）相关术语：receipt 收据；parcel receipt 包裹提单；goods receipt 货物收据；warehouse receipt 仓单；depository receipt 存托凭证；receipt voucher 收款凭证；duty receipt 完税收据；receipt notification 回执通知

**10. Waybill (WB)　运货单，提货单**

The statements in the air waybill relating to the weight, dimensions, and packing of the cargo, as well as those relating to the number of packages, shall be prima facie evidence of the facts stated.

航空货运单上关于货物重量、尺寸、包装和包裹件数说明，具有初步证据效力。

注：（1）prima facie evidence 初步证据，是"最终证据"的对称，又称"表面证据"。是指可解除其提供者举证责任，在没有相反证据的情况下可具有最终说服力的证据，即初步证据可以被充分的相反证据所推翻。（2）相关术语：prima facie case 表面上证据确凿的案件；initial evidence 初步证据；conclusive evidence 最终证据

A waybill (UIC) is a document issued by a carrier giving details and instructions relating to the shipment of a consignment of goods.

运单（UIC）是由承运人签发的文件，用来提供与托运货物有关的详细信息和说明。

注：（1）在货运合同中，承运人的责任一般说来主要是保证所运输的货物按时、安全地送达目的地。因此，承运人应对货物在运输过程中发生的货物灭失、短少、污染、损坏等负责。一旦发生此种情况，承运人应按实际损失给予赔偿。（2）相关术语：consignment 托运；consignment invoice 寄售发票；consolidated consignment 集运货物；manufacturing consignment 委托加工；consignment stock 寄售库存；consignment ledger 委托销售总账

## 4.4 Investment Bank（投资性银行）

本节首先介绍投资性银行的概念，其次介绍银行投资性金融工具和相关机构，并进一步分析相关机构的职能和作用。

投资性金融指以证券投资活动为核心的一系列金融活动。投资性金融的主体机构是在直接金融领域内为投资活动提供中介服务或直接参与投资活动的金融机构，主要包括投资银行、证券经纪和交易公司、金融公司、投资基金等。

### 4.4.1 投资性金融工具

**1. Home equity loan 房屋净值贷款**

You could also consider a home equity loan, which may offer a tax deduction, or a consolidation loan.

你还可以考虑房屋净值贷款，它可以提供税收减征，或考虑一下合并贷款。

注：（1）tax deduction 减税，又称税收减征，指的是按照税收法律、法规减除纳税义务人的一部分应纳税款。减税是对某些纳税人、征税对象进行扶持、鼓励或照顾，以减轻其税收负担的一种特殊规定。（2）相关术语：tax avoidance 逃税；tax evasion 避税；tax preference 税收优惠；tax rebate（出口）退税；tax refund 退还税款；tax exemption 免税

A home equity loan, also called a second mortgage, allows the borrower to pull equity out of their home. The loan amount is determined by the value of the property, and the value of the property is determined by an appraiser from the lending institution. The loan increases the lien on the borrower's house and reduces the amount of equity they have in their home. There are two types of Home Equity loans: a cash out loan and a HELOC loan.

房屋净值贷款也叫做二次抵押贷款，允许借款人从他们的房屋中提取净值。贷款金额由资产价值决定，资产价值由贷款机构估价师决定。贷款增加了对借款人房屋的留置权，减少他们在房子里的资产净值。房屋净值贷款有两种类型：现金流出贷款和 HELOC 贷款。

注：（1）second mortgage 二次抵押贷款；（2）first mortgage 第一抵押权；（3）second mortgage 的产生往往是当你需要借更多的钱时，原本贷款的银行（A 银行）拒绝再贷款给你，而 B 银行（通常是小型财务公司，private lender）愿意借钱给你，条件是你必须把房子也同时抵押给它。当你还不起贷款，房子被银行拍卖时，A 银行的利益将会先得到保证，因为它是 first mortgage。在 A 银行扣除你所欠的本息及与拍卖有关的费用后，剩下的钱才会再去还欠 B 银行的债务，因为它是 second mortgage。

**2. Hong Kong Inter Bank Offered Rate (HIBOR)　银行间市场对港元贷款的利率**

HSBC also said that it had executed its first CNH Hibor swap contract, providing an early indication of what the rate might be.

汇丰银行也表示，该行已执行首份 CNH Hibor 互换合约，初步表明它的利率可能会是多少。

注：（1）swap contract 互换合约，指两个或以上的交易当事人按照商定的条件，在约定的时间内交付一系列支付款项的金融交易合约，主要包括货币互换与利率互换两类。（2）相关术语：interest rate swap 利率互换；currency swap 货币互换；coupon swap 息票互换；basis swap 基础互换

HIBOR refers to the rate of interest offered on Hong Kong dollar loans by banks in the inter bank market for a specified period ranging from overnight to one year.

HIBOR 指的是银行在银行间市场对港元贷款的利率，规定的期限为隔夜至一年。

相关术语：（1）interbank market 同业拆借市场；（2）目前货币市场上较有代表性的同业拆借利率：Federal funds rate 美国联邦基金利率；London Inter bank Offered Rate（LIBOR）伦敦同业拆借利率；Singapore Inter bank Offered Rate（SIBOR）新加坡同业拆借利率；Hong Kong Inter bank Offered Rate（HIBOR）香港同业拆借利率；Shanghai Inter bank Offered Rate（Shibor）上海银行间同业拆借利率

**3. Hot money　热钱**

Others, not least London, have seen hot money inflows from China and other emerging markets.

其他地区，尤其是伦敦，已经有来自中国和其他新兴市场的大量热钱流入。

注：（1）emerging markets 新兴市场，指发展中国家的股票市场或能源市场。按照国际金融公司的权威定义，只要一个国家或地区的人均国民生产总值未达到世界银行划定的高收入国家水平，那么这个国家或地区的股市就是新兴市场。（2）相关术语：emerging market sovereigns 新兴市场主权国家；emerging market bonds 新兴市场债券；emerging market portfolios 新兴市场投资组合；emerging market economies 新兴市场经济体

Hot money is the flow of funds (or capital) from one country to another in order to earn a short-term profit on interest rate differences and/or anticipated exchange rate shifts. These speculative capital flows are called “hot money” because they can move very quickly in and out of markets, potentially leading to market instability.

热钱指从一个国家流向另一个国家的资金（或资本），目的是通过利率差异和/或预期汇率变化获得短期利润。这些投机性资本流动被称为“热钱”，因为它们可以非常迅速

地进出市场，同时有可能导致市场不稳定。

注：（1）投机性资本流动（speculative capital flow）是利用汇率、利率或其他金融资产（如黄金、股票等）价格的预期变动进行牟利的短期资本流动。以汇率变动而言，主要有以下四种投机：不抵补套利、对暂时性汇率变动所作的反应、对永久性汇率变动所作的反应及与贸易有关的投机性流动。（2）相关术语：speculative capital flows 投机性资本流动；短期资本流动：trade financing 贸易融资；hedging 保值；speculative capital flows 投机性资本流动；长期资本流动：direct investment 直接投资；securities investment 证券投资；international loans 国际贷款

**4. Interbank lending market 银行间拆借市场**

The draft rules, which are expected to take effect in some form in February, are aimed at the interbank lending market, usually used by banks to borrow at low interest rates from one another to cover their short-term funding needs.

该新规草案预计将在明年 2 月份以某种形式开始实施，它针对的是银行同业拆借市场，通常各大银行通过该市场以低利率相互拆借资金，以满足短期资金需求。

注：（1）funding 融资，从狭义上讲，指一个企业资金筹集的行为与过程。从广义上讲，融资也叫金融，就是货币资金的融通，指当事人通过各种方式到金融市场上筹措或贷放资金的行为；（2）银行间市场即银行间同业交易的市场，包括 interbank foreign exchange market（银行间的外汇市场）和 interbank money market（银行间的货币市场）；（3）相关术语：bank loans 银行贷款；equity financing 股票筹资；bonds financing 债券融资；finance leasing 融资租赁；overseas financing 海外融资；mortgage financing 典当融资

The interbank lending market is a market in which banks extend loans to one another for a specified term. Most interbank loans are for maturities of one week or less, the majority being overnight. Such loans are made at the interbank rate (also called the overnight rate if the term of the loan is overnight).

银行间拆借市场是银行在一定期限内相互发放贷款的市场。大多数银行间贷款期限为一周或更短，其中大多数为隔夜。这类贷款是按银行间利率发放的（如果贷款期限是隔夜，也称为隔夜利率）。

相关术语：overnight rate 隔夜利率；liquidity cycle 流动周期；money supply 货币供给

**5. Inactive account 非活跃账户**

Every major Wall Street broker now imposes an inactive account fee on investors who don't generate enough commissions.

现在，每个华尔街的主要经纪商都会对没有收到足够佣金的投资者征收非活跃账户费用。

注：（1）broker 经纪商，又称掮客，为买主与卖主之间签订买卖契约提供中介服务，从而收取手续费或佣金的人。在金融证券方面，从事经纪商活动的人不能直接进入交易所经营，他们的主要作用是接受投资者的委托，将委托人的证券转交给经纪人到交易所内买卖。（2）相关术语：inter-dealer brokers 交易商经纪；client or agency brokers 代理经

纪；real estate brokers 房地产经纪；insurance brokers 保险经纪

Inactive account is an account that has little or no activity; neither deposits nor withdrawals having been posted to the account for a significant period of time.

非活跃账户指很少有或根本没有活动的账户；在相当长的时间内，均未有存款或取款记入账户。

相关术语：（1）deposits 存款；（2）存款的种类：demand deposit 活期存款；time deposits 定期存款；notice deposits 通知存款；corporate deposits 单位存款

**6. Individual account 个人账户**

Accrual stores according to individual account computation of method of frontal accrual calculation.

利息按照个人账户储存额利息计算办法计算。

注：（1）accrual 计提，指计算和提取，按规定的比率与规定的基数相乘计算提取，列入某科目。计算方法是在一个规定的基数上乘以规定的比率）；（2）相关术语：build accrual 累积应计；accrual bonds 累息债券；accrual expense 应付费用；accrual concept 应计概念；accrual basis 权责发生制

Individual account is an account in the name of one individual.

个人账户是以一个自然人名义建立的账户。

注：相关术语：① individual 自然人；② 我国法律确认的民事主体：natural person 自然人；legal person 法人；unincorporated organization 非法人组织

**7. Import trade finance 进口贸易融资**

For import trade finance, it includes limit for letter of credit, trust receipt, inward bills receivables, delivery against banking guarantee, inward documentary collection advance and etc.

进口贸易融资涉及信用证限额、信托收据、进口票据、银行提货担保以及进口跟单托收预付款等业务。

注：（1）trust receipt 信托收据，委托人向受托人提供资金或信用，并以所提供的动产标的物之所有权作为债权担保，而受托人，例如进口商，则依据信托合同或其他信托约定对前述标的物进行处分，并把处分标的物的对价，即款项，交付给委托人，例如开证银行。（2）相关术语：settler 委托人；trustee 受托人；beneficiary 受益人；trust property 信托财产；trust document 信托文件；trust terms 信托条款

Import trade finance signifies financing for trade, and it concerns both domestic and international trade transactions. A trade transaction requires a buyer of goods and services. Various intermediaries such as banks and financial institutions can facilitate these transactions by financing the trade.

进口贸易融资指的是为交易提供资金，涉及国内和国际贸易交易。在贸易交易中，需要商品和服务的买方，同时银行、金融机构等各种中介机构可以通过提供资金来促进交易实现。

注：（1）financing 融资，指为支付超过现金的购货款而采取的货币交易手段，或为

取得资产而集资所采取的货币手段；（2）融资种类：internal financing 内源融资；external financing 外部融资；equity financing 股权融资；debt financing 股权融资；direct financing 直接融资；indirect financing 间接融资

**8. Individual retirement account (IRA)　个人退休金账户**

As of 2010, low savings rates, financial crises, and poor stock market performance had caused retirement savings account values to fall so low that 75% of Americans nearing retirement age had less than $30,000 in their retirement accounts, which Forbes called "the greatest retirement crisis in American history."

截至2010年，低储蓄率、金融危机和糟糕的股市表现导致退休储蓄账户价值偏低，以至于75%接近退休年龄的美国人的退休账户金额低于30 000美元，这被福布斯称为"美国历史上最大的退休金危机"。

注：（1）savings rates 储蓄率，是反映一个国家或地区储蓄发展水平的重要指标。它指储蓄存款的增加额占城乡居民、单位职工货币收入的百分比，可借以分析和研究一个地区城乡居民或一个单位职工在一定时期内参加储蓄的意愿和趋势，是制订储蓄计划的一项重要依据。（2）相关术语：personal savings rate 个人储蓄率；aggregate savings rate 总储蓄率；personal disposable income（PDI）个人可支配收入

An individual retirement account (IRA) in the United States is a form of "individual retirement plan", provided by many financial institutions, that provides tax advantages for retirement savings.

美国的个人退休金账户是一种"个人退休计划"，它由许多金融机构提供，可为退休储蓄提供税收优惠。

**9. Insufficient funds　资金不足**

Once the originator of the insufficient funds check is notified of the problem with the check, he or she is normally provided some time to cover the face value of the check, plus an fees or penalties that the depositor chooses to apply.

一旦资金不足支票的发起人被通知支票有问题，他或她通常会被给予一些时间来支付支票的面值和存款人要求的费用或罚款。

注：（1）face value（far value）票面价值，有价证券票面上标明的金额，由发行者规定。发行价格，也称行市，是证券公开发行的销售价格。发行价格的高低由市场上的供求关系决定。在票面价值确定后，发行价格将依据市场的利率、证券的利率水平、发行者信誉和资金供应状况来确定。（2）相关术语：negotiable securities/valuable papers 有价证券；at premium 溢价发行；at par 平价发行；at a discount 折价发行

Sometimes referred to as non-sufficient funds, insufficient funds is a term used to refer to a checking account that does not contain enough resources to process a check that is presented for payment.

non-sufficient funds 和 insufficient funds 都是资金不足的表达方式，指一个支票账户中没有足够的存款来处理待付款的支票。

注：（1）checking account 支票账户，也称支票存款，指存于银行或其他金融机构中，

能够开支票的账户，用专业术语来讲就是“活期存款及其他支票存款”。（2）相关术语：check clearance 支票结算；blank check 空白支票；check for transfer 转账支票；cash a check 支票兑现

**10. Insurance　保险**

The Obama administration says gov's error rate for transmitting health insurance applications to insurance companies has plunged.（NPR News）

奥巴马政府表示，联邦医保网站向保险公司提交医保申请表的错误率大幅下降。

注：（1）词义辨析：plunge 用来表示价格和温度等的暴降、骤降；plummet 可以表示数量、比率、价格等突然暴跌，骤然下降；slump 指价格、数量等的大幅度下降。（2）相关词汇：edge down 微降；rally 回升；climb 攀升；soar 猛增；surge 激增

Insurance is a means of protection from financial loss. It is a form of risk management, primarily used to hedge against the risk of a contingent or uncertain loss.

保险是一种防止经济损失的手段，它是一种主要用于对冲或有损失、不确定损失风险的风险管理形式。

注：（1）risk management 风险管理，指通过对风险的认识、衡量和分析，选择最有效的方式，主动地、有目的地、有计划地处理风险，以最小成本争取获得最大安全保证的管理方法。（2）相关术语：risk identification 风险识别；risk analysis 风险分析；risk tracking 风险跟踪

**11. Insured deposits　保险存款**

She was not the author of the (abortive) idea to raid insured bank deposits in Cyprus；that was the Cypriot government's attempt to spare offshore savers from bearing the entire bill for the island's rescue.（*The Economist*）

她并不是突袭塞浦路斯保险银行存款这个（这个想法未能实施）想法的始作俑者，塞浦路斯政府试图让海外储户免于承担整个岛国救助的费用。

注：（1）offshore savers 离岸储蓄者；offshore account 离岸账户，指在境外银行开立的账户，客户可以从离岸账户上自由调拨资金，而不受本国的外汇管制。只要银行客户披露了离岸账户的信息，并按个人收入缴纳了税收，那么持有离岸银行账户就是合法的。（2）相关术语：offshore banking 离岸银行；offshore outsourcing 离岸外包；offshore fund 离岸基金

Deposits held in financial institutions that are guaranteed by the Federal Deposit Insurance Corporation (FDIC) against loss due to bank failure.

保险存款是在联邦存款保险公司（FDIC）担保的金融机构中的存款，用来防止因银行倒闭而造成损失。

注：（1）Federal Deposit Insurance Corporation (FDIC) 联邦存款保险公司；（2）Deposit Insurance System 存款保险制度，指由符合条件的各类存款性金融机构集中起来建立一个保险机构，各存款机构作为投保人按一定存款比例向其缴纳保险费，建立存款保险准备金，当成员机构发生经营危机或面临破产倒闭时，存款保险机构向其提供财务救助或直接向存款人支付部分或全部存款，从而保护存款人利益，维护银行信用，稳定金融秩序

的一种制度。

**12. Interest 利息**

It pays no interest on these things, but it gets interest on some of its assets.

人们不用为此支付利息，但是能从部分资产中获取利息收入。

注：（1）asset 资产，指由过去的交易或事项形成的、由企业拥有或控制的、预期会给企业带来经济利益的资源；（2）相关术语：current assets 流动资产；non-current assets 非流动资产；fixed assets 固定资产；long-term assets 长期资产；deferred assets 递延资产；intangible assets 无形资产

Interest is payment from a borrower to a lender of an amount above repayment of the principal sum (i.e. the amount borrowed). It is distinct from a fee which the borrower may pay the lender or some third party.

利息是借款人向贷款人支付的款项，金额高于还本金额（即借款金额）。它不同于借款人可能向贷款人或某些第三方支付的费用。

注：（1）principal 本金，贷款、存款或投资在计算利息之前的原始金额。（2）相关术语：annual interest rate 年利率；draw/withdraw 提款；credit card 信用卡；overdraw/overdraft 透支

**13. Interest rate 利率**

In December 1988 the monthly real interest rate was 0.8%；by the following December it had risen to 4.3%.

1988 年 12 月，实际月利率为 0.8%。到了下一年的 12 月，实际月利率已经上涨到了 4.3%。

注：（1）real interest rate 实际利率，指剔除通货膨胀率后储户或投资者得到利息回报的真实利率。（2）不同程度的上升：climb 轻微上升；grow, increase, rise 程度一般的上升；leap, rocket, soar 程度比较强的上升，即迅速上升、飞升、激增；（3）相关术语：deposit interest rate 储蓄存款利率；overnight rate 隔夜利率；floating interest rate 浮动利率；nominal interest rate 名义利率

The percentage amount charged by a bank etc when you borrow money, or paid to you by a bank when you keep money in an account there.

利率是当你借钱时，银行等机构收取的百分比金额，或当你把钱存在银行账户时，银行向你支付的百分比金额。

注：（1）词义辨析：charge 主要用于一次性劳务所收取的费用，如服务费、行李超重费和旅馆费等；cost 常用来表示对已取得的货物或劳务所支付的费用；rent 指土地、建筑物、房舍和机器等定期的租费；toll 指道路、桥梁、港口、市场的捐税、通行费及电话费等。（2）相关术语：period charges 当期费用；fixed charge 固定抵押、固定费用、固定支出；discount charges 贴现利息、贴现费用；floating charge 浮动抵押

**14. Interest rate index 利率指数**

CMS rate defined and quoted by the International Swaps and Derivatives Association (ISDA), is widely used in the market as a reference interest rate index.

CMS 利率是由国家互换与衍生金融商品协会定义和引用的利率互换报价，在市场上被广泛用作利率指数的参考指标。

注：（1）CMS (Constant Maturity Swap) 固定期限掉期协议，又称恒定到期利率调期，是一种掉期协议形式。它使得购买者能够锁定所收到现金流的久期。（2）相关术语：London Inter Bank Offered Rate (LIBOR) 伦敦银行同业拆放利率；duration 久期；interest rate swap 利率互换

Interest Rate Index is a table of yields or interest rates being paid on debt that is used to determine interest-rate changes for adjustable-rate mortgages and other variable-rate loans.

利率指数是用于确定可变利率抵押贷款和其他可变利率贷款利率变化的债券收益率表或利率表。

注：（1）adjustable-rate mortgages (ARMs) 可变利率抵押贷款，指在贷款期限内允许根据一些事先选定的参考利率指数的变化，对合同利率进行定期调整的抵押贷款。（2）相关术语：fixed rate mortgages，FRMs 固定利率抵押贷款；conversion mortgage 可转换抵押贷款；graduated payment mortgages，GPMs 分级还款抵押贷款；constant payment mortgage 等额还款抵押贷款

**15. Interest rate swap　利率互换**

Such as foreign-exchange and interest-rate swaps, were becoming volume (or “flow”) businesses where scale and low costs were paramount.（*The Economist*）

诸如外汇和利率互换业务，在规模和低成本尤为重要的地区正逐渐发展为规模产业或流动性产业。

注：（1）foreign exchange 外汇，货币行政当局以银行存款、财政部证券或长短期政府证券等形式所持有的，在国际收支逆差时可以使用的债权；是国际贸易的产物，是国际贸易清偿的支付手段；（2）外汇分类：free convertible exchange 自由外汇；foreign exchange purchasing 购汇；trade foreign exchange 贸易外汇；non trade foreign exchange 非贸易外汇

An interest rate swap (IRS) is a liquid financial derivative instrument in which two parties agree to exchange interest rate cash flows, based on a specified notional amount from a fixed rate to a floating rate (or vice versa) or from one floating rate to another. Interest rate swaps can be used for both hedging and speculating.

利率互换（IRS）是一种流动金融衍生工具，该工具双方同意根据一种固定利率到一种浮动利率（反之亦然）或一种浮动利率到另一种浮动利率之间指定的名义金额来交换利率现金流。利率互换既可用于对冲，也可用于投机。

注：（1）hedge 对冲，指用于特意减低另一项投资风险的投资，它是一种在减低商业风险的同时仍然能在投资中获利的方法。一般对冲是同时进行两笔行情相关、方向相反、数量相当和盈亏相抵的交易。（2）相关术语：swap transaction 掉期交易；hedge options 对冲期权；risk hedging 风险对冲；selling hedge 沽空对冲，卖出对冲；hedge fund 对冲基金

**16. Trade finance 贸易融资**

The recent decline reflects both the steep drop in global demand as well as the evaporation of trade finance, essential to exporting and importing. (news.iciba.com)

最近贸易量下滑既反映出全球需求的急剧下降，也反映出对进出口至关重要的贸易融资的蒸发。

注：（1）demand 需求，指人们在某一特定的时期内在各种可能的价格下愿意并且能够购买某个具体商品的数量。（2）相关术语：market demand 市场需求；quantity demanded 需求量；derived demand 派生需求；demand shift 需求变动

Trade finance signifies financing for trade, and it concerns both domestic and international trade transactions. A trade transaction requires a seller of goods and services as well as a buyer. Various intermediaries such as banks and financial institutions can facilitate these transactions by financing the trade.

贸易融资指为交易提供资金，涉及国内和国际贸易交易。贸易交易需要商品和服务的买方，同时银行和金融机构等各种中介机构可以通过提供资金来促进交易实现。

注：（1）financial institutions 金融机构，指从事金融服务业有关的金融中介机构，为金融体系的一部分。金融中介机构包括银行、证券公司、保险公司、信托投资公司和基金管理公司等。（2）分类：financial regulator 金融监管机构；financial enterprises 金融企业 deposit financial institution 存款性金融机构；non-deposit financial institution 非存款性金融机构；policy financial institution 政策性金融机构；non-policy financial institution 非政策性金融机构；bank financial institutions 银行金融机构；non-bank financial institutions 非银行金融机构

**17. Triangular arbitrage 三角套汇**

Meanwhile the paper analyzes the relationship of RMB exchange rate against US Dollar and non-US Dollar from the view of the triangular arbitrage. (www.e-say.com.cn)

同时，文章从三角套汇的角度分析了人民币对美元和对非美元货币汇率之间的关系。

注：（1）exchange rate 汇率，又称外汇利率，外汇汇率或外汇行市，指的是两种货币之间兑换的比率，亦可视为一个国家的货币对另一种货币的价值。（2）相关术语：buying rate 买入汇率；selling rate 卖出汇率；medial rate 中间汇率；official rate 官定汇率；market rate 市场汇率

Triangular arbitrage involves the exchange of a currency for a second, then a third and then back to the original currency in a short amount of time.

三角套利指在短时间内将一种货币兑换成另一种货币，然后兑换成第三种货币，最后又兑换回原始货币。

注：（1）currency 货币，是购买货物、保存财富的媒介，是财产的所有者与市场关于交换权的契约，本质上是所有者之间的约定。（2）交易最多的货币：美元 US dollar；欧元 European Euro；日元 Japanese yen；英镑 Pound sterling；澳元 Australian dollar（排名来源：www.countries-ofthe-world.com）

**18. The gold standard　金本位**

Compared to the gold standard and the creation of super restore the sovereignty of the international monetary terms, the International Monetary oligarchs is more realistic.

相比金本位制和建立超主权国际货币而言，国际货币寡头更加现实。

注：（1）oligarch 寡头政治执政者；oligarchy 寡头政治，原指少数人掌握的政权，后通指由一小撮反动统治者操纵一切的政治制度。在政府事务中，服从少数人统治的政治，在任何团体中，诸如一个教堂、工会、学校或者任何其他机关，由少数人所管治者，均可称为寡头政治。（2）相关术语：oligopoly 寡头垄断；financial oligarch 金融寡头；economic monopoly 经济性垄断；natural monopoly 自然垄断

A gold standard is a monetary system in which the standard economic unit of account is based on a fixed quantity of gold.

金本位制是一种以一定数量的黄金作为标准经济计量单位的货币体系。

注：（1）monetary system 货币体系，指的是由两种或更多货币组成的有规律的货币整体。（2）相关术语：international monetary system 国际货币体系；Bretton Woods system 布雷顿森林体系；Jamaica system 牙买加体系；European Monetary System（EMS）欧洲货币体系

**19. Two-tier market　双向市场**

In this two-tier market, retail investors tend to buy and hold ETFs while traders and market-makers move in and out of funds rapidly for many different reasons. (*Forbes*: Cyprus, Anything But Unique and Why to Worry)

在双向市场中，散户投资者倾向于购买并持有 ETFs，而交易员和做市商则出于诸多不同的原因迅速吃进、卖出基金。

注：（1）ETFs（Exchange Traded Funds）交易型开放式指数基金，是一种跟踪“标的指数”变化、且在证券交易所上市交易的基金。投资者既可以在二级市场买卖 ETF 份额，也可以向基金管理公司申购或赎回 ETF 份额，不过申购或赎回必须以一篮子股票或少量现金，换取基金份额，反之亦可。（2）相关术语：Listed Open-Ended Fund，LOF 上市型开放式基金

Exchange rate system in which a country sets one rate for capital flows and another one for current account (import-export) transactions.

双向市场（Two-tier market）是国家为资本流动设定一种汇率，为经常账户（进出口）交易设定另一种汇率的汇率制度。

注：（1）capital flows 资本流动，是资本由货币形式转变为商品形式，再由商品形式转变为货币形式的运动过程。（2）相关术语：international capital flows 国际资本流动；short-term international capital movements 短期国际资本流动；long-term international capital flows 长期国际资本流动；globalization of capital flows 资本流动全球化

**20. Elegraphic transfer　电汇**

Inward and outward remittances are usually carried out by a mail transfer, demand draft, or telegraphic transfer.

汇进和汇出通常通过信汇，即期汇票或电汇方式进行。

注：（1）demand draft 即期汇票，指以提示日为到期日，持票人持票到银行或其他委托付款人处，后者见票必须付款的一种汇票，这种汇票的持票人可以随时行使自己的票据权利，在此之前无须提前通知付款人准备履行义务。（2）相关术语：time bill 远期汇票；bank drafts 银行汇票；commercial bill of exchange /commercial draft 商业汇票

Telegraphic transfer is a term used to refer to an electronic means of transferring funds. A transfer charge is often charged by the sending bank and in some cases by the receiving bank.

电汇代指电子转账方式，它产生的汇款费用通常由汇款银行收取，在某些情况下由收款银行收取。

注：（1）funds 资金，定义：①指的是资金管理；②垫支于社会再生产过程，用于创造新价值，并增加社会剩余产品价值的媒介价值；③以货币表现，用来进行周转，满足创造社会物质财富需要的价值，体现着以资料公有制为基础的社会主义生产关系；④用于社会主义扩大再生产过程中的有价值的物资和货币；⑤国民经济中财产物资的货币表现。（2）相关术语：financial funds 财政资金；credit funds 信贷资金；fixed funds 固定资金；liquidity 流动资金

**21. Joint and several liabilities　连带负债，共同及连带责任**

The right of contribution, corresponding to joint and several liability, is different from the right of indemnification.（*Science of Law*, 2010, 30-4:761-780.）

与连带责任相对应的出资权不同于赔偿权。

注：（1）contribution 出资，指股东，包括发起人和认股人，在公司设立或者增加资本时，为取得股份或股权，根据协议的约定以及法律和章程的规定向公司交付财产或履行其他给付义务。（2）相关术语：monetary contribution 货币出资；investment in labor 劳务出资；investment in kind 实物出资

Under joint and several liability or all sums, a claimant may pursue an obligation against any one party as if they were jointly liable and it becomes the responsibility of the defendants to sort out their respective proportions of liability and payment.

根据连带责任或全部责任，索赔人可以向任何一方追究赔偿，就好像他们负有连带责任，由被告负责理清各自的赔偿责任和付款比例。

注：（1）claimant 索赔人；claim 索赔，指受到损失的一方当事人，向违约的一方当事人提出损害赔偿的要求，相对而言，违约的一方受理另一方的索赔要求，即称为理赔（settlement of claim）。（2）相关术语：counter claim 反索赔；claims settling agent 理赔代理人；insurance claims 保险理赔

**22. Junior mortgage　次级抵押贷款**

Life insurance companies and savings and loan associations have not been permitted to make junior mortgage loans.（*The Journal of Finance*/March, 1956/Junior Mortgages In Real Estate Finance—A Case Study）

人寿保险公司以及储蓄贷款协会不得发放次级抵押贷款。

注：savings and loan associations 美国储贷协会，是在美国政府支持和监管下，专门从事储蓄业务和住房抵押贷款的非银行金融机构。

A junior mortgage is a mortgage that is subordinate to a first or prior (senior) mortgage, and often refers to a second mortgage, but it could also be a third or fourth mortgage.

次级抵押从属于第一顺位或优先（高级）抵押，通常指第二顺位抵押，但也可能是第三或第四顺位抵押。

注：（1）mortgage 抵押，指抵押人和债权人以书面形式订立约定，不转移抵押财产的占有，只将该财产作为债权的担保。当债务人不履行到期债务时，债权人有权依法以该财产折价或者以拍卖、变卖该财产的价款优先受偿。（2）抵押种类：real estate mortgage 不动产抵押；chattel mortgage 动产抵押；right mortgage 权利抵押；consortium charge 财团抵押；common mortgage 共同抵押；the maximum mortgage 最高额抵押；junk bond 风险债券，垃圾债券

## 4.4.2 投资性金融相关机构

### 1. Joint venture　合资企业

For instant, China Banking Regulatory Commission liberalized a number of business qualifications to foreign banks in March this year. Such as, the foreign-owned banks and joint venture banks can underwrite treasury bonds… (China Banking Association/May 27, 2018/http://www.china-cba.net/bencandy.php?fid=43&id=16512)

今年三月银监会向外资银行开放若干业务资格，如外商独资银行和中外合资银行可以承销国债等

注：（1）treasury bonds 国债，指由国家发行的债券，是中央政府为筹集财政资金而发行的一种政府债券。由于国债的发行主体是国家，所以它具有最高的信用度，被公认为是最安全的投资工具。（2）相关术语：corporate bond 公司债券；real estate mortgage bonds 不动产抵押债券

A joint venture (JV) is a business entity created by two or more parties, generally characterized by shared ownership, shared returns and risks, and shared governance.

合资企业（JV）是由两个或两个以上主体创建的商业实体，通常具有共同所有、共享收益、共担风险以及共同治理的特点。

注：（1）business entity 商业实体，是为了从事商业活动、慈善工作或其他允许的活动，而根据商法成立和管理的实体。大多数情况下，企业实体是为了销售产品或服务而成立的。（2）相关术语：在各国的法律体系中，定义了多种类型的企业实体。这些实体包括公司 corporations、合作社 cooperatives、合伙企业 partnerships、个人贸易商 sole traders、有限责任公司 limited liability company 和其他明确许可和标明的实体类型。具体规则因国家、州或省而异。

### 2. Joint stock company　股份公司

In an official announcement on Friday, the Saudi government said Aramco was converted into a joint-stock company—one in which shares can be bought and sold—on January 1.

(Marketplace Middle East/January 5, 2018/http://money.cnn.com/2018/01/05/investing/saudi-aramco-ipo-plans/index.html)

在周五的一份官方声明中，沙特政府表示阿美公司在 1 月 1 日被改制成了一家可以买卖股份的股份公司。

A joint-stock company is a business entity in which shares of the company's stock can be bought and sold by shareholders.

股份公司是股东可以买卖公司股票的商业实体。

## 4.5 World Banking（国际金融）

本节首先介绍国际金融的概念，其次介绍国际金融工具和相关机构，并进一步分析相关机构的职能和作用。

国际金融是指国家和地区之间由于经济、政治、文化等联系而产生货币资金周转和运动，由国际收支、国际汇兑、国际结算、国际信用、国际投资和国际货币体系构成，各体系之间相互影响，相互制约。

### 4.5.1 国际金融工具

**1. Money supply　货币供应**

The inflation would be reduced through controlling the money supply.

可以通过控制货币供应量来缓解通货膨胀。

相关术语：austerity budget 紧缩财政；pricing policy 价格政策；supply policy 供给政策

It is the entire stock of currency and other liquid instruments circulating in a country's economy as of a particular time. Also referred to as money stock, money supply includes safe assets, such as cash, coins, and balances held in checking and saving accounts that businesses and individuals can use to make payments or hold as short-term investments.

货币供应是在一个特定时间内，一国经济中流通的全部货币和其他流通票据，也称为货币库存。货币供应包括安全资产，例如现金、硬币和企业及个人可用于支付或短期投资的支票存款和储蓄存款。

注：liquid instruments 流通票据，仅凭背书或交付即能易主，特点是通过单纯交付或背书交付，无须告知原债务人。

**2. Margin　保证金**

deposit of transaction margin

存入交易保证金

注：refundable deposits 存出保证金，企业按规定交存的保证金，包括交易保证金、存出分保准备金、存出理赔保证金、存出共同海损保证金、存出其他保证金等。存出保证金应按实际存出的金额入账，一般金融企业会使用存入保证金和存出保证金这两个科目。

It is the difference between a product or service's selling price and its cost of production or to the ratio between a company's revenues and expenses. It also refers to the amount of equity contributed by an investor as a percentage of the current market value of securities held in a margin account. Margin is the portion of the interest rate on an adjustable-rate mortgage added to the adjustment-index rate.

这是产品或服务销售价格与其生产成本之间的差额，或公司收入与支出的比例。它也指投资者保证金账户所持有的股本金额，占证券当前市场价值的百分比。保证金是可调整利率抵押贷款利率加上调整指数利率的部分。

注：equity 股本，股份资本是经公司章程授权、代表公司所有权的全部股份，既包括普通股也包括优先股，为构成公司股东权益的两个组成部分之一。股本的大小会随着送股和配股而增加，但它的市价不会改变，这是由于送配股后除权的原因所致。

**3. Maturity　到期**

Important characteristics of bonds include face value, maturity date, and coupon rate.

债券的重要特征包括面值、到期日和票面利率等。

相关术语：int payment 付息方式；repayment 偿还方式；credit rating 信用评级

The date on which the principal balance of a loan, bond, or other financial instrument becomes due and payable.

贷款、债券或其他金融工具本金余额到期和应付的日期。

注：principal balance 本金余额，即贷款、存款或投资在计算利息之前的原始金额。企业本金作为整体，是同时的、在空间上并列地处在它的各个不同阶段上，以不同的本金占用形态表现。本金的每一种占用形态又都不断地依次由上一阶段过渡到下一阶段，由一种形态转化为另一种形态。

**4. Minimum balance　最小余额**

Like our standard checking account, which features no minimum balance, no monthly fees, and lets you write up to 300 checks a month.

与我们的标准支票账户一样，该账户没有最低余额，没有月费，并且可以让您每月填写多达 300 张支票。

注：saving account 储蓄账户，指存款人办理日常转账结算和现金收付而开立的银行结算账户，是存款人的主办账户；支票账户，指在商业银行或其他金融机构中的存款，允许以支票方式提款，故属于交易货币，也称为支票存款。

The amount of money required to be on deposit in an account to qualify the depositor for special services or to waive a service charge.

为使存款人有资格获得特别的服务或免除服务费而需要存入账户的金额。

注：waive 放弃（权利、要求等）

**5. Money market deposit account　货币市场存款账户**

A money market deposit account often offers limited check-writing privileges and pays an interest rate that is typically higher than a regular savings account but lower than a certificate of deposit or other time deposit.

货币市场存款账户提供的支票填写权限通常是有限的，利率通常高于普通储蓄账户，但低于存款证或其他定期存款利率。

A savings account that offers a higher rate of interest in exchange for larger than normal deposits. Insured by the FDIC, these accounts have limits on the number of transactions allowed and may require higher balances to receive the higher rate of interest.

货币市场存款账户是提供更高利率，以换取比正常情况下更多存款金额的储蓄账户。由 FDIC 承保，这类账户对交易次数有限制，还可能要求只有大额存款才能享受高额利率。

注：FDIC 联邦存款保险公司，是美国联邦政府的独立金融机构，负责办理存款保险业务，根据 1933 年银行法设立。从 1934 年 1 月 1 日起，对联邦储备系统所有会员银行以及申请参加联邦储备保险并符合条件的州银行，实行有法定限额的存款保险制度。

**6. Money market fund 货币市场基金**

Money market funds are widely (though not necessarily accurately) regarded as being as safe as bank deposits yet providing a higher yield.

人们广泛认为（尽管未必如此）货币市场基金与银行存款一样安全，但它的收益却更高。

相关术语：contractual fund 契约型投资基金；corporate funds 公司型投资基金

An open-ended mutual fund that invests in short-term debts and monetary instruments such as Treasury bills and pays money market rates of interest. Money market funds usually offer check writing privileges. They are not insured by the FDIC.

货币市场基金是一个开放式共同基金，投资于短期债务和短期国债等货币工具，利率等同于货币市场利率。货币市场基金通常会提供支票填写权限，联邦存款保险公司不为其承保。

注：check 支票，指由出票人签发的，委托办理支票存款业务的银行或者其他金融机构在见票时无条件支付确定的金额给收款人或者持票人的票据。同样，支票制度也适用汇票的有关规定。支票的特征表现在：其一，支票是委付证券，但支票的付款人比较特殊，必须是有支票存款业务资格的银行或非银行金融机构；其二，我国的支票只有即期支票，支票无承兑制度。

**7. Mortgage 抵押**

A debt instrument used in a real estate transaction where the property is the collateral for the loan. A mortgage gives the lender a right to take possession of the property if the borrower fails to pay off the loan.

抵押是房地产交易中使用的债务工具，其中房产是贷款的抵押品。如果借款人未能清偿贷款，则贷款人有权占有该房产。

注：collateral 抵押品，又称担保品，指银行发放贷款时作为抵押的实物，主要有土地、房屋、有价证券和商品等。

Solving “Goldie Complex” of Chattel Mortgage—On the System Improvement of Chattel Mortgage of Property Law

破解动产抵押“戈尔迪之结”——论《物权法》动产抵押制度的完善

注：（1）Chattel Mortgage 动产抵押；（2）相关术语：其他类型抵押包括 real estate mortgage 不动产抵押；right mortgage 权利抵押；inventory mortgage 库存抵押；joint mortgage 财团抵押/共同抵押；the maximum mortgage 最高额抵押。

**8. Negotiable Order of Withdrawal Account (NOW) 面议提款账户**

Negotiable Order of Withdrawal Account is an interest-bearing account for which the bank must reserve the right to require the depositor to provide at least seven days notice of his/her intent to withdraw funds.

面议提款账户（NOW）是一种计息账户，对于此类账户，银行必须保留权利，要求存款人至少提前七天通知提款意向。

注：non-interest bearing account 无息账户

A savings account from which withdrawals can be made by negotiable orders of withdrawal (functional equivalent of checks).

面议提款账户是可通过可转让提款单（功能等同于支票）提款的储蓄账户。

注：（1）deposit account 存款账户，是存款人因借款或其他结算需要，在基本存款账户开户银行以外的银行营业机构开立的银行结算账户。（2）相关术语：savings account 个人储蓄账户，指自然人凭个人有效身份证件，以自然人名称，在银行储蓄机构开立的办理资金存取业务的人民币储蓄存款账户。

**9. Official check 本票**

Official check are treated as guaranteed funds because the bank, rather than the purchaser, is responsible for paying the amount.

本票被视为有担保的资金，因为支付金额的是银行而不是买方。

相关术语：cash cheque 现金支票；cheque for transfer 转账支票

A check drawn on a bank and signed by an authorized bank official.

由授权的银行官员署名的银行支票。

注：bank official 银行官员，一般来说，全国性股份制商业银行董事长、行长均由正厅（局）级担任，可视为正厅（局）级。

**10. Online banking 网上银行**

Online banking, filling out job applications, and even using a smart phone, all require functional literacy.

使用网上银行，填写工作申请，甚至使用智能手机时，都需要功能性识字能力。

注：functional literacy 功能性识字，指个人所获得的知识与读写技巧，可以使其在所处的文化或团体中，正常地从事各种活动。

A service that allows an account holder to obtain account information and manage certain banking transactions through a personal computer via the financial institution's web site on the Internet.

网上银行是一项允许账户持有人用个人电脑，通过互联网在金融机构的网站上获取账户信息，并办理某些银行业务的服务。

注：financial institution 金融机构，指从事金融业有关的金融中介机构，为金融体系的一部分，金融业包括银行、证券、保险、信托、基金等行业，金融机构包括银行、证券公司、保险公司、信托投资公司和基金管理公司等。

**11. Open-end credit　开放式信用**

Open-end credit agreements are good for borrowers because it gives them more control over when and how much they borrow.

开放式信用协议对借方有好处，因为它给予了借方更多对借贷的时间和金额的控制权。

注：borrower 借方，或借款人，向贷方（尤其是银行）借款的个人或组织机构。

A credit agreement (typically a credit card) that allows a customer to borrow against a preapproved credit line when purchasing goods and services. The borrower is only billed for the amount that is actually borrowed plus any interest due.

一种允许客户在购买商品和服务时借用预先批准的信用额度的信用协议（通常是信用卡），借款人只需支付实际借款金额加上到期利息。

注：credit card 信用卡，又称贷记卡，是由商业银行或信用卡公司对信用合格的消费者发行的信用证明。持有信用卡的消费者可以到特约商业服务部门购物或消费，再由银行同商户和持卡人进行结算，持卡人可以在规定额度内透支。

**12. Operating subsidiary　运营子公司**

An operating subsidiary is a business term frequently used within the United States in corporate profile descriptions.

在美国，运营子公司是公司简介中常用的商业术语。

注：independent legal entity 独立法人

National banks conduct some of their banking activities through companies called operating subsidiaries. These subsidiaries are companies that are owned or controlled by a national bank and that, among other things, offer banking products and services such as loans, mortgages, and leases.

各国家银行都通过运营子公司开展一些银行业务。这些子公司由国家银行拥有或控制，提供银行产品和贷款、抵押、租赁等服务，此外也办理其他业务。

注：subsidiaries 子公司，在国际商务中，指由母公司投入全部或部分股份，依法在世界各地设立的东道国法人企业。子公司在法律上独立于母公司，并拥有独立而完整的公司管理组织体系，因而在经营方面具有较大的独立性和一定的灵活性。

**13. Outstanding check　未兑现支票**

An outstanding check represents a liability for the payor. The payor must be sure to keep enough money in the account to cover the amount of the outstanding check until it is cashed, which could take weeks or even months.

未兑现支票对付款人来说是一项负债，在支票未兑现的数周甚至数月中，付款人必须确保在账户中存有足够款项来支付支票金额。

相关术语：cheque to transfer 转账支票；canceled cheque 已付支票

A check written by a depositor that has not yet been presented for payment to or paid by the depositor's bank.

未兑现支票是由存款人填写的，尚未提交给存款人银行，或银行尚未支付的支票。

注：depositor 存款人，指向银行存储人民币用户的主体，分为企业法人、非法人企业、个体工商户、个人用户。

**14. Overdraft　透支**

If there is a prior agreement with the account provider for an overdraft, and the amount overdrawn is within the authorized overdraft limit, then interest is normally charged at the agreed rate.

如果事先与账户提供商达成透支协议，并且透支金额在授权透支限额内，则通常按商定的利率收取利息。

注：benchmark interest rate 基准利率

When the amount of money withdrawn from a bank account is greater than the amount actually available in the account, the excess is known as an overdraft, and the account is said to be overdrawn.

当从银行账户中提取的金额大于该账户中实际可用金额时，该超出部分被称为透支额，该账户被称为透支账户。

注：overdrawing account 透支账户，是银行为企业单位开设的一种账户类型，透支是银行放款的一种形式。银行允许存款户，在彼此约定的限额内，超过其存款金额继续签发支票。存款户对透支放款应支付利息，并有随时偿还的义务。

**15. Minimum payment　最低付费**

This credit card minimum payment calculator will show you how long it would take to pay off your credit card if only the minimum payment was made.

这个信用卡最低支付计算器会告诉您，如果只支付最低金额的话，需要多久才能还清您的信用卡。

注：interest calculator 利息计算器

The minimum dollar amount that must be paid each month on a loan, line of credit, or other debt.

最低付费是每月必须要为贷款，信用额度或其他债务支付的最低金额。

注：debt 债务，"债权"的对称，指债的法律关系中，债务人依法对债权人所承担的为一定行为或不为一定行为的义务。如在买卖合同中，出卖人有将出卖的物品交付买受人的义务，这就是为一定行为的债务。

**16. Overlimit　超限**

If the balance owing on the account for the revolving loan exceeds the credit limit, we may charge an overlimit fee as set out in the service fee table or loan agreement.

倘若循环贷款账户上的结欠超过信贷限额，我们可按服务收费表或贷款协议书征收超限费用。

注：loan agreement 贷款协议，是中长期贷款中，借贷双方之间签订的贷款协议。

An open-end credit account in which the assigned dollar limit has been exceeded.

一个开放式信用账户，其中结欠已超过指定的限额。

注：trading limit 货币交易限额，一个交易商、一组交易商或一个交易室被允许做某种货币交易的最大额度。

**17. Payment method　付款方式**

Payment method refers to the specific practice adopted by the payer to perform the obligation of the bill.

付款方式指付款人履行票据义务的具体做法。

注：paying agent 付款代理人

For years, agreements that retailers have signed with third-party payment processors prohibited merchants from selling products at different prices depending on payment method.

多年来，零售商与第三方支付平台签订协议，禁止商家根据不同的付款方式，以不同价格销售产品。

注：third-party 第三方，通常指合同关系双方的两个主体之外，相对独立的，有一定公正性的第三主体，一般引入第三方的目的是为了确保交易的公平、公正，避免纠纷和欺诈。

**18. Presenting bank　提示银行**

Presenting Bank is the bank that points to the payer to draw the draft and the documents.

提示银行指向付款人出具汇票和单据的银行。

相关术语：online banking 网上银行

If the remitting bank does not nominate a specific presenting bank, the collecting bank may utilize a presenting bank of its choice. (www.dictall.com)

如果汇出行未指定某一特定提示行，代收行可自行选择提示行。

注：remitting bank 汇出行，指接受汇款人的委托，办理汇出汇款业务的银行。在国际贸易中，通常为进口地银行。

**19. Packing loan　信用证抵押贷款**

Packing loan: the exporter applies for a short-term loan under original letter of credit used as guarantee. The loan is used to ensure funds for production and shipping.

信用证抵押贷款：出口商以信用证正本作抵押，申请短期贷款，贷款用于确保生产和运输的资金。

相关术语：housing mortgage loan 住房抵押贷款

The bank usually asks the applicant to pledge the original true L/C against packing loan. (danci.911cha.com)

银行在办理信用证抵押贷款业务中通常都要求申请人提供信用证正本作抵押。

注：L/C 信用证，指银行根据进口人（买方）的请求，开给出口人（卖方）的一种保证承担支付货款责任的书面凭证。在信用证内，银行授权出口人在符合信用证所规定的条件下，以该行或其指定的银行为付款人，开具不得超过规定金额的汇票，并按规定随附装运单据，按期在指定地点收取货款。

**20. Renewal　转存**

Renewal is a kind of capital turnover of the bank.

转存是银行的一种资本周转方式。

注：capital turnover 资本周转

The specific measures for the stipulated or automatic renewal shall be formulated and promulgated by the department in-charge of savings. (dictsearch.appspot.com)

约定转存、自动转存的具体办法由经营储蓄的主管部门自行制定、公布。

注：renewal 转存，指定期存款自动转存，在客户存款到期后，客户如果不前往银行办理转存手续，银行可自动将到期的存款本息按相同存期一并转存，不受次数限制，续存期利息按前期到期日利率计算。

**21. Period　时间长度**

We shall be pleased to receive a fixed deposit for any amount more than $1, 000, for a period over six months at the rate of 6% p.a. (www.ebigear.com)

定期存款条件为年利 6%，存期 6 个月以上，只要存款金额超过 1 000 美元我们均乐意接受。

注：（1）fixed deposit 定期存款，同义词：time deposit, term deposit；反义词：current deposit, demand deposit, liquid deposit；（2）相关术语：deposit account 存款账户；open an account 开账户

Period is a particular length of time with a beginning and an end.

时期是从开始到结束的特定时间长度。

**22. Passbook　存折**

A passbook or bankbook is a paper book used to record bank transactions on a deposit account.

The current balance is held by the passbook, which also keeps a record of the transactions on the account. (www.ibm.com)

存折是用于记录存款账户上银行交易的纸本。

存折上记录了该账户当前的存款余额，和交易记录。

注：（1）transaction 交易，业务；（2）相关术语：transaction cost 交易成本；transaction tax 交易税，流通税；transaction code 交易代码；transaction exposure 产品交易风险；transaction journal 交易日志；transaction time 交易时间；transaction proceed 进行交易

**23. Reserve ratio　存款准备金率**

The reserve ratio is the percentage of reserves a bank is required to hold against deposits. (*Forbes:* How Has The Fed Evolved?)

存款准备金率指的是，银行需要针对存款而持有的准备金所占百分比。

Reserve ratio is a central bank regulation employed by most, but not all, of the world's central banks, that sets the minimum fraction of customer deposits and notes that each commercial bank must hold as reserves (rather than lend out).

存款准备金率是世界上大多数（但不是所有）央行采用的一项央行监管措施，规定了每一家商业银行必须作为准备金持有的，占客户存款和票据的最低比例（而不是贷款）。

**24. Proceeds 收益**

It banned them from competing with the banks by lending out the proceeds to other companies. (*Forbes*: The sun also rises)

相关规定禁止他们通过将收益借给其他公司来与银行竞争。

注：（1）ban *v.* 禁止；取缔；把……逐出；*n.* 禁止；禁令；逐出令；褫夺公民权的判决；诅咒；（2）相关词组：ban on 禁止……；ban for 禁止对……

Proceeds is the money that is obtained from doing something or selling something.
收益指通过做某事或出售某物而获得的钱。

## 4.5.2 国际金融相关机构

**1. National bank 国家银行**

A bank that is subject to the supervision of the Comptroller of the Currency. The Office of the Comptroller of the Currency is a bureau of the US Treasury Department.

国家银行是一家受货币监理署监督的银行，其中货币监理署隶属于美国财政部。

注：（1）Office of Comptroller of Currency 美国货币监理署，是联邦政府五个主要的监管机构之一。货币监理署（OCC）隶属美国财政部，1863 年《国家货币法》（National Currency Act of 1863）赋予货币监理署监管美国联邦注册银行（国民银行）的职能。货币监理署主要负责对国民银行发放执照并进行监管，具体监管职能包括：检查、审批监管对象设立分支机构、资本等变更的申请；对其违法违规行为或不稳健经营行为采取监管措施；制定并下发有关银行投资、贷款等操作的法规。（2）相关术语：Federal Reserve Bank 美国联邦注册银行；Office of the Comptroller of the Currency (OCC) 货币监理署

A national bank can be recognized because it must have "national" or "national association" in its name.

国家银行可以得到认可，因为它的名称中必须有"国家"或"国家协会"字样。

注：完全由国家投资设立的银行，除中央银行外，可以是商业银行，也可以是各种专业银行。世界上有些国家的中央银行虽非全部由国家投资或完全按股份制组织，但也称为国家银行。

**2. National Credit Union Administration (NCUA) 国家信用社管理局**

The Federal regulatory agency that charters and supervises Federal Credit Union. NCUA also administers the National Credit Union Share Insurance Fund, which insures the deposits of Federal credit unions.

国家信用社管理局是包括并监督联邦信用社的总联邦监管机构，它还负责管理国家信用社股票保险基金，该基金为联邦信用社存款提供保险。

注：insurance fund 保险基金，指专门从事风险经营的保险机构，根据法律或合

同规定，以收取保险费的办法建立的、专门用于保险事故所致经济损失的补偿或人身伤亡的给付的一项专用基金，是保险人履行保险义务的条件。广义上的保险基金指整个社会的后备基金体系。从狭义上来讲，保险基金是指由保险机构集中起来的后备基金，由保险机构根据大数据法则，经过科学的测算，订出各种不同的保险费率。

**3. National bank examiner　国家银行审查员**

An employee of the Comptroller of the Currency whose function is to examine federally chartered financial institutions.

国家银行审查员是一名通货监理官，其职能是监查联邦特许金融机构。

注：audit 审计，是由国家授权或接受委托的专职机构和人员，依照国家法规、审计准则和会计理论，运用专门的方法，对被审计单位的财政、财务收支、经营管理活动及其相关资料的真实性、正确性、合规性、合法性、效益性进行审查和监督，评价经济责任，鉴证经济业务，用以维护财经法纪、改善经营管理、提高经济效益的一项独立性的经济监督活动。

National Bank Examiners evaluate bank activities and management processes to ensure national banks operate in a safe and sound manner and comply with laws and regulations.

国家银行审查员对银行活动和管理流程进行评估，以确保国家银行安全、健康地运作并遵守法律和法规。

**4. Zurich Stock Exchange　苏黎世证券交易所**

The financial sector is an important part of Zurich's economy and the city is home to the Swiss Stock Exchange and companies such as Credit Suisse and Swiss Re.

金融业是苏黎世经济的一大支柱，瑞士证交所以及瑞士信贷、瑞士再保险等公司均位于这里。

Zurich Stock Exchange was the first stock exchange in the world to incorporate a fully automated trading, clearing and settlement system in 1995.

苏黎世证券交易所在 1995 年成为世界上第一个采用全自动交易、清算和结算系统的证券交易所。

注：（1）苏黎世证券交易所是瑞士最大的证券交易市场，其业务量占瑞士全国证券交易总额的 65%。每年约有 40 000 多人出入于该交易所，买卖双方还可通过电话或电视屏幕进行交易。（2）相关术语：Berne Exchange 伯尔尼证券交易所

# Chapter 5

# Terminologies of Insurance（保险篇）

## 5.1 Basics of Insurance（保险的基本概念）

本章重点介保险基本原理。

保险有广义和狭义之分。

广义保险：无论何种形式的保险，都可以根据其自然属性概括为是将具有同类风险的单位和个人集合起来，以合理的方式计算风险分担金，向经济损失者提供保险经济保障的一种行为。

狭义保险：通常而言的保险均是狭义保险，即商业保险。《中华人民共和国保险法》明确指出：本法所称保险，是指投保人根据合同约定，向保险人支付保险费，保险人对于因合同约定的可能发生事故发生所造成的财产损失承担赔偿保险金责任，或者当被保险人死亡、伤残、疾病或者达到合同约定的年龄、期限时承担给付保险金责任的商业保险行为。

**1. Insurance　保险**

The Obama administration says gov's error rate for transmitting health insurance applications to insurance companies has plunged.

奥巴马政府表示，联邦医保网站向保险公司发送医保申请表的错误率大幅降低。

Insurance to protect the homeowner and the lender against physical damage to a property from sources such as but not limited to fire, wind, or vandalism.

保护房主和贷款人免受火灾、风或故意破坏等原因对财产造成的实际损害的保险。

注：（1）insurance 保险，指投保人根据合同约定，向保险人支付保险费，保险人对于合同约定的可能发生的事故因其发生所造成的财产损失承担赔偿保险金责任，或者被保险人死亡、伤残、疾病或者达到合同约定的年龄、期限等条件时承担给付保险金责任的商业保险行为。从经济角度看，保险是分摊意外事故损失的一种财务安排；从法律角度看，保险是合同一方同意补偿另一方损失的一种合同安排；从社会角度看，保险是社会经济保障制度的重要组成部分，是社会生产、生活“精巧的稳定器”；从风险管理角度看，保险是一种风险管理的方法。（2）相关术语：property insurance 财产保险；personal insurance 人身保险；liability insurance 责任保险；credit insurance 信用保险；subsidized insurance 补贴保险；maritime insurance 海上保险

**2. Voluntary insurance　自愿保险**

At that time the insurance industry was split into compulsory insurance and voluntary insurance.（*Forbes*: Life Insurance in China）

保险业分为强制保险和自愿保险。

注：compulsory insurance 强制保险，指根据国家颁布的有关法律和法规，凡是在规定范围内的单位或个人，不论是否愿意都必须参加的保险。比如，世界各国都将机动车第三者责任强制保险规定为强制保险。由于强制保险在表现为国家对个人意愿的干预，所以强制保险的范围受到严格限制。我国《保险法》规定，除法律、行政法规规定必须保险外，保险公司和其他任何单位都不得强制他人订立保险合同。

voluntary insurance 自愿保险，也称任意保险，是指保险双方当事人通过签订保险合同，或是需要保险保障的人自愿组合、实施的一种保险。自愿保险是当事人之间自由决定并彼此协商后订立的合同关系。投保人可以自行决定是否投保、向谁投保、中途退保等，也可以自由选择保障范围、保障程度和保险期限等。保险人也可以根据情况自愿决定是否承保、怎样承保，自由选择保险标的和投保条件等。

The insurance form of the insurance contract is concluded on a voluntary basis by the insurer and the insured.

保险合同是由保险人和被保险人自愿订立的一种保险形式。

## 5.2　Life Insurance（人身险）

本节主要介绍现代保险制度下人身险的分类以及各种分类的依据和主要业务种类。

### 5.2.1　人寿保险

人寿保险，简称寿险，是人身保险的一种，是以被保险人的寿命为标的，以被保险人的生存或死亡为给付条件的保险。寿险和所有保险业务一样，被保险人将风险转嫁给保险人，同时接受保险人的条款并支付保险费。与其他保险不同的是，人寿保险转嫁的是被保险人生存或死亡的风险。

#### 5.2.1.1　人寿保险基本概念

**1. Cash value　现金价值**

Cash values are usually associated with whole life insurance or endowment life insurance and other forms of permanent life insurance. The contract determines for each possible cancellation date the related cash value. (https://en.wikipedia.org/wiki/Cash_value)

现金价值通常与整个人寿保险、养老保险或其他形式的永久性人寿保险联系在一起。合同明确了保险每个可注销日的现金价值。

注：whole life insurance 终身人寿保险，是现金价值人寿保险之一。除了提供人寿保

险，还建立了现金价值或者投资价值，称为内部建设，这种价值建设不受制于税收，即资本利得和收入都是免税的。现金价值可以撤回，保单所有者可以以此举债。投保人撤回现金价值，保单即失效，否则保单终身有效。在保单期间投保人支付的保费是不变的。

The cash value of an insurance contract, also called the cash surrender value or surrender value, is the cash amount offered to the policyowner by the issuing life carrier upon cancellation of the contract. This term is normally used with a life insurance contract.

保单现金价值，也称为解约退还金或退保价值，是在保险合同解除时，保险人提供给投保人的现金金额。这个术语通常与人寿保险合同一起使用。

注：life insurance contract 人寿保险合同，指投保人和保险人约定，当被保险人在合同规定的年限内死亡或生存时，保险人按照合同约定向被保险人或受益人给付保险金的合同。人寿保险合同多为定额给付型的长期保险合同，不适用损失补偿原则，也不存在重复保险或者超额保险的问题。人寿保险合同以按照保险金给付的条件不同，可以分为死亡保险合同、生存保险合同和生死两全保险合同三种类型。死亡保险合同是被保险人死了，保险公司就赔钱的合同。有权指定被保险人的是投保人，保险公司赔付的对象是受益人。保险公司是保险人，预期死亡的人是被保险人。

**2. Life insurance 人身保险**

When you take out a life insurance policy, you pay premiums in the expectation that when you die your spouse or your children will receive the benefit. But audits of the nation's leading insurance companies have uncovered a systematic, industry-wide practice of not paying significant numbers of beneficiaries.

当你购买人寿保险时，你会支付保险费，期望当你死后，你的配偶或你的孩子会得到保险金。但是，通过对全国大型保险公司审计发现，全行业存在着一种统一的做法，，即不向大量的受益人支付保险金。

注：insurance premium 保险费，是指被投保人参加保险时，根据其投保时所定的保险费率，向保险人交的费用。当保险财产遭受灾害和意外事故而造成全部或部分损失，或人身保险中被保险人发生意外时，保险人均要付给保险金。保险费由保险金额、保险费率和保险期限构成。保险费的数额同保险金额的大小、保险费率的高低和保险期限的长短成正比，即保险金额越大，保险费率越高，保险期限越长，保险费越多。交纳保险费是投保人的义务。如果被保险人不按期交纳保险费，在自愿保险中，则保险合同失效；在强制保险中，则要附加一定数额的滞纳金。

相关术语：insurance rate 保险费率，是保险人按保险金额向投保人或被保险人收取费用的比例，通常用“‰”或“%”表示。保险费率是计算保险费的依据。保险费率由纯费率和附加费率两部分构成。

Life insurance (or life assurance, especially in the Commonwealth of Nations) is a contract between an insurance policy holder and an insurer or assurer, where the insurer promises to pay a designated beneficiary a sum of money (the benefit) in exchange for a premium, upon the death of an insured person (often the policy holder).

人寿保险是保单持有人与保险人或保险公司之间的合同，在合同中，保险人收取保险费并承诺在被保险人（通常是保单持有人）死亡后，向指定受益人支付保险金。

相关术语：personal insurance 人身保险；health insurance 健康保险；personal accident insurance 人身意外伤害保险

**3. Indemnity　赔偿**

Several studies (e.g., Sinn, 1982; Keeton and Kwerel, 1984) show that under limited liability, individuals will not always demand full insurance, even if the premium equals the expected indemnity payment (referred to as actuarially fair premium). (The journal of risk and insurance / March 23,2018/https://doi.org/10.1111/jori.12247)

一些研究（例如，Sinn，1982; Keeton 和 Kwerel，1984）表明，在有限责任下，即使保费等于预期赔款（称为精算公平保费），个人也不会总是购买全额保险。

Indemnity is a contractual obligation of one party (indemnitor) to compensate the loss occurred to the other party (indemnitee) due to the act of the indemnitor or any other party.

赔偿是一方（赔偿方）的合同义务，用来补偿另一方（受偿人）因赔偿人或其他方行为而遭受的损失。

**4. Insured　被保险人**

The potential loss of insured can be affected by many nondeterministic factors, in which uncertainty always coexists with randomness. (Insurance: Mathematics and economics/Sep, 2015/ https://doi.org/10.1016/j.insmatheco.2015.06.004)

被保险人的潜在损失可能受许多不确定性因素的影响，其中不确定性总是与随机性共存。

The insured is a person whose interests are protected by an insurance policy.

被保险人是指其利益受到保单保护的人。

**5. Insurance claim　保险索赔**

However, a validation on the basis of insurance claims might be more conservative in cases where model errors are more pronounced in areas with a high density of values at risk. (Insurance: Mathematics and economics/February, 2018/https://doi.org/10.1016/j.jhydrol.2017.12.042)

但是，在高风险值密度区域模型误差更为明显的情形下，基于保险索赔的验证可能会更保守。

An insurance claim is a demand for payment in accordance with an insurance policy.

保险理赔是根据保险单的要求付款。

**6. Juvenile life insurance　青少年人寿保险**

In recent years, juvenile life insurance has become a popular college savings, lifetime savings, investment, and estate planning tool. It is increasingly popular with financial planners and insurance professionals.

近年来，青少年人寿保险已成为一种流行的大学生储蓄、终身储蓄、投资和财产规划的工具，越来越受到财务规划师和保险专业人士的欢迎。

Juvenile life insurance is permanent life insurance that insures the life of a child (generally under age 18). It is a financial planning tool that provides a tax advantaged savings vehicle with potential for a lifetime of benefits.

青少年人寿保险一般是为不满 18 岁的儿童提供的永久性人寿保险。它是一种财务规划工具，能够提供一个具有终身受益潜力的税收优惠储蓄工具。

#### 5.2.1.2 人寿保险实务

**Claim settlement 理赔**

Solvency margin is an important leading indicator of benefit payment or claim settlement ability of life insurance companies. (http://www.doc88.com/p-6126780551568.html)

偿付能力是反映寿险公司保险给付或理赔能力的重要指标。

A claim settlement is an agreement between two or more parties to settle a legal claim with payment and other terms.

理赔是指两个或两个以上的当事方之间以付款和其他条款解决法律索赔的协议。

### 5.2.2 意外伤害险

意外伤害保险是指以被保险人的身体作为保险标的，以被保险人因遭受意外伤害而造成的死亡、残疾、医疗费用支出或暂时丧失劳动能力为给付条件的保险项目。其保障的项目有死亡赔偿、残疾赔偿、支付医疗费用以及误工补贴等。

#### 5.2.2.1 意外伤害险基本概念

**1. Personal insurance 人身保险**

The scale of personal insurance business increases constantly, but it is an extensive development model and this kind of model causes the product structure of the insurance to be unreasonable.（dict.cnki.net）

人身保险业务规模不断扩大，但由于其发展模式较为粗放，必然会导致保险产品结构不合理。

Personal insurance is a type of insurance you buy to protect you from risks that could create financial losses that you would not be able to afford to cover on your own. Personal insurance relates to risks that you as an individual may face, due to accidents, illnesses, death, or damage to property you own.

个人保险是购买一种保险，旨在保护免受可能造成的个人无法独自承担的经济损失。个人保险涉及个人可能因事故、疾病、死亡或拥有的财产损失而面临的风险。

**2. Tourist accident insurance 旅游意外保险**

Visitors to the insured when the insured person during the tour because suffer accident harm accident caused casualties, according to the stipulations of the contract of insurance payment of death, disability, medical expenses insurance.

被保险人在旅行期间因遭遇意外伤害事故造成人员伤亡时，根据保险合同规定支付死亡、伤残、医疗费用的保险。

Tourism accident insurance, that is, tourism insurance, refers to the insured in the international or domestic tourism process of the insurance contract agreed to the accident or other accidents, the insurance company will be in accordance with the agreement of the insurance contract, it is a form of insurance business compensation.

旅游意外保险即旅游保险，指被保险人在国际或者国内旅游过程发生保险合同约定的意外或者其他事故时，保险公司将依据保险合同约定，对其予以保险金赔偿的一种保险业务形式。

**3. Time on risk　保险期限**

The period when the risk premium is greater than zero. With the increase of the policy year, the investment account value of the investment linked insurance and the reserve level of the bonus risk may exceed the insured amount, so that the risk premium is zero.

风险溢价大于零的期间。随着保单年度增加，投资连结保险的投资账户价值和分红风险准备金水平可能超过保险金额，使风险溢价为零。

The term of insurance is also known as "insurance period" and the period of protection provided by the insurance policy. That is, from the beginning of the insurance liability to the time of termination. Different insurance contracts have different insurance deadlines.

保险期限指保险单所提供的保障期限，即从保险责任开始到终止的时间。不同保险合同有着不同的保险期限。

#### 5.2.2.2　意外伤害险实务

**Time of payment of claim　索赔期限**

The time limit for the insurance company to pay the insurance is stipulated.

索赔期限规定了保险公司支付保险金的时限。

The period of claim refers to the period during which the injured party has the right to file a claim with the defaulting party. In accordance with the law and international practice, the injured party can only file a claim within a certain period of claim, otherwise it loses its right to claim.

索赔期限，是指受损害方有权向违约方提出索赔的期限。按照法律和国际惯例，受损害方只能在一定索赔期限内提出索赔,否则就会丧失索赔权利。

### 5.2.3　健康险

#### 5.2.3.1　健康险基本概念

**1. Endowment insurance　养老保险**

The Decision of the State Council on Improving the Basic Pension Insurance System for Enterprise Employees was released and implemented. China's basic pension insurance system will be improved from ten major aspects, including ensuring the basic pension of retirees is paid in full and on time, no default on basic pensions will occur and so on.

《国务院关于完善企业职工基本养老保险制度的决定》发布实施。我国基本养老保险制度将从十大主要方面予以完善，其中包括确保离退休人员基本养老金按时足额发放，不得发生基本养老金拖欠等内容。

Endowment insurance is a type of life insurance that pays a particular sum directly to the policyholder at a stated date, or to a beneficiary if the policyholder dies before this date.

养老保险是种人寿保险，在规定日期直接向投保人支付保险金如果投保人在规定日期前死亡，则直接向受益人支付保险金。

**2. Health insurance 健康保险**

There have been criticisms that the changes would cause many people to drop their private health insurance, causing a further burden on the public hospital system and a rise in premiums.

有人批评这些改革会使很多人放弃私人健康保险，进而加重了公立医院的负担，并导致保费上涨。

Health insurance is insurance that covers the whole or a part of the risk of a person incurring medical expenses, spreading the risk over a large number of persons. By estimating the overall risk of health care and health system expenses over the risk pool, an insurer can develop a routine finance structure, such as a monthly premium or payroll tax, to provide the money to pay for the health care benefits specified in the insurance agreement.

健康保险是涵盖一个人发生医疗费用全部或部分风险的保险，将风险分散到大量人身上。通过估计风险池中医疗和医疗系统支出的总体风险，保险公司可以制定常规财务结构，如每月的保费或工资税，用来支付保险协议中规定的医疗福利。

**3. Insurance broker 保险经纪人**

In the United States, insurance brokers are regulated by the individual U.S. states. Most states require anyone who sells, solicits, or negotiates insurance in that state to obtain an insurance broker license, with certain limited exceptions.

在美国，保险经纪人受美国各州监管。除某些有限的例外情况外，大多数州要求在该州销售、招揽或协商的保险人需要获得保险经纪人执照。

An insurance broker sells, solicits, or negotiates insurance for compensation.

保险经纪人通过出售、招揽或协商保险获得收益。

### 5.2.3.2 健康险实务

**1. Deductibles 免赔额**

Several states mandate first-dollar coverage for certain types of health insurance benefits, no deductibles permitted. (*Forbes*: Fact and Comment)

有几个州要求对某些类型的健康保险福利实行全额给付保险，不允许扣除免赔额。

Deductibles is a clause in an insurance policy that relieves the insurer of responsibility to pay the initial loss up to a stated amount.

免赔额是保险单中的一项条款，它免除了保险人支付初始损失责任，最高可达规定数额。

**2. Insurance coverage　保险范围**

While social insurance provided to the poor has a negative incentive effect, it also increases their otherwise insufficient insurance coverage. (Insurance: Mathematics and economics/ February 2017/ https://doi.org/10.1016/j.jpubeco. 2016.12.009)

虽然向穷人提供的社会保险具有负面的激励效应，但这也扩大了保险范围。

Insurance coverage is the amount of risk or liability that is covered for an individual or entity by way of insurance services.

保险范围是指通过保险服务为个人或实体承保的风险或赔偿责任金额。

**3. Insurance premium　保险费**

The US health insurance industry is highly concentrated, and health insurance premiums are high and rising rapidly. (Insurance: Mathematics and economics/July, 2015/https://doi.org/ 10.1016/j.jhealeco.2015.03.009)

美国医疗保险行业高度集中，医疗保险费用不仅高且增长迅速。

Insurance premium is a payment for insurance.

保险费是对保险的一种支付。

## 5.3 Property Insurance（财产险）

本节主要介绍现代保险制度下财产险的分类，并简要介绍财产险的各种分类依据和业务类型。

**财产保险**是指投保人根据合同约定，向保险人交付保险费，保险人按保险合同的约定对所承保的财产及其有关利益因自然灾害或意外事故造成的损失承担赔偿责任的保险。

### 5.3.1 财产损失险

#### 5.3.1.1 财产损失险基本概念

**1. Actuary　精算师**

The CMS Office of the Actuary (OACT) released an update today regarding their annual National Health Expenditures report. (WHITEHOUSE: Health Care Blog/The White House)

精算师 CMS 办公室（OACT）今天发布了关于年度国民健康支出的最新消息。

An actuary is a person who is employed by insurance companies to calculate how much they should charge their clients for insurance.

精算师是指受雇于保险公司的人，主要负责计算应向客户收取多少保险费。

**2. Annuity　年金**

Given costly and limited annuity products, we investigate how annuity market innovation could improve participation and increase individual welfare. (*Journal of Risk and Insurance*/

August 2010/https://doi.org/10.1111/j.1539-6975.2010. 01381.x )

考虑到年金产品成本昂贵且有限，我们将研究年金市场创新如何提高参与度同时增加个人福利。

An annuity is a series of payments made at equal intervals.

年金是以相等时间间隔支付的一系列款项。

**3. All–risks insurance　全保险**

We offer all risk insurance for domestic, air and ocean shipments.

我们提供国内、国际、海上和航空全保险。

All-risks insurance is the insurance that covers all risks to property except any types that are specifically excluded or limited in the policy.

全险保险是一种承保财产全部风险的保险，但保单中明确排除或限制的类型除外。

**4. Act of God　不可抗力**

In the law of contracts, an act of God may be interpreted as an implied defense under the rule of impossibility or impracticability.

在合同法中，不可抗力指不能预见、不能避开并不能客服的客观情况。

An act of God is a natural hazard outside human control, such as an earthquake or tsunami, for which no person can be held responsible. An act of God may amount to an exception to liability in contracts or it may be an “insured peril” in an insurance policy.

天灾是人类无法控制的自然灾害，如地震或海啸，任何人都不能为此承担责任。天灾可能构成合同责任的例外，也可能构成保险单中的“保险风险”。

**5. Beneficiary　受益人**

The Office of the Beneficiary works for the beneficiary, to mentor the beneficiary in such areas as work, relationships, and communication. (*Journal of Risk and Insurance*/October 2015/ https://doi.org/10.1002/9781119118312.ch20)

受益人办公室为受益人工作，在工作、交往和沟通等领域为受益人提供指导。

A beneficiary in the broadest sense is a natural person or other legal entity who receives money or other benefits from a benefactor.

从广义上讲，受益人是从捐赠人处获得金钱或其他利益的自然人或其他法律实体。

**6. Free from particular average (FPA)　平安险**

The three basic risks are Free from Particular Average (FPA), With Particular Averaged (WPA) and All Risks (AR). (www.qzr.cn)

这三种基本险是平安险、水渍险和一切险。

Marine insurance provision which limits the liability of an insurance company to only those losses that exceed a specified percentage of the value of the goods. FPA conditions are applied where the goods are extremely susceptible to damage, or are rendered almost worthless from exposure to water or heat.

海上保险条款，该条款将保险公司赔偿责任限制在超过货物价值一定比例的损失。平安险适用于货物极易受损或因接触水或热而失去价值的情况。

**7. Risk aversion　风险规避**

We study the relative risk aversion of an individual with particular social preferences: his wellbeing is influenced by his relative wealth, and by how concerned he is about having low relative wealth. (*Journal of Risk and Insurance*/February 26, 2018/https://doi.org/10.1111/jori.12239)

我们研究具有特定社会偏好的个人相对风险厌恶：他的健康受其相对财富以及他对自己相对财富较低的担忧程度的影响。

Risk aversion is the behavior of humans (especially consumers and investors), when exposed to uncertainty, in attempting to lower that uncertainty.

规避风险是人类（特别是消费者和投资者）在面临不确定性时试图降低不确定性的行为。

**8. Finite risk insurance　有限风险保险**

Finite risk insurance excludes products expressly sold as annuities. (https://en.wikipedia.org/wiki/Finite_risk_insurance)

有限风险保险不包括以年金形式出售的产品。

Finite risk insurance is the term applied within the insurance industry to describe an alternative risk transfer product that is typically a multi-year insurance contract where the insurer bears limited underwriting, credit, investment and timing risk. The assessment of risk is often conservative.

有限风险保险是保险业中用来描述替代风险转移产品的术语，该产品通常是一项多年期的保险合同，在这种合同中，保险公司承担有限的承保、信贷、投资和时间风险。风险评估通常是保守的。

**9. Marine hull insurance　船舶保险**

At present，domestic shipping industry is under booming state , but river and marine hull insurance as shipping industry safeguard runs difficultly , due to the high loss ratio.

目前，我国航运业正处于大力发展时期，但作为航运业保障的沿海内河船舶保险却因为赔付率高而经营困难，这不利于国内航运业的发展。

Marine hull insurance covers the loss or damage of ships, cargo, terminals, and any transport or cargo by which the property is transferred, acquired, or held between the points of origin and the final destination.

船舶船体保险包括船舶、货物、码头以及在原产地和最终目的地之间转让、获取或持有财产的任何运输或货物损失或损坏。

**10. Moral hazard　道德风险**

By insuring against loss, all forms of insurance can lead to moral hazard and inefficient increases in risky behavior. (*Journal of Risk and Insurance*/February 11, 2018/https://doi.org/10.1111/jori.12240)

通过承保损失，所有形式的保险都可能导致道德风险以及风险行为的无效增加。

Moral hazard occurs when someone increases their exposure to risk when insured. This can happen, for example, when a person takes more risks because someone else bears the cost of those risks.

当投保人增加风险敞口时，道德风险就发生了。例如，当一个人因为别人承担风险的成本而承担更多风险时，就可能发生这种情况。

**11. Claims adjuster 索赔核算员**

Claims adjusters work long hours including work nights and weekends. Their work is appointment based and must revolve around the needs of clients.

理赔员工作时间长，包括夜班和周末。他们的工作以预约为基础，必须围绕客户的需要展开。

Claims adjuster (claim adjuster), or claims handler (claim handler), investigates insurance claims by interviewing the claimant and witnesses, consulting police and hospital records, and inspecting property damage to determine the extent of the company's liability.

理赔员或索赔处理人通过采访索赔人和证人，查阅警察和医院记录，检查财产损失以确定公司损失程度，来确定保险索赔责任。

**12. Material fact 重要事实**

Misrepresentation of a material fact on an application for insurance may allow an insurance company grounds to rescind an insurance policy.

保险申请中歪曲重大事实是，保险公司有理由撤销保险单。

A material fact is a fact that a reasonable person would recognize as germane to a decision to be made, as distinguished from an insignificant, trivial, or unimportant detail.

重要事实是一个理性人会认识到与决策密切相关的事实，有别于无关紧要、琐碎或不重要的细节。

**13. Kidnap and ransom insurance 绑架和赎金保险**

Kidnap and ransom insurance policies are indemnity policies – they reimburse a loss incurred by the insured. The policies do not pay ransoms on the behalf of the insured.

绑架和赎金保险单是用来赔偿被保险人遭受的损失的。保单不代表为被保险人支付赎金。

Kidnap and ransom insurance or K&R insurance is designed to protect individuals and corporations operating in high-risk areas around the world.

绑架和赎金保险（K&R 保险）旨在保护世界各地高风险地区经营的个人和公司。

**14. Open policy（open cover） 预约保险单**

The open cover shall be evidenced by an open policy to be issued by the insurer.（http://dict.cn/open%20policy）

预约保险合同应当由保险人签发预约保险单来确定。

Marine cargo insurance that provides open policy against loss or damage to all goods transported by a specific carrier, or by a specific shipper, during a stated period. Under its terms, the insured is required to periodically provide the insurer with the description, quantity, and value of goods shipped during that period.

海运货物保险，为特定承运人或特定托运人在规定期间运输所有货物的损失或损坏提供预约保单。根据其条款，被保险人必须定期向保险人提供在此期间装运货物的种类、数量和价值。

**15. Particular average　单独海损**

The FPA clause does not cover partial loss of the nature of Particular Average, whereas the WPA clause covers such losses.（www.chinaqking.com）

平安险条款不包括单独海损性质部分的损失，但水渍险条款包括。

Particular Average is a partial loss in marine insurance that must be borne by the interest or goods sustaining it without benefit of contribution from other interests—compare General Average.

单独海损是海上保险中的部分损失，相较于共同海损而言，它必须由维持该损失的权益或货物承担，而不受其他权益或共同海损分摊的影响。

**16. Partial loss　部分损失**

For the cover of All Risks the insurance company shall be liable for total or partial loss on land or sea of the insured goods within the period covered by the insurance.（www.crazyenglish.org）

投保“一切险”，在承保期内，保险公司应承担投保货物在海上或陆上产生的部分或全部损失。

Partial loss is a damage that neither destroys the insured good or property nor renders it useless for its designed purpose. It is of two types which are Particular Average Loss and General Average Loss.

部分损失是指既不毁坏被保险人的利益或财产，也不使其无法用于其设计目的的损害。它分为单独海损和共同海损两种。

**17. Premium rebate　保费回扣**

Usually we receive a handsome premium rebate from our underwriter at regular interval.（provided by jukuu）

通常，我们可定期从保险公司拿到一笔可观的保险费回扣。

Premium rebate is a kind of discount offered by the insurance company who is willing to surrender part of the profits in order to attract more purchasers and then the policyholder is able to pay less premium.

保费回扣是保险公司提供的一种折扣，他们愿意放弃部分利润以吸引更多客户，使投保人能够支付更少的保费。

**18. Policyholder　投保人**

If the policyholder conceals the actual circumstances of the insured property, the insurer shall have the right to rescind the contract or shall not be liable for making indemnity.（provided by jukuu）

投保人如隐瞒被保险财产的真实情况，保险方有权解除合同或不承担赔偿责任。

Policyholder is an entity that owns an insurance policy and has the right to exercise all privileges under the contract of insurance, except where restricted by the rights of an assignee (see assignment). A policyholder-also called policyowner- may or may not be the insured, or the sole or one of the beneficiaries of the policy.

投保人是拥有保险单并有权行使保险合同项下所有特权的实体，除非受到受让人权利的限制 （见转让）。保单持有人也称为投保人——可能是也可能不是被保险人，或是保单唯一受益人或受益人之一。

**19. Proportional reinsurance 比例再保险**

Proportional reinsurance is composed of quota share reinsurance and surplus reinsurance.

比例再保险又分为成数分保方式和溢额分保方式。

Proportional reinsurance is based on original liability and proportional cession, whereby in the case of non-proportional reinsurance, it is the amount of loss and the cover-limited in amount-which is significant. It is also referred to as "excess of loss reinsurance".

比例再保险是以原始责任和比例转换为基础的，而非比例再保险的基础是损失数额和承保限额，因此也被称为"超额损失再保险"。

**20. Proximate cause 近因原则**

Principle of proximate cause is the fundamental in the phase of claiming damages and claiming setting for marine insurance.（dict.cnki.net）

近因原则是在海上保险中索赔理赔阶段应当遵循的原则。

In the law, a proximate cause is an event sufficiently related to an injury that the courts deem the event to be the cause of that injury. There are two types of causation in the law: cause-in-fact, and proximate (or legal) cause.

在法律中，近因是指与伤害充分相关的事件，法院认为该事件是该伤害的原因。法律中有两种因果关系：事实原因和近因。

**21. Property insurance 财产保险**

An insurer shall not concurrently engage in business of both property insurance and insurance of persons.（www.dictall.com）

同一保险人不得同时经营财产保险业务和人身保险业务。

Property insurance provides protection against most risks to property, such as fire, theft and some weather damage. This includes specialized forms of insurance such as fire insurance, flood insurance, earthquake insurance, home insurance, or boiler insurance. Property is insured in two main ways—open perils and named perils.

财产保险对财产的大多数风险提供保护，如火灾、盗窃和一些天气损害。包括专门保险形式，如火灾保险、洪水保险、地震保险、家庭保险或锅炉保险。财产保险主要有两种方式——公开危险和指定危险。

**22. Primary insurance amount 基本保险金额**

Whether the benefit is for the worker or for a spouse, child or other relative, it is necessary to compute a "primary insurance amount" or "PIA" that is based on the worker's earnings averaged over much of his or her career. (3920 Computing The Primary Insurance

Amount For Social Security /2008/Human resources management. Employment relations)

无论是为劳动者还是为配偶、子女或其他亲属提供福利，都必须依据劳动者在其职业生涯中的平均收入计算一个“基本保险金额”或“PIA”。

The Primary Insurance Amount (PIA), is a component of Social Security provision in the United States. For the purposes of the United States Social Security Administration, PIA is used as the beginning point in calculating the annuity payment of benefits that is provided to an eligible recipient each month during retirement until the recipient's death.

基本保险金额，简称 PIA。是美国社会保障制度的组成部分。根据美国社会保障局的规定，在计算向符合条件的受益人退休直至其死亡期间每月提供的福利年金支付时，使用 PIA 作为起点。

**23. Right of subrogation　代位求偿权**

The insurer may deduct a corresponding sum from the amount of indemnity if it is not able to exercise the right of indemnity by subrogation due to the fault of the insured.（www.dictall.com）

由于被保险人的过错致使保险人不能行使代位赔偿权利（代位求偿权），保险人可以相应扣减保险赔偿金。

Subrogation is a term describing a legal right held by most insurance carriers to legally pursue a third party that caused an insurance loss to the insured. This is done in order to recover the amount of the claim paid by the insurance carrier to the insured for the loss.

代位权是大多数保险公司拥有的合法权利，即依法追索对被保险人造成保险损失的第三方。这样做是为了收回保险公司为被保险人支付的损失索赔金额。

**24. Salvage charge　救助费用**

Expenses incurred by or on behalf of the assured for the safety or preservation of the subject matter insured, other than general average and salvage charges, are called particular charges.（averageadjusting.net ）

除共同海损和救助费用外，由被保险人或为保险标的的安全或保存所产生的费用，叫作特别费用。

Salvage charge means the charges recoverable under Maritime Law by a salvor independently of contract. Expense incurred in recovering the salvage value of an asset or property.

救助费用是救助人根据海商法可以独立于合同而收回的费用。为回收资产或财产的残值而发生的费用。

### 5.3.1.2　财产损失险实务

**1. General average　共同海损**

Under the BIMCO Standard General Average Absorption Clause, hull insurers pay the costs of general average up to an agreed sum thus eliminating low value claims where the costs are often disproportionate to the eventual recovery. (BIMCO: Changes To Specialist

General Average Clauses.2017.07.05 海商法研究中心)

根据 BIMCO 标准通用条款，船舶保险公司按照约定金额支付共同海损费用，从而消除了低价值索赔，因为索赔费用往往与最终赔偿不成比例。

General average is loss or damage to a ship or its cargo that is shared among the owners of the ship and cargo.

共同海损是指船舶和货物所有人共同分担船舶或货物的损失。

**2. Hedge 对冲**

We find that unless the risk premium on the bond is close to zero, the robust optimal hedge is significantly less sensitive to variations in the underlying probability distribution. (*Journal of Risk and Insurance*/January 2017//https://doi.org/10.1111/jori.12201)

我们发现，除非债券风险溢价接近于零，否则稳健的最优套期保值会对潜在概率分布变化不太敏感。

A hedge is an investment position intended to offset potential losses or gains that may be incurred by a companion investment.

对冲是一种投资头寸，旨在抵消配套投资可能产生的潜在损失或收益。

**3. National Insurance Company Limited 印度国家保险有限公司**

National Insurance Company Limited was spun off as a distinct company under the General Insurance Business (Nationalisation) Amendment Act in 2002.

印度国家保险有限公司是根据 2002 年《一般保险业务（国有化）修正案》剥离出来的一家独立公司。

National Insurance Company Limited (NICL) is a state owned general insurance company in India. Its catchline is “Trusted Since 1906” in italic. The company headquartered at Kolkata was established in 1906 and nationalised in 1972.

印度国民保险有限公司是印度的一家国有保险公司。其标语用斜体写着“自 1906 年就被信任”。公司总部设在加尔各答，成立于 1906 年，1972 年被收归国有。

**4. Insurable interest 保险利益**

In summary, for indemnity insurance other than marine the lack of an insurable interest will not render the contract unenforceable. (*Journal of Business Law*/May, 2005/Insurable Interest: As Intended?)

总而言之，除海运保险以外的赔偿保险，缺少可保利益合同依然可以执行。

Insurable interest exists when an insured person derives a financial or other kind of benefit from the continuous existence, without impairment or damage, of the insured object (or in the case of a person, their continued survival).

当被保险人从标的物持续存在（就个人而言，其继续生存）中获得经济利益或其他种类的利益时，就存在可保险利益。

**5. Valued insurance contract 定值保险合同**

Chapter 3 “Current situation of valued insurance contract in China and suggestion on perfection” is the essence of analysis and research in this paper, and is also the key point of this paper.

第三章“我国定值保险合同现状及完善建议”是本文研究的实质，也是本文的研究重点。

The parties of the two parties first determine the insurance value of the insurance subject and specify the insurance contract in the insurance policy. When making an insurance contract, the policyholder and the insurance personnel first agree on the value of the insured object, that is the insurance value, as the sum of the insurance sum, and write the two points in the insurance contract. In the event of an insurance accident, no matter whether the actual value changes or not, the insurance per person takes the amount of insurance as the basis of the compensation.

双方首先确定保险标的的保险价值，并在保险单中明确保险合同。在订立合同时，投保人和保险人员首先约定保险标的价值，即保险价值，作为保险金额总和，并写在保险合同中。在发生保险事故时，无论实际价值是否变化，人均保险均以保险金额作为赔偿依据。

## 5.3.2 责任保险

责任保险，是指保险人在被保险人依法应对第三人负赔偿责任，并被提出赔偿要求时，承担赔偿责任的财产保险形式。责任保险以被保险人对他人依法应负的民事赔偿责任为保险标的，在合同中无保险金额，而规定赔偿限额。责任保险仅承保被保险人的过失侵权民事责任，对故意行为造成的损害不负责任，除特别约定外，通常不包括合同违约责任。

### 5.3.2.1 责任保险基本概念

**1. Business interruption insurance　营业中断保险**

Business interruption insurance differs from property insurance in that a property insurance policy only covers the physical damage to the business, while the additional coverage allotted by the business interruption policy covers the profits that would have been earned.

营业中断保险与财产保险区别在于财产保险单只承保企业的有形损害，而营业中断保单附加保险范围覆盖了应获得的利润。

Business interruption insurance (also known as business income insurance) is a type of insurance that covers the loss of income that a business suffers after a disaster. The income loss covered may be due to disaster-related closing of the business facility or due to the rebuilding process after a disaster.

营业中断保险（即营业收入保险）是一种涵盖企业在灾后遭受的收入损失的保险。涵盖的收入损失可能是与灾害有关的商业设施关闭，或由于灾后的重建过程。

**2. Claims adjuster　理赔核算员**

Our purpose here is to consider one aspect of automobile bodily injury liability claims management: the assignment of fault across parties as judged by the insured defendant's claims adjuster. (*Journal of Risk and Insurance*/May 2003/https://doi.org/10.1111/1539-6975.00055)

我们的目的是考虑汽车人身伤害赔偿责任管理的一个方面：由被告保险理赔人判断各方责任的分配。

Claims adjuster investigates insurance claims by interviewing the claimant and witnesses, consulting police and hospital records, and inspecting property damage to determine the extent of the company's liability.

理赔核算员通过约谈索赔人和证人、查阅警察和医院记录、检查财产损失以确定公司赔偿责任从而调查保险索赔。

**3. Coinsurance clause　共同保险条款**

The advantage of buying insurance with a coinsurance clause is the policy's premium will generally be lower than a similar policy without the coinsurance clause. (Interpreting the Coinsurance Clause in a Builder's Risk Policy)

用共同保险条款的好处是，保单保费通常低于没有共同保险条款的类似保单.

Definition of coinsurance clause: Insurance policy stipulation that a building must be insured for at least a certain percentage (usually 80 percent) of its insurable value (appraised or market value of the property less value of land) in order to collect the full amount of a partial-loss claim on it.

共同保险条款的定义：保险单规定，建筑物至少按其可保价值(估价或市场价值减去土地价值)的一定比例（通常是 80%）投保，以获得索赔的全部金额。

### 5.3.2.2　责任保险实务

**1. Insurance regulatory law　保险管理法**

Historically, the insurance industry has been regulated almost exclusively by the individual state governments. The first state commissioner of insurance was appointed in New Hampshire in 1851 and the state-based insurance regulatory law grew as quickly as the insurance industry itself.

历史上，保险业几乎由各州政府监管。1851 年，新罕布什尔州任命了第一位州保险专员，以州为基础的保险监管法发展和保险业一样快。

Insurance regulatory law is the body of statutory law, administrative regulations and jurisprudence that governs and regulates the insurance industry and those engaged in the business of insurance. Insurance regulatory law is primarily enforced through regulations, rules and directives by state insurance departments as authorized and directed by statutory law enacted by the state legislatures. However, federal law, court decisions and administrative adjudications also play an important role.

保险监管法是对保险业和从业人员进行监管的成文法、行政法规和判例的总称。保险监管法主要通过州立法机关制定的成文法授权和指示的州保险部门条例、规则和指示执行。联邦法律、法院裁决和行政裁决也发挥着重要作用。

**2. Liability insurance　责任保险**

The confirming of responsibility of liability insurance depend on the agreement of contract of insurance.

责任保险责任的确定取决于保险合同的约定.

Liability insurance is a part of the general insurance system of risk financing to protect the purchaser (the "insured") from the risks of liabilities imposed by lawsuits and similar claims. It protects the insured in the event he or she is sued for claims that come within the coverage of the insurance policy. Originally, individual companies that faced a common peril formed a group and created a self-help fund out of which to pay compensation should any member incur loss (in other words, a mutual insurance arrangement).

责任保险是风险融资保险制度的一部分，旨在保护买方（“被保险人”）免受诉讼和类似索赔带来的责任风险。当被保险人因保单范围内的索赔被起诉时，它可以保护被保险人。最初，面临共同风险的个别公司组成团体并设立自助基金，如果成员发生损失，则从该基金中支付赔偿 ，换言之，是种相互保险安排。

## 5.3.3　信用保险

信用保险，是指保险人对被保险人信用放款或信用售货，债务人拒绝履行合同或不能清偿债务时，所受到的经济损失承担赔偿责任的保险方式。主要有出口信用保险、抵押信用保险等形式。

### 5.3.3.1　信用保险基本概念

**1. Compulsory insurance　强制保险**

The Chinese government has released a guideline promoting a compulsory insurance pilot program in heavy industries and other enterprises posing high environmental risks. (Compulsory insurance to cover more high-risk industries/www.chinadaily.com.cn)

中国政府发布在重工业和其他高环境风险企业中推行强制保险试点的指导方针。

Compulsory insurance is any type of insurance individual or business is legally required to buy.

强制保险是法律要求购买的个人或企业保险。

**2. Cargo insurance　货物保险**

In international cargo insurance, the insured must be interested in the subject matter insured at the time of loss though he need not be interested when the insurance is effected. ( edu.sina.com.cn)

在国际货物保险中，被保险人在损失发生时必须对保险标的有利益关系，在保险生效时可以没有利害关系。

Cargo insurance is an activity aiming at moving the burden of risk from the exporters and importers to the underwriters.

货物保险是将风险从出口商和进口商转移给承保人。

**3. Ceding insurance company　再保险分出人**

The ceding insurance company shall not decline or delay fulfilling its obligation of the direct insurance on the basis that the reinsurer fails to fulfill the reinsurance obligation.

再保险分出人不得以再保险人未履行再保险责任为由，拒绝履行或者迟延履行其原保险责任。

A ceding insurance company is an company that passes the part or all of its risks from its insurance policy portfolio to a reinsurance firm. Passing off risk in this manner allows the ceding company to hedge against undesired exposure to loss and frees up capital to use in new insurance contracts.

再保险分出人是将部分或全部风险从保单组合转移给再保险公司。以这种方式规避风险，可以让分出公司对冲损失敞口，将资本用于新保险合同。

**4. Deposit premium　存款保险**

Deposit premiums are unique from regular insurance premiums, as they are refundable should if either the insured or the insurer chooses to terminate the perpetual insurance.（https://en.wikipedia.org/wiki/Deposit_insurance）

存款保险费与一般保险费的不同之处在于：如果被保险人或保险人选择终止保险，保险费应予退还。

A deposit premium is a type of insurance premium where the insured deposits money with the insurer to obtain perpetual insurance against the risk of a loss.

存款保险费是被保险人为获得永久保险而向保险人存款发生的保险费。

### 5.3.3.2　信用保险实务

**1. Interest rate insurance　利率保险**

Monetary Policy Committee member Professor David Miles first highlighted interest rate insurance in *the Miles Review* in 2004 commissioned by Gordon Brown. Professor Miles suggested that it would provide greater security in housing finance.

货币政策委员会成员戴维·迈尔斯教授在 2004 年戈登·布朗委托的《迈尔斯评论》中首次强调了利率保险，并表示这将为住房融资提供更大的保障。

Interest rate insurance protects the holder of a variable rate mortgage or loan from rising interest rates. It is generally offered independently of the original borrowing and typically as an alternative to a remortgage onto a fixed rate.

利率保险使可变利率抵押贷款或贷款持有人免受利率上升的影响。它独立于原始借款，通常作为固定利率再抵押的替代方案。

**2. Solvency　偿付能力**

Solvency is essential to staying in business as it asserts a company's ability to continue operations into the foreseeable future. While a company also needs liquidity to thrive, liquidity should not be confused with solvency. A company that is insolvent must often enter bankruptcy.（https://www.investopedia.com/terms/s/solvency.asp）

偿债能力对于维持经营至关重要，因为它体现了公司在可预见未来持续经营的能力。虽然公司需要流动性才能运营，但流动性不应与偿付能力混为一谈。资不抵债的公司通常会进入破产程序。

Solvency, in finance or business, is the degree to which the current assets of an individual or entity exceed the current liabilities of that individual or entity.Solvency can also be described as the ability of a corporation to meet its long-term fixed expenses and to accomplish long-term expansion and growth. This is best measured using the net liquid balance (NLB) formula.

在金融或商业领域，偿付能力是指个人或实体流动资产超过流动负债的程度。偿付能力也是公司满足长期固定支出、实现扩张和增长的能力。最好用净流量余额 (NLB) 来衡量。

**3. Reinsurance　再保险**

Traditional reinsurance operates efficiently in managing relatively small, uncorrelated risks and in facilitating efficient information sharing between cedants and reinsurers. (*Journal of Risk and Insurance*/August 2009/https://doi.org/10.1111/j.1539-6975. 2009. 01319.x)

传统再保险在管理较小的不相关风险和促进再保险分出人和再保险人之间信息共享较为有效。

Reinsurance is insurance that is purchased by an insurance company.

再保险是由保险公司购买的保险。

# Appendix　Acronyms（缩略词）

A/P（account payable）　应付账款（花费时记账，未来付款）
A/R（account receivable）　应收账款（销售时记账未来收款）
ABC（The Agricultural Bank of China）　中国农业银行
ABS（Asset-backed securities）　资产支持证券
ACCA（Association of Chartered Certified Accountants）　特许公认会计师
ACE（Amex Commodities Exchange）　美国商品交易所
ACG（Asia-Pacific Central Securities Depository Group）　亚太区中央证券存管处组织
ACH（Automated Clearing House）　自动票据交换所；自动清算所
ACRS（Accelerated Cost Recovery System）　加速成本回收制度
ACU（Asia Currency Unit）　亚洲货币单位
ACV（Actual Cash Value）　实际现金价值
ADB（Adjusted Debit Balance）　调整负债余额
ADB（Asian Development Bank）　亚洲开发银行
ADBC（Agricultural Development Bank of China）　中国农业发展银行
ADL（Advance-Decline Line）　腾落指数
ADR（Advance-Decline Ratio）　股票价格涨跌比率
ADR（American Depositary Receipt）　美国存托凭证
ADS（American Depository Share）　美国存托股票
AE（Account Executive）　客户经理
AGI（Adjusted Gross Income）　调整后毛利，调整后总收入
AGM（Annual general meeting）　股东周年大会，年度股东大会
AIB（Audit Investigation Board）　审计调查委员会
AIBD（Association of International Bond Dealers）　国际债券交易商协会
AIM（Alternative Investment Market）（UK）　另项投资市场（英国）
AIMR（Association for Investment Management and Research）　投资管理与研究协会
AM（Active Management）　积极性管理
AMA（Asset Management Accounts）　资产管理账户
AMBAC（American Municipal Bond Assurance Corporation）　美国市政债券保险公司
AMCHAM（American Chamber of Commerce）　美国商会
AMEX（American Stock Exchange）　美国证券交易所
AMIs（Alternative Mortgage Instruments）　替代抵押信用工具
AMOS（Amex Options Switching System）　美国证交所期权转换系统

AOSEF（Asian and Oceanian Stock Exchanges Federation） 亚洲及大洋洲证券交易所联会

APM（Average Propensity to Import） 平均进口倾向

APT（Arbitrage Pricing Theory） 套利定价理论

APV（Adjusted Present Value） 调整后现值

APX（Average Propensity to Export） 平均出口倾向

ARM（Adjustable rate mortgage） 调息按揭，调整式利率抵押贷款

ARPS（Adjustable Rate Preferred Stock） 可调股息优先股

ASAC（Asian Securities' Analysts Council） 亚洲证券分析员公会

ASAF（Asian Securities Analysts Federation） 亚洲证券分析家协会

ASC（Accounting Society of China） 中国会计学会

ASE（Australian Stock Exchange） 澳大利亚证券交易所

ATI（Account Transfer Instruction） 账户转移指示

ATM（Automated Teller Machine） 自动出纳机，自动柜员机

ATS（Automated Trade System） 自动交易系统

BO（Buyer's Option） 买方选择权

B/L（Bill of Lading） 提单

B/P（Bills Payable） 应付票据

B/R（Bills Receivable） 应收票据

BA（Bank Acceptance） 银行承兑汇票

BA&TA（Banker's and Trade Acceptances） 银行及商业承兑汇票

BAS（Block Automation System） 巨额交易自动报价制度

BOC（Bank of China） 中国银行

BOLL（Bollinger Bands） 布林线指标

C&F（Cost&Freight） 成本加运费价

CIC（China Insurance Clause） 中国保险条款

CO（Certificate of Origin） 原产地证

C/D（Customs Declaration） 报关单

CAPEX（Capital Expenditures） 资本支出

CAPI（China Association for the Promotion of Investment） 中国投资发展促进会

CAR（Capital Adequacy Ratio） 资本充裕/充足比率

CASIF（The Chinese Association of Securities Investment Funds） 中国证券业协会基金公会

CBIRC（China Banking and Insurance Regulatory Commission） 中国银保监会

CBOE（Chicago Board Options Exchange） 芝加哥期权交易所

CBOT（Chicago Board of Trade） 芝加哥交易所

CCB（China Construction Bank） 中国建设银行

CCMS（Common Collateral Management System） 共同抵押品管理系统

CCP（Central Counterparty） 中央结算对手
CCSD（Conference of Central Securities Depositories） 中央证券存管处国际会议
CCSS（Central Clearing and Settlement System） 中央结算及交收系统（中央结算系统）
CDB（China Development Bank） 国家开发银行
CDO（Collateralized Debt Obligation） 债务抵押债券
CDR（Chinese Depositary Receipt） 中国预托证券；中国存托凭证
CDS（Credit Default Swap） 信用违约互换
CDs（Negotiable Certificates of Deposit） 可转让存单
CDSC（Contingent Deferred Sales Charge） 递延申购手续费
CFA（The Corporate Finance Association） 企业融资协会
CFD（Contract for Differences） 合同利差
CFETS（China Foreign Exchange Trade System） 中国外汇交易中心
CFFEX（China Financial Futures Exchange） 中国金融期货交易所
CGSDTCCL（China Government Securities Depository Trust & Clearing Co. Ltd. 中央国债登记结算有限责任公司（中央国债登记结算公司）
CHATS（Clearing House Automated Transfer System） 票据交换所自动转账系统
CI（Cost and Insurance） 成本加保险
CIA（Certified Internal Auditor） 注册内部审计员
CICC（China International Capital Corporation） 中国国际金融有限公司
CICPA（Chinese Institute of Certified Public Accountants） 中国注册会计师协会
CIF（Cost, Insurance & Freight） 成本、保险加运费价
CIMA（Chartered Institute of Management Accountants） 特许管理会计师公会
CIRC（China Insurance Regulatory Commission） 中国保险监督管理委员会
CIs（Certificate of Indebtedness） 负债证明书
CIS（Collective Investment Scheme） 集体投资计划
CLF（Central Liquidity Facility） 中央流动资金机制
CLO（Collateralized Loan Obligation） 贷款抵押债券
CMA（Cash Management Account） 现金管理账户
CMB（China Merchants Bank） 中国招商银行
CME（Chicago Mercantile Exchange） 芝加哥商品交易所
CML（Capital Market Line） 资本市场线
CMO（Collateralized Mortgage Obligation） 担保抵押贷款债务
COD（Cash/Collect on Delivery） 货到付款
COGS（Cost of Goods Sold） 销货成本；主营业务成本
CPI（Consumer Price Index） 消费者物价指数
CPSS（The Committee on Payment and Settlement Systems） 支付及结算系统委员会
CPT（Continuous Professional Training） 持续专业培训课程
CR（Cash Receipts） 现金收入

CR（Current Rate） 当日汇率、现行汇率
CRB（Commodity Price Index） 物价指数
CRD（Central Registration Depository） 中央登记保管机制
CRM（Customer Relationship Management） 客户关系管理
CRT（Charitable Remainder Trust） 慈善信托
CS（Convertible Securities） 可转换证券
CSRC（China Securities Regulatory Commission） 中国证券监督管理委员会
CUs（Credit Unions） 信用合作社
D/A（Document Against Acceptance） 承兑交单
D/P（Document Against Payment） 付款交单
DCI（Direct Credit Instruction） 直接存款/存账指示
DCP（Direct Clearing Participant） 直接结算参与者
DCSS（Derivatives Clearing and Settlement System） 衍生产品结算及交收系统
DDI（Direct Debit Instruction） 直接扣款/扣账指示
DJIA（Dow Jones Industrial Average） 道琼斯工业平均指数
DPI（Disposable Personal Income） 个人可支配收入
EEMU（European Economic and Monetary Union） 欧洲经济及货币联盟
EFIL（Exchange Fund Investment Limited） 外汇基金投资有限公司
EFN（Exchange Fund Note） 外汇基金债券
EFP（Exchange for Physicals） 期货与现货互转交易
EFT（Electronic Funds Transfer） 电子资金转账
EFTPS（Electronic Funds Transfer at Point of Sale） 销售点电子资金转账
EGM（Extraordinary General Meeting） 股东特别大会
EIB（Export-Import Bank） 进出口银行
EIPOS（Electronic Initial Public Offering Service） 电子认购首次公开招股服务
ELI（Equity Linked Note） 与股票挂钩票据；高息票据
EM（Equity Multiplier） 权益乘数
EMF（European Monetary Fund） 欧洲货币基金
EMIP（Equivalent Mean Investment Period） 等值平均投资期
EMP（End of Month Payment） 月末付款
EMS（Express Mail Special） 特快专递
EMS（European Monetary System） 欧洲货币体系
EMU（European Monetary Union） 欧洲货币联盟
EOE（European Options Exchange） 欧洲期权交易
EPI（Electronic Payment Instruction） 电子收付款指示
EPS（Earnings Per Share） 每股收益额，每股盈利额
ER（Exchange Rate） 外汇汇率
ERM（Exchange Rate Mechanism） 欧洲汇率机制

ES（Exempt Securities） 免税证券
ESOP（Employee Stock Ownership Plan） 员工购股计划
ESS（Electronic Submission System） 电子提交系统
ETC（Exchange-traded Commodity） 交易所买卖商品
ETD（Exchange-traded Derivatives） 股票交易所
ETF（Exchange-traded Fund） 交易所买卖基金；组合股；交易所交易基金
ETN（Exchange-traded Note） 交易所买卖票据
EU（European Union） 欧盟
EUA（European Units of Account） 欧洲记账单位
FAI（Fixed Asset Investment） 固定资产投资
Fannie（Mae Federal National Mortgage Association） 美国联邦国民抵押贷款协会
FASB（Financial Accounting Standard Board） 美国财务会计准则委员会
FC（Fixed Cost） 固定成本
FCA（Free Carrier） 货交承运人
FCG（Foreign Currency Guarantee） 外币担保
FCI（Factors Chain International） 国际应收账款联盟
FDI（Foreign Direct Investment） 国际直接投资
FDIC（Federal Deposit Insurance Corporation） 联邦储蓄保险公司
FI（Fixed Investment） 固定投资
FIBV（Federation International Des Bourses De Valeurs） 国际证券交易所联会
FICA（Fellow of the Institute of Chartered Accountants） 特许会计师学会会员
FOB（Free on Board） 离岸价
FOE（Futures and Options Exchange） 期货和期权交易所
FOMC（Federal Open Market Committee） 美国联邦公开市场委员会
FOREX（Foreign Exchange） 外汇；外汇交易
FP（Floating Policy） 浮动政策
FRA（Forward Rate Agreement） 远期利率协议
FRB（Federal Reserve Board） 联邦储备局
FRBs（Federal Reserve Banks） 美国联邦准备银行
FRC（The Financial Reporting Council） 财务汇报局
FRCD（Floating Rate Certificate of Deposit） 浮动利率定期存单，浮息存款证
FREF（Fixed Rate Export Finance） 固定利率出口融资
FREIT（Finite-Life Real Estate Investment Trust） 有限寿命不动产投资信托
FRN（Floating Rate Note） 浮动利率债券，浮息票据
FRR（Financial Resources Rules） 财政资源规则
FRRC（Financial Reporting Review Committee） 财务汇报检讨委员会
FRS（Federal Reserve System） 联邦储备系统
FRS（Flexible Rate System） 灵活的汇率制度

FSA（Financial Services Authority）（UK） 英国金融业管理局
GW（Gross Weight） 毛重
GM（Gross Margin） 毛利
GSP（Generalized System of Preferences） 普惠制
IBP（International Balance of Payments） 国际收支平衡
ICBC（Industrial and Commercial Bank of China） 中国工商银行
ICL（Investment Corporate Ltd.） 中国投资有限责任公司
IPO（Initial Public Offering） 首次公开募股
IRA（Interest Rate Agreement） 利率协议
IRR（Interest Rate Risk） 利率风险
IRR（Internal Rate of Return） 内部收益率
ISD（Investment Services Directive）(European Union) 投资服务指令（欧盟）
ISFO（International Stock Futures and Options） 国际股票期货及期权
ISIN（International Securities Identification Numbers） 国际证券号码
ISMA（International Securities Markets Association） 国际证券市场协会
ISSA（International Securities Services Association） 国际证券服务业联会
L/C（Letter of Credit） 信用证
LAF（Liquidity Adjustment Facility）(HKMA) 流动资金调节机制（金管局）
LAW（Liquidity Adjustment Window） 流动资金调节窗
LB（Leverage Buyout） 杠杆购并，融资买下
LB（Licensed Bank） 许可银行
LBO（Leveraged Buy Out） 杠杆买断交易；借贷融资收购，杠杆收购
LIBOR（London Inter-bank Offered Rate） 伦敦同业拆借利率
LIFFOE（London International Financial Futures and Options Exchange） 伦敦国际金融期货及期权交易所
LSE（London Stock Exchange） 伦敦证券交易所
LTOM（London Traded Options Market） 伦敦期权市场
LYON（Liquid Yield Option Note） 流动收息权利票据
M&A（Mergers & Acquisitions） 企业并购
MBS（Mortgage-backed Security） 抵押贷款支持证券
MC（Marginal Cost） 边际成本
MEI（Marginal Efficiency of Investment） 投资的边际效率
MFN（Most Favoured Nation） 最惠国
MMDAs（Money Market Deposit Accounts） 货币市场存款账户
MMI（Major Market Index） 主要市场指数
MMMFs（Money Market Mutual Funds） 货币市场共同基金，货币市场信托基金
MR（Marginal Revenue） 边际收入
MSRP（Manufacturer Suggested Retail Price） 厂商建议零售价

NW（Net Weight） 净重
NI（Net Income） 净收入
NASDAQ（The National Association of Securities Dealers Automated Quotation System）国家证券经纪商协会自动报价系统（纳斯达克）
NDF（Non-Deliverable Forward） 无本金交割远期外汇
NNP（Net National Product） 国民生产净值
NYSE（New York Stock Exchange） 纽约证券交易所
OF（Ocean Freight） 海运费
OMO（Open Market Operation） 公开市场操作
OSP（Official Selling Price） 官方售价
OTC（Over the Counter） 场外交易
PBOC（The People's Bank of China） 中国人民银行
PMI（Purchase Management Index） 采购经理指数
PPI（Producer Price Index） 生产价格指数
QE（Quantitative Easing） 量化宽松
QFI（I-Qualified Foreign Institutional Investor） 合格境外机构投资者
RAN（Return Authorization Number） 退货号
RGA（Return Goods Authorization） 退货授权/许可
RMA（Return Material Authorization） 退货授权/许可
ROA（Return on Assets） 资产收益率
ROC（Return on Capital） 资本收益率
ROE（Ratio of Equity） 股本利润率
ROE（Return on Equity） 股本回报率
ROI（Return on Investment） 投资回报率
RPI（Retail Price Index） 零售物价指数
RRP（Reverse Repurchase Agreement） 逆回购协议
RTA（Reciprocal Trade Agreement） 互惠贸易协定法
S&Ls（Savings and Loan Institutions） 储蓄与贷款机构
S&P 500（Standard & Poor's 500 Composite Price Index） 标准普尔股票价格指数
SC（Sales Contract） 销售合同
SAFE（the State Administration of Foreign Exchange） 国家外汇管理局
SAR（Stock Appreciation Rights） 股票增值权益
SBU（Strategic Business Unit） 战略业务单位；事业部
SEC（US Securities and Exchange Commission） 美国证券交易委员会
SITC（Standard International Trade Classification） 国际贸易标准分类
SOEs（State-owned Enterprises） 国有企业
T/T（Telegraphic Transfer） 电汇
TC（Total Cost） 总成本

TPP（Trans-Pacific Partnership） 跨太平洋伙伴关系协定

TPRM（Trade Policy Review Mechanism） 贸易政策审议机制

USM（Unlisted Securities Market） 非上市证券市场

USP（Unique Selling Proposition） 独特销售主张

VAT（Value Added Tax） 增值税

VC（Variable Cost） 变动成本

VC（Venture Capital） 风险资本

VC（Venture Capitalist） 风险投资

VER（Voluntary Export Restraint） 自愿出口限制

VIX（Chicago Board Options Exchange Volatility Index） 芝加哥期权交易所波动率指数

VIX（Volatility Index） 恐慌指数

VRM（Variable Rate Mortgage） 可变利率抵押贷款

VT（Voting Trust） 表决权信托

WB（World Bank） 世界银行

WBEIL（WB Economic Integration Loan） 世界银行经济一体化贷款

WEF（World Economic Forum） 世界经济论坛

WFOE（Wholly Foreign-owned Enterprise） 外资独资企业

WRI（War Risk Insurance） 战争险

XBRL（Extensible Business Reporting Language） 可扩展商业报告语言

YLD（Yield） 收益，收益率

YoY（Year over Year） 按年（度）计

YTC（Yield to First Call） 第一次通知赎回时收益

YTD（Year to Date） 年初至今

YTM（Yield to Maturity） 全期收益，到期收益，到期收益率

Z（Zero） 零，零单位，无报价

ZBA（Zero-balance Account） 零余额账户

ZBB（Zero-based Budgeting） 零基数预算法，免税金额，免征点

ZCI（Zero Coupon Issue） 零息发行

ZCS（Zero Coupon Security） 零息票证券